The GUINNESS Guide to

Feminine Achievements

Joan & Kenneth Macksey

GUINNESS SUPERLATIVES LIMITED

2 CECIL COURT, LONDON ROAD, ENFIELD, MIDDLESEX

Published in Great Britain by
Guinness Superlatives Ltd, 2 Cecil Court,
London Road, Enfield, Middlesex

ISBN 0 900424 31 1

Set in 'Monophoto' Bembo Series 270
Printed and bound in Great Britain by
Jarrold and Sons Ltd, Norwich

155.304 / 920.72.

CONTENTS

ACKNOWLEDGEMENTS

Section heading illustrations reproduced by kind permission of the following:

Sections: 2, 3, 4, 6, 7, 8, 9, 10, 11, 12, 13, 14, 16, 17, 21, 22, Mary Evans. Sections: 15, 19, Radio Times Hulton Picture Library. Section: 18, Mansell Collection.

Other photographs and illustrations reproduced by kind permission of:

Associated Press: pages 12, 254, 259 (left), 263 (bottom). *Mansell Collection:* 14, 15, 19, 20, 25, 26, 29 (right), 31, 34, 51 (left), 64, 67 (right), 89, 94, 95, 96, 98, 146 (bottom), 153 (top), 171, 179, 231. *Mary Evans:* 29 (left), 32, 35, 51, 56, 67 (left), 71, 80, 85, 91, 93, 100, 102, 108, 112 (top and bottom), 115, 123, 132, 134, 135, 142, 145, 163, 178, 180, 183, 185, 187, 207, 208 (top), 212, 225, 226, 228 (top), 229, 239. *Popperfoto:* 17, 37, 60, 75, 138, 156 (top and bottom), 172, 189, 191, 192 (bottom), 215, 217, 218, 232, 235, 243, 263 (left), 269, 270, 271. *Keystone:* 44, 121, 127, 130, 153, 174, 175, 219 (right), 220, 249, 257, 267, 268. *Radio Times Hulton Picture Library:* 36, 69, 119 (left), 162, 213, 224, 247 (bottom), 262. *Cinema Bookshop:* 233, 236. *Durand-Ruel & Son:* 205, 206. *Women's Home Journal:* 42 (right), 157. *Bettmann Archive:* 149, 165, 219 (left). *Monitor Press:* 208 (bottom). *Muller:* 42 (bottom), 251. *Novosti:* 58, 74, 192 (top). *Harcourt, Brace and Co:* 42 (left). *Bodley Head:* 253. *Haddam Press:* 65, 140. *News Chronicle:* 256. *Clement & Co:* 204. *Madame Tussaud's London:* 202. *London Express:* 103. *Harrap:* 240, 241, 242. *Hutchinson:* 53, 146 (top). *Sport & General:* 261. *National Federation of Women's Institutes:* 275. *Children and Youth Aliyah:* 119 (right).

I INTRODUCTION

This book aims to collect between two covers the names and achievements of as many important women as is possible, well realising that to include every woman who has made a contribution to history is impossible. In any case, our wish is as much to entertain as to inform though it is hoped that a useful reference work results. For it is one of the absurdities of our time that, in the midst of a struggle for women's equality, the immense sum of feminine achievement tends rather to be tucked into the background except in so far as it helps by propaganda to stimulate the case for emancipation. A search for records of feminine achievement inevitably, and immediately, reveals a score of celebrities, but one has to delve deeply through a vast bibliography before the multitudes who have performed usefully and well in relative obscurity come to light. Selection became a major problem. No work such as this can be fully comprehensive: the final choice of characters is ours. It is as objective and international as we can make it.

Above all we put people before events and causes. Primarily we searched for the genuine originators, those who were either first in their field of endeavour or at least first among the ladies. Having established the beginnings of a lasting activity we were then compelled to omit those thousands who appeared after pioneering was complete, and mention only the subsequent outstanding successes. For example, we give prominence to the first female doctors and thereafter only describe those of their sex who have, in our opinion, significantly advanced medical science – though sometimes we indulged ourselves by including incidents out of sheer interest as much as for their importance.

It has been our delight to rediscover many women who were celebrated in their day but who are now largely forgotten. Who could imagine that a book by Mrs E. Ellet written in 1859 could detail over 500 women artists? How many people know that the world's first full novel was written by a Japanese woman? So many dynamic and creative women who dominated and acquired recognition in their time are pushed out of sight as the later generations thrust forward into prominence.

We rated versatility as a governing factor in our selection process. There is, for example, a chorus of distinguished sopranos, but priority goes to one such as Lotte Lehmann who can also claim distinction as an opera producer, a notable teacher and a music critic, as well, incidentally, as being a sculptress, a painter and the author of ten books including a novel. And yet, while emphasising the extraordinary, the creative and the famous, we have mentioned those who carry on everyday jobs and make that humble contribution to life which is essentially feminine in its application to the common good. Some we have selected are quite ordinary people who have hardly caught the public eye. Fame is not an essential qualification of achievement, neither is it a measure; some women who have achieved fame, have, in fact, achieved little else.

It is undeniable that even when women have been most ruthlessly exploited by the opposite sex they have persevered to achieve remarkable attainments by the application of intelligence and determination. Often in the past the scales have been heavily weighed against them. Today things are easier. Women have reached the heights in politics, the arts, in science and commerce. They have also plumbed the depths in crime and intrigue. In liberal societies they will continue to do most things, though proportionally in much larger numbers. The extremists among them will steal the headlines and the moderates play their essential role in causing steady evolution as they all improve their education, gain more experience of men's techniques, and impose their own methods.

A Suffrage Pilgrimage

Fewer women are born live than men, a disparity for which there is no convincing explanation. There are racial variations of the disparity but world-wide, on average, it amounts to 106 men to 100 women. Every continent has an excess of males except Australia, which has equality of sexes, and Europe which has a deficiency of men – a condition brought about by the higher death-rate of males after birth and losses during the Second World War which, in Russia for example, engineers a present surplus of 19 000 000 women out of a 1971 population of 243 000 000. Fecundity is both stimulated and controlled by modern methods to which women have made their contribution, but the greatest number of children produced by a mother in an independently attested case in the days prior to mass contraception is 69 by **Madame Vassilet** (Russian, 1816–72). In 27 confinements she gave birth to 16 pairs of twins, 7 sets of triplets and 4 sets of quadruplets and, what is more, nearly all the offspring reached their majority. Extraordinarily unusual pregnancies there always will be.

The oldest recorded mother was **Ruth Kistler** (American) who, in 1956, gave birth to a daughter when aged 57 years and 129 days.

The largest recorded live multiple birth was of octuplets (four boys and four girls) on 10 March 1967 to **Maria de Sepulveda** (Mexican). All died within 14 hours. Many more multiple births have been recorded, but first survival of the largest complete group is reserved for the sextuplets – three boys and three girls – born to **Sue Rosenkowitz** (South African) on 11 January 1974. A fertility drug, known as 'HCG', apparently caused this multiple birth.

Sandy Allen the world's tallest living woman at more than 7 ft 5 in

The heaviest normal new-born child is credited to **Saadat Cor** (Turkish) with a boy, born on 3 June 1961, who weighed 24 lb 4 oz (11 kg).

The lowest birth weight for a surviving child was the 10 oz (283 g) daughter born to **Marion Chapman** (British) on 5 June 1938.

Once a child has survived its first few days the essential differentiation of dimensions between the sexes start to become apparent, notably in the nature of their size.

In Western civilisations:

Height: Women average 5 ft 3 in (159 cm) compared with 5 ft 7 in (170 cm) for men. The tallest woman, on substantiated evidence, was **Jane Bunford** (British, 1895–1922) who stood at 7 ft 7 in (231 cm), but might have been 7 ft 11 in (241 cm) but for spinal curvature. She also wore her hair to the record length of 8 ft (284 cm). The shortest mature woman on record was **Pauline Husters** (Dutch, 1876–95) who was 24 in (60·9 cm) long at death.

Weight: On average women are lighter than men by 10 to 15 lb (4·5–6·8 kg). Their muscles are smaller (27 lb (12 kg) compared with 47 lb (21 kg) for men), giving a ratio in strength of about 75 to 100 for men. Their hearts are 10 to 15 per cent smaller and brain volume is also lower at about 1300 cc to 1500 cc for men. While these figures, subject to enormous individual variations, account for lower performances by women in physical pursuits it would be unwise to suggest that they cause a correspondingly reduced intellectual capacity. For example, the brain of the male writer Anatole France was among the smallest recorded at 1017 g (2 lb 4 oz).

The heaviest woman ever accurately recorded, was the negress, **Flora Jackson** (American, 1930–65) who once turned the scales at 60 stone (381 kg). The lightest adult human on record was **Lucia Zaratè** (Mexican, 1863–89) who seems to have reached her maximum weight of 13 lb (5 kg 900 g) when aged 20.

Women live longer on average than men, though age at death varies considerably by race and due to the effects of environment. The average life-span of North American and western European people in 1959–61 was 70 years and rising. In Russia, for example, it was stated in 1971 as being 74. The oldest woman, fully authenticated among many uncon-firmed claimants, was **Alice Stevenson** (British, 1861–1973) with 112 years 39 days. In fact, of 28 authenticated national longevity records quoted by the *Guinness Book of Records* in 1974 19 were held by women.

Women have their fair share of the bizarre and sometimes acquire, by immense efforts, physiological attributes such as nature did not intend.

For example:

The smallest waists ever recorded, probably as the result of hard dieting and tight corsetry, came about as the result of a feminine royal decree when the ladies of **Catherine de Médicis's** (French, 1519–89) court reduced to 13 in (33 cm). Yet this was less of a feat than the same measure-ment acquired by **Ethel Granger** (British, b 1905) because women in the 15th century were of smaller stature than those of today.

The longest necks are those of the Padaung or Mayan women of Burma (up to $15\frac{3}{4}$ in (40 cm)) produced by wearing copper coils – the practice serving not only to enhance the ladies' beauty (in the eyes of their men) but as an assurance of fidelity. Unhappily it can cause atrophy of the neck muscles to the extent that, if the coils are removed, asphyxia can result.

Medically, too, women have caused sensations. The most notorious example of medical infection ever recorded was that of **Mary Mallon** (Typhoid Mary) (American, d 1938) who as the carrier of typhoid, was the source of the 1903 outbreak and 1300 cases. She would never suffer control of her activities and tried to go on working with food, often under an assumed name. Eventually she was put into detention from 1915 until her death in 1938.

The longest coma has been endured so far by **Elaine Esposito** (American) who remained unconscious after an appendicectomy on 5 August 1941 and is still in that condition.

Both the highest and lowest temperatures recorded in a living human go to the credit of women. *The Lancet* of 31 October 1970 quoted a high of 112 °F (44·4 °C); **Vickie Davis** (American) after being found unconscious in an unheated room with an air temperature of -24 °F ($-31\cdot1$ °C), registered only 60 °F (15·6 °C) and may actually have been one degree lower.

One can continue indefinitely finding a host of significant and bizarre facts about women. For example, there is the claim by the Soviet Union that, probably, as a nation, it has the highest utilisation of women's talents in the world with 51 per cent women in the labour force, 49 per cent of all university and college students, 71 per cent of all teachers, over 25 per cent of members in the Supreme Soviet (Parliament), one-third of the judges and 91 as winners of the highest military honour, Hero of the Soviet Union: or the calculation by an Italian court in 1973 that the value of a housewife is £2·85 a day.

Statistics can be awfully dull and extremely misleading as to the true measure of performance. The deeds described in the ensuing Sections are more revealing of woman's constructive achievements.

HOMEMAKERS

Mrs Beeton

When Field-Marshal Sir William Slim dedicated his book *Defeat into Victory* 'To Aileen, a soldier's wife, who followed the drum and from mud-walled hut or Government House made a home', he voiced the appreciation of millions of men for their homemakers; the women who shun the limelight in order to provide a happier and more comfortable background to support their mate's struggle for basic survival or great achievement.

As civilisation has advanced so has the demand for more sophisticated living accommodation – and the difference between the 'haves' and the 'have nots' has widened. Can a woman in an impoverished country who spends a day gleaning grains of rice, so enabling her family to eat enough to exist until the next day, be considered an inferior homemaker to the more privileged woman who spends her day baking, rug-making and house-decorating?

The gap between the two situations is epitomised in that famous mis-quotation 'First catch your hare'. This was made by the Marchioness of Londonderry and further publicised by Metternich in 1747, but what **Hannah Glasse** (British, *c* 1720) actually said in her *The Art of Cookery made Plain and Easy*, published in 1747, was 'Take your hare when it is cased.' This book also gave medicaments as well as recipes.

Hannah Glasse was far from being the first woman to write upon specific aspects of homemaking. For example **Ann (or Hannah) Woolley** (English, *c* 1650) who wrote *The Ladies Delight* in 1672 also produced cook-books and pamphlets on the preparation and uses of cosmetics. Probably the first part-works on cookery and domestic science were written by **Isabella Beeton** (British, 1836–65) between 1859 and 1860.

She died after the birth of her fourth son, when she was 29 years old, but her book, consolidated in 1861 by her publisher husband and titled *Household Management*, lived on and was the first to include all aspects of home management.

As women became better educated, so their advice on homemaking acquired a new authority based upon sound scientific knowledge. **Catharine Beecher** (American, 1800–78) was an educationalist (see section on Education) and also a pioneer of home economics with her books *A Treatise on Domestic Economy* (1841) and *The American Woman's Home or Principles of Domestic Science* (1869). The latter presented a plan for running an economical, hygienic and attractive home and stressed the importance of a scientific basis for an intelligent study of the subject. Catharine Beecher herself benefited by being the daughter of a brilliant clergyman, Lyman Beecher, whose large family included numerous brainy children, one of whom was **Isabella Beecher** (American, 1822–1907) who was to be a pioneer of women's legal rights.

However, the foremost leader of home economics was **Ellen Richards** (American, 1842–1911) who received her education at Vassar College, Poughkeepsie, and graduated from the Massachusetts Institute of Technology in 1873 with a B Sc and an MA in chemistry. Not only was she the first woman from that institute to receive a degree in chemistry, she also represented that vitally inquisitive and systematic sort of individual in whom scientific training implants both method and ambition.

Cookery class in England 1885

Ellen Richards maintained that chemistry was for people's well-being and concentrated her studies and teaching as an instructor in sanitary chemistry upon air, water and food. At this time campaigns to improve water-supplies and stamp out the typhoid which ravaged the closely packed industrial cities with their poor or non-existent sewage systems, were on the upsurge. She took 10 000 samples of water to prove cases for re-coursing water-supply and sewage disposal; showing that if the two were so sited that drainage and sewage could seep into the water-supply, that water-supply would become polluted and typhoid fever result. In a report submitted in 1879 she exposed adulterations in different foods with the result that, a few years later, Massachusetts passed its first Food and Drug Act with full reference to her.

By 1880 she was an established authority and widening her horizons. Projects in work study led to proposals to improve home design, and save drudgery. For example, in 1893 the National Household Economic League came into being and at the Chicago World Fair the US Department of Agriculture displayed an analysis of food along with a model kitchen which could be owned by a family in receipt of $500 a year. Ellen Richards was the kitchen's director and its impact made her into a minor celebrity. While continuing with research (in looking for a non-combustible oil at the request of an insurance company she discovered the process of cleaning wool with naphtha and thus became a pioneer of dry-cleaning) she began to establish organisations that would extend the influence of her teaching. As a dietary consultant to hospitals she virtually created the profession of dietician and home economist, and in due course she was to expand her activities into the study of environment by trying to improve the quality of life. It was she who coined the word 'euthenics' and in a lecture on the subject 'Carbon Dioxide as a Measure of the efficiency of Ventilation' gave fundamental meaning to her pursuit of purification. Her chairmanship in 1899 of the first conference on home economics had world-wide consequences, for the only man and the ten women who attended were to lay the foundations of the American Home Economics Association (1908) which, 50 years later, was 20 000 strong. Ellen Richards was its first president.

The final years of her life brought an honorary Doctorate of Science to this dynamic and purposeful personality who managed, as did Florence Nightingale, to persuade governmental committees to act.

Complementary to Ellen Richards's work was that of **Candace Wheeler** (American, 1827–1923) who made vast improvements to the appearance of homes. As a founder-member in 1879 of the Associated Artists she specialised in embroidery and collage for room hangings, helped re-decorate rooms in the White House and won a first prize for wallpaper design that led to the development of traditional American designs to replace the English and French designs then in use. At the Columbia Exposition in 1893 she designed the Women's Building, but in addition she wrote a great deal in propagating her ideas to a large public.

A world-wide influence in advancing home economics also came from **Adelaide Hoodless** (Canadian, 1857–1910) (see section on Clubs and Institutes) who, after introducing the subject into Canadian public schools in 1892, established the Women's Institute in 1897, a movement which has concentrated on improving homecraft skills.

Emily Post

Beautiful gardens to surround the home were encouraged by **Gertrude Jekyll** (British, 1843–1932) who, having received an art school training in London, Paris and Rome, saw gardening as a fine art and used her artistic training in a gardening career. She advocated colour harmonies instead of the old garish colour contrasts when planning a garden, prompting the evolution of the modern garden. In 1907 she wrote a book on flower decoration in the home.

A different means whereby the home could become more attractive was publicised when the gentle art of flower arranging made the Irish-educated **Constance Spry** (British, 1886–1960) a household name in England, America and Australia where she was famed as a lecturer and author. Her flower-arranging business was opened in London when she was 42 and her unorthodox and open-minded choice of 'material' once brought Bond Street's traffic to a halt due to an arrangement of purple cabbages and red roses. As the first person to arrange exotic hot-house and common hedgerow flowers together, she taught her pupils and audiences to see the beauty and possibilities of blending many flowers and foliages previously overlooked; she inspired thousands of women to aim for artistic flower arrangements in their own homes. She also became the joint principal of the Cordon Bleu Cookery School in England.

The correct ways to invite, to entertain and to thank for hospitality in the home were all established by **Emily Post** (American, 1872–1960), the writer on etiquette and proper behaviour. It was her publisher's idea that she write on the subject and her book *Etiquette*, published in 1922, was an immediate success running to 10 editions and 90 printings. The success also led to a syndicated newspaper column to answer queries on etiquette and Emily's own successful radio programme. Manners maketh man and they also 'madeth' Emily rich.

There have been few revolutions in homemaking. As knowledge was made available to women so the scope of home economics evolved. Women educationalists, architects and artists, social reformers and scientists have played their part in raising the standard of living and are still doing so.

4

IN POLITICS AND STATECRAFT

Women have been indirectly involved in the art of statecraft since communities first took root. That they have not played a more prominent part may well have been due to the difficulty of the physically weaker sex imposing itself in days when sheer brute force was the final arbiter of power. In the face of traditional subservience the handful of women who have risen to the peaks of political influence have had to possess quite extraordinary qualities which transcended even the respect due to Divine Right: after all, some male monarchs who claimed the inviolability of Divine Right have been known to go to the chopping-block.

The first recorded women of political power were, however, of royal blood or had married into the royal line. Among the first of distinction was **Hatshepsut** (Egyptian, 18th Dynasty), the only woman Pharaoh in history, who reigned between 1503 and 1482 BC. Whereas previous Egyptian consorts had been content to use indirect influence in government, Hatshepsut, who was married to her half-brother, the Pharaoh, and was a real power behind his throne, ruled openly when he died. She was sufficiently influential to achieve the unprecedented position, for a woman, of exercising supreme power when she took over the government as Regent to her husband's six-year-old son by a concubine.

She surrounded herself with men of outstanding administrative and intellectual abilities, manipulating her council and strengthening her position by marrying the boy to her daughter. Then she renounced the Regency and successfully declared herself Pharaoh. Thus, as a female Pharaoh, she had broken the 2000 year masculine principle of Nilotic government in an extremely conservative civilisation: she also broke the traditional Pharaoh's major occupation of war-making. Her reign of

Queen Hatshepsut

about 20 years was devoted to peace and prosperity of her country, she encouraged agriculture and trade and new sea trade routes were found to replace long, arduous, overland journeys so facilitating the import of exotic and rare merchandise. The arts, especially architecture, flourished under her patronage as the construction of her funerary temple at Deir el-Bahri and the two obelisks at Karnak demonstrated. When she died her constructive administration came to an end, and the usurped half-nephew cum stepson cum son-in-law at last became Pharaoh. He systematically smashed her statues and hid or erased her name from monuments, thus belittling Queen Hatshepsut who, to this day, is less renowned and yet was of greater calibre than the later, much-publicised Cleopatra of Egypt.

Not all women rulers were precursors to peaceful co-existence, however, and high on the roll of those female monarchs who ruled by violence was **Arsinoe** (Greek–Macedonian, *c* 316–270 BC). She married the aged King of Thrace as his third wife and had many domains bestowed upon her. She is said to have persuaded her husband to execute his son and heir on a false charge in order to further her ambitions for her own three sons. Later, when her husband had been killed in battle and Arsinoe had been tricked into another marriage, she escaped to Egypt where her brother, Ptolemy II, a weaker character than her, reigned with his wife, also called Arsinoe. This wife was soon ousted by her and she married her own brother to become Arsinoe II.

From then on Arsinoe II exerted even greater influence in this kingdom than she had in Thrace, being in every way the dominant partner in joint rule. She was not only responsible for many of Egypt's military and political successes, but her importance was shown by her head being figured on the coinage and her possession of a throne-name. No other queen in the Hellenistic world received so many honours. She encouraged people to worship her as a Goddess, a cult that became widespread in Egypt and overseas, overshadowing her husband's image.

Nearly 300 years later Egypt was to have another queen who, although not beautiful, practised much more expertly the art of self-display and fascination. She was **Cleopatra VII** (Greek-Macedonian, 69–30 BC), an unscrupulous, well-educated woman who channelled all the charm, energy and intelligence she could muster to further her two ambitions. One was to recover all the territories round Egypt that had once belonged to her ancestors, so reviving the Greater Egypt, and the other to personally become a great power in the Roman world.

It was a measure of her capability that she recognised potential greatness when she saw it, for she captivated Julius Caesar when he conquered Egypt in 47 and was settled by him in Rome where she produced a son, said to be his. In 44 Caesar was murdered and three years later she was summoned to Tarsus, in Asia Minor, to be questioned by Mark Antony on charges that she had given support to the war effort of the men who had murdered him. She arrived bejewelled and glamorised, surrounded by a lavish display of wealth and gifts, well knowing that with Caesar dead, Mark Antony was now the most powerful man in the Roman world. Her 'show business' spectacle was well timed, for she kept him waiting in anticipation and then arrived unheralded and with dramatic impact. She captivated Antony and they spent the winter together at Alexandria.

Cleopatra VII

It must not be supposed, however, that he was immediately enslaved by her, for he had as much to gain from an alliance with her as she with him, because Egypt was a good supply base and shipbuilding country. After the winter he went away for three years leaving her to produce their twin children while he married Octavia, sister of Octavian, an influential Roman who later became Augustus Caesar.

In 37 Antony returned to Cleopatra and they underwent a form of marriage recognised in Egypt but not Rome. He accorded her more power than was, for a Roman, ordinarily the case: their heads appeared jointly on Antony's Roman coins and he proclaimed her 'Queen of Kings' over the Eastern Empire. So the generals interpreted such acts as the alienation of territories which rightly belonged to Rome.

When a war between Octavian and Antony became inevitable it was due to Cleopatra's foresight that Antony made preparations: she supplied a great sum of money and 200 ships to aid him. Many of his supporters resented her presence at the military headquarters at Ephesus, thinking she made Antony appear nothing more than a foreign woman's paramour. But she was obstinate and her will prevailed. This probably cost her the battle for many leading supporters, among them senators and foreign kings, deserted and went over to the other side, taking with them valuable information. The outcome was a foregone conclusion. Antony's ships were destroyed while he and Cleopatra escaped in her fleet.

As Octavian's force converged on Egypt Antony committed suicide and Cleopatra, after meeting Octavian privately, decided upon the same fate. She chose a snake bite, the snake being the minister of the sun god of the country's religion and died, dressed in full regalia, with the typical superb showmanship with which she had lived.

As Roman civilisation faded and the barbarians started to move in from the north and east, woman's hold upon power demanded even greater cunning and ferocity than before. To take the most celebrated examples:

Amalasuntha (Italian, 498–535) who, on her young son's accession to the throne of the Ostrogoths in Rome in 526, became Regent. Intelligent and well educated herself, she insisted on giving her son a more academic and civilised education than was usual for Ostrogoths to receive. This, plus her leanings towards the later Roman capital at Byzantium (Istanbul) and her desire to stay on good terms with both Rome and the Church, brought about plotting by her people. Ruthlessly she ordered the deaths of three of her nobles. Her son's early death, however, brought an end to her reign: she was exiled, then murdered.

Fredegund (French, d 597), the former mistress of the Frankish King, Chilperic I, became his consort by first persuading him to give up one wife and later to order the murder of his second wife, the sister of another royal lady called:

Brunhilda (French, d 613). So was generated a lifetime of hatred between Fredegund and Brunhilda who were both renowned for their violence. Fredegund became a legend for her countless cruelties and several assassinations, though there is no proof it was she who arranged for the disposal of Chilperic in 584. She rather surprisingly died of natural causes. Brunhilda, however, who had fought against Fredegund and her successors ceaselessly but with a singular lack of success, was finally captured when her army would no longer give battle. For three days she was tortured and then dragged to death tied to a horse's tail.

Irene (Greek, 752–803), a beautiful and unscrupulous Athenian married Leo IV of Byzantium and later became an autocratic Regent during her son's minority. She gave rein to her ambition of restoring the use of icons in the Orthodox Church, in supporting monasteries and then in attempting to hold on to government after her son's maturity. She was banished from 790 to 792, but five years after her return successfully conspired to have her son deposed and, at her orders, blinded. She ruled as 'Emperor' until 802, when she was exiled by a clique of politicians and generals to Lesbos and allowed to die in peace, if not contentment.

Olga (Russian, d 969), widow of Prince Igor and Regent of Kiev from 945 to 964 had the distinction, by adopting the Greek Orthodox faith herself, of introducing Christianity to Russia. She had to fight hard to retain the Regency after her husband was killed and her counter-measures were, by necessity, ruthless, though backed up by sound administration. She has, too, the distinction of becoming the first Russian saint of the Orthodox Church.

The Far East also saw its female rulers, though in Japan only as a front behind whom others wielded power. Such was the case when **Suiko** (Japanese) reigned from 593 to 628 as the earliest known Japanese Empress. She was put on the throne by the all-powerful Sogo family while the real man in power, Shotoku Taishi, carried out sweeping reforms. This was not true in China, however, when the only woman Emperor gained power by her own exertions. At 14 **Wu Chao** (Chinese, 624–705) became a fifth-grade concubine to the Emperor. Luckily for her his heir fell in love with her and after the Emperor's death rescued her from a convent where all the late Emperor's concubines were supposed to end their days. Installed by the new Emperor as his second-grade concubine she soon bore him a son and became a threat to both his son-less wife and his favourite concubine (who had borne a son). These two women conspired together, but Wu Chao succeeded in getting them imprisoned and, later, murdered. Now aged 31 years she achieved, by manœuvre and by bribing officials, in becoming Empress – and promptly had the late concubine's son sent away.

In 660 the Emperor, a person mentally inferior to his intelligent Empress, suffered a paralytic illness and from then on for the next 45 years she was virtual ruler of China, ruthlessly removing or executing anyone who threatened her. She raised the intellectual level of the bureaucracy and became a patron of literature. All religions were given free rein and, under Wu Chao's planning, Korea was conquered and annexed by China.

In 683 the Emperor died and after seven years of complex political juggling she was proclaimed Emperor – Wu Hou Huang-ti, Holy and Divine. Now the arts really flourished and pagodas and temples sprang up. She collected pottery, sculptures and paintings and is reported to have been presented with an accurate clock. Buddhist hospitals and dispensaries were founded and the mentally ill provided for. In 701 Wu Chao created a lay organisation to administer to the sick through State hospitals. She reformed and strengthened the Government by loosening the old aristocratic families' control and women enjoyed greater freedom than before or after her reign. So, in her 50 years' rule over the vast Chinese Empire, Wu Chao prepared the way for the supreme T'ang Dynasty, famed for its culture.

Throughout the medieval period chivalry did nothing to strengthen women's rights, in fact quite the opposite. The fluctuations of women's political power epitomised the instability of the age. Many queens played crucial parts, but only a few became prominent by their own achievements. One such queen was **Eleanor of Aquitaine** (French, *c* 1122–1204) who attained immortality as a beautiful and passionate woman. She felt compelled to end her marriage to Louis VII of France on grounds of consanguinity and in the same year, 1152, married Henry II of England. A politician to the bone, she demonstrated her independence by supporting the remaining two sons of their marriage in a rebellion in France against their father. Then, after Henry's death, she supported her son Richard Cœur de Lion against her younger son, John, who had been Henry's favourite. Nevertheless, when Richard was killed in 1199, Eleanor decisively supported John in his claim to Anjou and Aquitaine against her grandson Arthur of Brittany (whose father had been her deceased son, Geoffrey). When Arthur joined in a general war against John, she held Mirabeau, near Poitiers, in the face of his attack (despite the fact that she was then aged about 80) until John came to her relief and captured him.

Warring and intrigue may make dramatic reading but steady constructive rule is of infinitely greater benefit to a country. And such was the rule of **Margaret** (Danish, 1353–1412), daughter of King Valdemar IV of Denmark, who was married when aged ten to Haakon VI of Norway. On the death of her father and her husband in 1375 and 1380 respectively she ruled both kingdoms as Regent for her young son Olaf. But seven years later Olaf also died and in 1388 she was chosen as 'sovereign lady and ruler' of the two countries.

Neighbouring Sweden was in a mutinous state under an unpopular king and its nobles accepted all Margaret's conditions to extend her realm to encompass it. She kept her promise to the three countries to provide them with her nearest male kinsman as king and chose her infant cousin, remaining as Regent. Even after he was declared of age in 1401 she continued as the real ruler, maintaining for appearance a Council of State taken from the three realms.

Under her supreme reign the territories displayed a diplomatic neutrality in foreign politics. She retrieved by purchase Gotland and Schleswig, previously lost to Denmark and, by decree, estates in Denmark and Sweden alienated from the Crown since 1360. She also reformed Danish currency.

A very different namesake, one almost entirely destructive in her achievements, was **Margaret of Anjou** (French, 1429–82), the Queen of Henry VI of England, who was a vigorous woman of aggressive temperament and immense tactlessness in times leading up to and during civil war. Hampered by an insane husband, she passionately defended the succession of her son in the struggle between York and Lancaster until he was killed at the Battle of Tewkesbury in 1471. She was seemingly inexhaustible both in her ability to raise armies, to create enemies and to liquidate her opponents when they fell into her hands. Her actions were partly responsible for starting, for raising the intensity of and also prolonging, the Wars of the Roses, and so it is all the more remarkable that, when captured, she was not herself executed but, instead, returned to France for a ransom.

John Knox's 'monstrous regiment of women' played their full part in launching the Renaissance throughout Europe. Italian women frequently were the reason for, as well as the resolvers of, political confrontations. Marriages of convenience (sometimes brother to sister) might bring about a typical settlement of family alliances and the history of the Borgia family epitomises the system – but the women themselves could rise to heights of government if their men happened to be weak or the circumstances demanded. **Isabella d'Este** was renowned for creating the first *salon* devoted to literature and the arts (see section on Mistresses, Courtesans and Salonnières), but she also ruled as Regent of Mantua.

Anne of France (French, 1461–1522), the eldest daughter of Louis VI, had the difficult job, as Regent after her strong father's death, of neutralising those he had offended during his lifetime. With the help of her Bourbon husband and a judicious mixture of astute give and take, talk and war, she preserved what Louis had created until his son, Charles VIII, came of age. She was then faced with the problem of defending the Bourbon estates against the designs of Charles's wife, **Anne of**

Brittany (French, 1477–1514). These, the two most sophisticated politicians of their day, fought for power regardless of offending the King's authority – and in the end reached a sort of impasse from which a new unity in France gradually emerged. There began, as the Dark Ages gave way to enlightenment, a period of petticoat domination of French affairs. **Louise of Savoy** (French, 1476–1531) was twice Regent during the reign of Louis XII and governed well: it was she who, in 1529, during the reign of her son, Francis I, negotiated the 'Ladies' Peace' between France and the Netherlands with **Margaret of Austria** (Austrian, 1480–1530). And it was Louise's daughter, **Margaret of Angoulème** (French, 1492–1549), who was to marry Henry II of Navarre in 1527 and, as his Queen, assert a moderating influence when Lutheranism was beginning to cause one of the greatest religious upheavals of all time.

Catherine de Médicis (Italian, 1519–89), in search of religious peace, achieved by vaccillation precisely the opposite of what she intended. She had married the future Henry II in 1533 but initially was virtually excluded from politics by Henry's mistress **Diane de Poitiers** (French, 1499–1566) (see section on Mistresses, Courtesans and Salonnières). Although Henry's senior by 20 years Diane absorbed the King's attention until his death in 1559 when Catherine, a coarse and unattractive woman of great zest, became Regent and was increasingly engrossed by the complex struggles for power surrounding the throne, a struggle involving rival family groups, the bitter Catholic and Protestant factions and her own utter determination to secure her sons' accessions. She dealt with the religious factions by alternating displays of conciliation and force. However, when the pressure became too great it was she who ordered the appalling Massacre of St Bartholomew's Day in 1572. This murder of hundreds of Protestants was a decisive factor in an already explosive situation which was finally to culminate in the Wars of Religion. Eventually Catherine achieved the accession of all three of her surviving sons but in an age of mounting violence, fanned by her own actions.

Although in England none of Henry VIII's six wives were of personal political importance, his eldest daughter became so as **Mary I** (English 1516–58). For, by her insistence on marrying Philip of Spain, she drew England into the Spanish war against France and, when attempting to restore Catholicism to England, fanatically executed 300 equally fanatical Protestants, stirring up further antagonism among her people. So it was with relief and enthusiasm that, upon her death, most English people welcomed her half-sister and successor, **Elizabeth I** (English, 1533–1603) to the throne. For, although Elizabeth had attended Mass, as was politically necessary in her precarious first 25 years of life before her accession, she was a Protestant. And, because of necessity she had so tactfully and carefully taken no sides and kept her own counsel, no one knew what to expect of the new Queen.

At her coronation this reddish haired, tall, regal figure with an air of vitality captivated and held the onlooker's attention as well as any actress and immediately gained popular support. But it did not end there, for she was a self-reliant and intelligent politician who made sure no man, nor council of men, would be her master. So she reigned for 45 years,

Elizabeth I

served devotedly by her councillors (whom she generally consulted individually and encouraged to vie for her favour, so avoiding an amalgam by them) and developed the much-weakened England she had inherited into a country to be reckoned with. According to her opponent, Pope Sixtus V, 'She is a great woman; and were she only Catholic she would be without her match. . . . Just look how well she governs; she is only a woman, only mistress of half an island, and yet she makes herself feared by Spain, by France, by the Emperor, by all.'

At home Protestantism was restored though not allowed to become politically all powerful, while action against Catholics was not vigorously enforced unless treason was proved, for Elizabeth was not dogmatic over religion. In fact she is known to have been bored with sermons and often supposedly listened to them behind closed windows of an alcove while actually carrying on her business instead. So she played down the political importance of differing religions and many Catholics came to feel they could pay allegiance to her, their Protestant Queen, as well as to Rome without a clash of conscience.

Trade flourished, with cloth as the largest single export. Voyages of discovery were undertaken and joint-stock companies set up to find more markets for this commodity with exotic treasures as return cargo. Profit – and a big one – was the motive. The shareholders, merchants and manufacturing middle classes grew prosperous. Their affluence spread and England became a wealthy nation.

Her knowledge of languages enabled Elizabeth to deal personally with foreign envoys and she showed herself an astute statesman. When war with Spain became unavoidable she proved an inspiring leader, too, and was at times clearer sighted as to which way success lay than her military and naval advisers. Spain was beaten. England, which had been rich enough to weather the war, even though there followed a period of disillusionment and high taxation, was soon embarked upon many years of renewed prosperity. However, Elizabeth was growing old. With her choice of James of Scotland as her successor she went some way to uniting Scotland with England at her death.

From Sweden was to come one of the most remarkable monarchs ever to reign. She was **Christina** (Swedish, 1626–89), the daughter and heir

Christina of Sweden

CRISTINA REGINA SVECIÆ, ETC.

of an illustrious father, Gustavus II Adolphus, who was killed when she was only six. A prodigy, and courageously strong willed, she developed immense curiosity and intellectual ability both in statecraft and the arts, besides having an insatiable desire for learning and sheer hard work – to the exhaustion of those who surrounded her. Known as the 'Minerva of the North', she was educated as a prince, was not physically attractive (since her face was pockmarked and she had a hump on her right shoulder) and liked to dress in men's clothing. This stickler for protocol and truthfulness was an unmitigated, bad-tempered liar and, like so many brilliant people, unstable and liable to exaggerated swings of policy. She was also immensely extravagant.

Suddenly, at the age of 27, having been secretly converted to Catholicism which was forbidden in Sweden, she announced her abdication and moved, lock, stock and barrel, to Rome where she proceeded to indulge all her extra-mural talents, including intrigue, in the affairs of the Church and other countries. Her achievements were formidable and included:

● The ability to attend State council meetings when only 14.
● Making it possible, at a time of great financial difficulty at the end of the Thirty Years War, for Sweden's education, industry and trade to expand, and for the nation's first newspaper to be published in 1645.
● The protection of paintings from destruction in war and the assembling of the largest collection of Venetian paintings and sculpture at her palace in Rome – part of it acquired by dubious means.
● The discovery of Scarlatti and his music which involved starting the first public opera-house in Rome. Her choir master was Corelli.
● Founding the Arcadia Academy and the collection of a superb library, which is now lodged in the Vatican.

For the next 100 years the Western world saw a succession of queens and politically motivated women whose achievements pall to mediocrity by comparison but who, taken in aggregate, represent a period in which women dominated the councils of Europe:

Marie Anne Ursins (French, 1642–1722) helped arrange the marriage of Philip V of Spain to **María Luisa of Savoy** (Italian, d 1714) and, in so doing, obtained strong influence over the new Queen who, for her part, ruled the weak Philip. This was at the time of the War of Spanish Succession. Marie Ursins acted in concert, though not always in agreement, with Louis XIV of France and from 1701 to 1714 virtually dictated Spanish affairs. When María Luisa died in 1714, Marie Ursins promptly arranged a marriage between Philip and **Isabel de Farnesio** (Italian, 1692–1766), but this was a miscalculation since, warned in advance of her power, Isabel purposely picked a quarrel at their first meeting and dismissed her, taking over the reins of government herself. For the next 30 years she engaged in fostering her sons' fortunes to the detriment of the nation.

Anne (English, 1665–1714), Queen of England, also had her problems with feminine favourites. Even if the dominance of the Queen by her close friend **Sarah Jennings** (English, 1660–1744), the wife of John

Churchill, who was to become Duke of Marlborough and Britain's greatest general, was to the benefit of Sidney Godolphin's and Marlborough's policy in waging the War of the Spanish Succession, she was really only the tool of these men just as Sarah's usurper, **Abigail Masham** (English, d. 1734) was the tool of the anti-war party. Yet these three women formed a joint contribution to the petticoat government of a volatile kind which could never be ignored.

Sophia (Russian, 1657–1704), the sixth child of Tsar Alexis, governed Russia as Regent from 1682 to 1689 during her half-brother's minority. In holding the throne for the man who, as Peter the Great, was to set Russia on a fresh course, she performed good service in turbulent times. **Catherine I** (Russian, 1684–1727) and **Anna Ivanovna** (Russian, 1694–1740) also each ruled Russia on their own for short periods but with little or no impact. In 1741, in the aftermath of the failure of Anna Ivanovna as Empress, **Elizabeth Petrovna** (Russian, 1709–62) was thrust upon the throne. The *coup d'état* which brought her to power was not entirely of her own making, but her dynamic performance of the role allotted to her, in haranguing the crowd and leading the soldiers, showed beyond doubt that she was a true daughter of Peter the Great. Although she leaned heavily upon her Chancellor, Aleksei Bestuzhev-Ryumin, who ended the war with Sweden and the War of the Austrian Succession and who later was partly responsible, by miscalculation, for the beginning of the Seven Years War, it was Elizabeth's single-minded dislike and fear of Frederick the Great of Prussia which largely made the latter war possible. She also, despite declining health, played the vital role in maintaining the alliance of Russia, France and Austria. At that time the latter country also had a woman ruler, **Maria Theresa** (Austrian, 1717–80), Archduchess of Austria and, as the wife of Francis I, Queen of Hungary and Bohemia after 1740.

Maria Theresa had to face a combined attack by Prussia, Bavaria and France during the War of the Austrian Succession and, despite lack of help from her husband and ministers and the subsequent loss of Silesia, she fought back at all times. After the war she began the reorganisation of her country's administration and army, combined Bohemia with Austria, formed the defensive treaty with Elizabeth of Russia (mentioned above) in 1746 and allowed her minister, Wenzel Kaunitz, to negotiate an alliance with an old enemy, France. The Seven Years War, which began in 1756, went against Austria and was irrevocably lost when Russia withdrew. Silesia was not recovered. Maria Theresa's husband died in 1765 and thereafter she ruled jointly with her son, Joseph II. Her main concern became the improvement of her people's lot, particularly the easing of the serf's life. She concentrated upon education (making primary education compulsory and encouraging secondary and university level), social reform and the stimulation of the Austrian economy, to good effect.

Catherine II (German, 1729–96) emulated the Empress Elizabeth in 1762 by taking power in Russia through a *coup d'état* in which she was prominently assisted by the Princess **Ekaterina Dashkova** (Russian, 1744–1810) whose sister would have come to power if Catherine had been deposed. (Ekaterina Dashkova was to achieve a success when, in 1783, she became the founder and first President of the Russian Academy.)

Maria Theresa and *Catherine II*

Catherine had moved to Russia in 1744 for an arranged marriage with the future Peter III, a mentally and physically subnormal man, and ousted him from power a few months after his succession. As a usurper, dependent upon the aristocracy who supported her and conscious of her precarious position as a foreigner with no lineal claim to the throne, Catherine had to trim her most ambitious plans for Russia to fit the circumstances. So, despite an innate liberalism fed by deep-reaching and high intelligence, a tendency towards republicanism and leanings towards religious toleration, she was compelled to act as a despot, suppressing serfs and rebels with a heavy hand while withholding the radical reformation of law she had evolved after much study. Restricted by the rules of political 'possibility', she was very much dependent upon the goodwill of her closest advisers and ministers, and helped assure their loyalty by making many of them her lovers – but none her master. It was perhaps fortunate that she may have been sterile, although she owned to one son born in 1753 who certainly looked like her husband.

Catherine firmly believed that all her plans for progress were dependent on education. She founded medical schools and, in 1764, the first girls-only school in Russia. She also wrote innumerable letters, some plays and an uncompleted history of Russia, often working 15 hours a day. When the French Revolution began the European swing towards republicanism, she busily strengthened the monarchy and aristocracy of Russia and exacted her sternest repressions. All along her foreign policy was one of expansion, in line with the practice adopted by most monarchies that, to do otherwise, was retrograde. As a result she twice brought Russia into war with Turkey, gaining the Crimea and access to the Black Sea, and annexed large parts of Poland. She was a charming woman who used her charm to flatter and pick the brains of such thinkers as Voltaire and Diderot and had the insight to choose the most able advisers.

On the day of her death from apoplexy on 17 November 1796, Napoleon Bonaparte completed his victory at Arcola in Italy. Within a few years, as First Consul of France, he would be embarked upon a scheme of military conquest and judicial reform while cancelling the rights granted to women at the commencement of the Revolution. Many women were to become deeply involved in the Revolution in France. From queens to the market women, who later marched on Versailles and were to sit at the steps of the guillotine, many thought they recognised their opportunity for equality. But only two personally actuated the vital decisions of the Revolution – both through marriage.

The first, **Marie–Antoinette** (Austrian, 1755–93), was married to Louis XVI as a means to consolidate Franco-Austrian political ties. A warm-hearted, pleasure-loving woman she found her dull husband unsatisfactory. Thus began her search for entertainment – though not at

Marie–Antoinette
by *Marie–Louise Vigée–le Brun*

such a cost as to place a fatal burden upon the national exchequer as is sometimes suggested. After the fall of the Bastille and in the face of Louis's indecision, it was Marie-Antoinette who took the initiative and who was largely responsible for arranging the abortive escape of the Royal Family.

Inevitably her subsequent role in the Revolution was as a conspirator in league with counter-revolutionary forces, both internally and with the Austrian Ambassador. She was regarded as the most potent threat to the Republican cause and, indeed, it was Marie-Antoinette who rejected a constitutional monarchy after Louis had agreed it. When the mob invaded the Tuileries in August 1792 it was the Queen more than the King they most wished to see in prison. She was guillotined nine months after the King.

Manon Roland

The other woman whose actions had positive effect on the French Revolution was **Manon Roland** (French, 1754–93), a cool-headed, intelligent woman of patriotic zeal and great forcefulness. She, with her husband, welcomed the Revolution and took a leading part in the formation of the right-wing Gironde Party, made up of educated professional and middle-class men who wanted political equality for all, but desired ability to be favoured and wealth protected. This party gained 136 seats in the Legislative Assembly and Manon Roland's husband was made Minister of the Interior. However, he was largely dominated by her, and she wrote his letters and speeches.

The Gironde Party secured a war against Austria, thinking the Austrians would join them in revolution. But the French forces were rebuffed, French nationalistic feelings were renewed and counter-revolutionary forces from the working population appeared. Manon Roland's husband sent a request (drafted by her) to the King asking him to withdraw his veto on the formation of a national guard to protect the new administration; it did not succeed. The counter-revolutionaries gained in force and were mob ruled. They forced an entry into the Tuileries and captured the Royal Family. From then on violence and terror reigned. Manon Roland's husband was accused of favouring the King and resigned, she was arrested and followed the Royal Family to the guillotine. She is renowned for her bravery and the words 'Oh Liberty! Oh Liberty! What crimes are committed in your name', which she is said to have uttered as she journeyed in the tumbril. Of these two women Manon Roland was the trend-setter, the first of many such politically and idealistically committed women to follow.

It was generally in the Christian nations that women attained viable political power. Muslims virtually banned their participation as did most of the Far Eastern religions. Yet, political power was not entirely restricted to Western woman. Where the Coptic Church operated in Ethiopia, notably in Gondar, some women governed. There was, for example, **Mentuab**, the Regent from 1730 to 1760 and, later, **Menen**, an ambitious Muslim girl turned Christian who became Empress of Gondar in the mid 19th century. Yet not even Menen nor her able son, Ali, could win the imperial crown of Ethiopia; their Muslim connections forbade that. Incidentally, the Koran rules that women must be treated with justice and that, because they hold a man's honour, they must be guarded!

As the pace of political and industrial revolution increased in parallel with improved communication systems, centralised bureaucracies began to appear with legislative powers that were strengthened in favour of the males who staffed the ministries and made the laws. Women were largely deprived of what little equal opportunities for education they already possessed and, therefore, lost even more of their competitive position in a world of growing technology, where specialised education became essential. Hence a constriction was applied to women's political growth. They hardly realised that their privileges were being removed by restrictive practices which favoured men in nearly all the professions (see in particular the section dealing with the Fight for Equality).

Organisations with political, suffrage and social connotations started to appear under female motivation, heralding the beginning of organised co-operation by women. One woman to be the driving force of such an organisation was **Frances Willard** (American, 1839–98), who started as a teacher in 1859, became President of Evanston College for Ladies in 1871 (and Dean of Women when it merged with Northwestern University two years later) and then was Secretary of the US National Woman's Christian Temperance Union from 1874 until she became its President in 1879. She organised and became President of the World's Woman's Christian Temperance Union in 1883. These organisations, and several others in which she became involved, had suffrage aims. Not only was Frances Willard an excellent speaker and an inveterate lobbyist, but she was also among the first members, as one might expect, of the Prohibition Party and later the Populist Party which arose out of the Industrial Conference of 1892. Prohibition and the demand for the vote went together in the USA. In due course they led to changes in the Constitution which, for both good and evil, had profound political consequences. In a way women became the conscience of America.

Frances Willard

Other women bypassed the necessarily slow, democratic methods of political action and opted for more direct means of achieving their aim. There were times when the dividing-line between political action and, by the classification of law, crime, was often narrow (see the section on Crime for a description of the assassination of Tsar Alexander II in 1881). However, it must be remembered that in the 'Will of the People' organisation were women who have been called 'the apotheosis of emancipated Russian womanhood' – such as:

Vera Figner (Russian, 1852–42) who went to Zürich University in 1872 to study medicine because there were no such facilities for women in Russia at that time. Here she joined a group of Russian women, the Frichi Circle, who, in their discussions, contemplated a Socialist revolution. At first she thought persuasion a better way than violence to achieve change in Russia, but the peasants were slow to react to persuasion. She later adopted a policy of force during the wave of Government repression and took a part in the political murders which culminated, in 1881, in the assassination of Alexander II. Two years later, while still organising terrorist activities, she was arrested and spent the next 20 years in solitary confinement. The effort by **Vera Zasulich** (Russian, 1851–1919) to kill General Trepov, the Governor of St Petersburg, as her protest against his treatment of revolutionaries and her subsequent acquittal in a celebrated trial by jury, set in motion a feeling of popular support for her action.

The opposite view to that of the revolutionaries was taken by **Bertha von Suttner** (Austrian, 1843–1914) who worked through literature for a *détente* in world politics. She was the daughter of Field-Marshal von Kinsky, well educated and perceptive. As a young girl she was driven to an obsession with pacifism by the horrors of war from the Crimea and Piedmont, in 1859, and her own sufferings from war when the Prussians invaded her homeland in 1864. In 1876, as secretary-housekeeper to Alfred Nobel, the armament-manufacturer, she worked with this man who was a sponsor of both war and peace. There is a theory that she influenced him in his decision to institute the Nobel Peace Prize. The impact upon the world of her anti-war book *Die Waffen nieder!* (Lay Down Your Arms), written in 1889 and translated into many languages, was positive: it became second only in sales to the anti-slavery book, *Uncle Tom's Cabin* by **Harriet Beecher Stowe**. *Die Waffen nieder!* is a study of the effects of war upon an Austrian woman whose first husband is killed in the Piedmont War of 1859 and whose second husband takes part in the wars of 1864, 1866 and, finally, the Franco-Prussian War of 1870, in which he is arrested and shot on suspicion of being a Prussian spy.

Bertha von Suttner founded the Austrian Peace Organisation in 1891 and was editor of a peace journal, *Die Waffen nieder!* from 1892 until 1899, when she published her definitive work *Das Maschinenzeitalter* (The Machine Age). In 1905 she became the first woman to be awarded the Nobel Peace Prize. Her belief was that, 'First the world must be released from the threat of world war and the armaments race, then the other social problems can be solved more easily and more justly.' She died on 21 June 1914, ironically just a week before the assassination at Sarajevo of Franz Ferdinand, and his wife Sophie acted as the trigger for the First World War.

The last ruling Empress of China was one of the most powerful yet least productive of all. She was the Dowager Empress **Tz'u hsi** (Chinese, 1835–1908), a Manchu who was first called Yehonala and sent, with 27 other girls, as a concubine to the court of the Emperor Hsien Feng. She became favourite and the birth of a boy in 1856, which she claimed as hers, secured her position. Even though still in her early twenties she offered advice on State affairs, and when the Emperor died in 1861 the infant T'ung-chih, her claimed son, became Emperor. From then on her dominant personality overrode that of the late Emperor's widow and she ruled as Regent. T'ung-chih died when only 19 years and without leaving an heir – there is evidence to suggest Tz'u hsi murdered him. Choosing her sister's son to be the new Emperor Te-tsung, she ruled China herself with a rod of iron until her death.

However, this iron rule could not entirely suppress the unrest felt throughout rural China: although the T'ai P'ing Rebellion which had begun in 1851 was eventually suppressed in 1864, the discontent remained and fermented. Only once, for a short spell, did she appear to relinquish the reins of power. That was in 1889 when she decided to rebuild the Peking Summer Palace and, for this purpose, purloined money which had been allotted to rebuild the fleet at a time when the

大清國當今慈禧端佑康頤昭豫莊誠壽恭欽獻崇熙聖母皇太后

Tz'u hsi

foreign threat, above all that of Japan, was increasing. War with Japan, in 1895, ended in China's defeat. Despite attempts by enlightened advisers to reform the government, Tz'u hsi would have none of it and encouraged xenophobia to distract attention from its failures, thus drifting into the Boxer Uprising of 1900 with its attacks upon foreign legations and consequent quelling by foreign troops.

Her firm grip upon government, upon maintaining the old régime, and stubbornly refusing evolutionary change within her country, left China as a breeding-ground for Communist revolution.

The last Empress of Russia, **Alexandra** (German, 1872–1918), was also a disaster for her country in that her domination of her husband, Nicholas II, contributed to the undermining of the Royal House. Her own reliance upon the unscrupulous monk Rasputin, as the one person she thought could cure her son's haemophilia, was bitterly resented. As Russia's fortunes declined in the First World War, Alexandra persuaded Nicholas to dismiss the Commander-in-Chief and take personal command at the front. She then ruled at home under Rasputin's spell, sacking the most able ministers and ruining the Government's credit at home and abroad. After Rasputin had been murdered in December 1916, Nicholas and Alexandra tried to make contact with him at seances. Believing implicitly in their autocratic rule by Divine Right, neither would listen to reason and so, quite inevitably, in March 1917 the Russian Revolution began and swept the monarchy from power. In due course Alexandra found herself in detention at Ekaterinburg, where she and her family were executed.

Thousands of women took part in the Russian Revolution and all the other revolutions world-wide which grew from it. Very few of them played a dominant part and yet, from out of Russia almost at a stroke, emerged their greatest recognition and actuation of equality that had ever appeared. At first their outstanding successes were largely in the field of war (see section on Women at War) and in politics. The first Russian female Cabinet Minister and, later, the first female foreign Ambassador, was **Aleksandra Kollontai** (Russian, 1872–1952), the daughter of an army general who became a member of the Social-Democratic Party. After the uprisings of the mid 1900s she left Russia and did not return until the Revolution began. Then she joined the Communist Party, becoming commissar for Public Welfare and gaining enough influence for Lenin to save her from execution after an indiscreet affair with a Russian seaman led to charges against her for dereliction of duty. In 1922 she was sent to the Commissariat for Foreign Affairs and, in 1923, became Minister in Norway for 2 years. After a brief spell as Minister in Mexico, she returned, in 1927 as Minister to Norway for another 3 years, then as Minister to Sweden for 15 years, when she received the rank of Ambassador. It was she who negotiated an end to the Soviet-Finnish War in 1944.

Of the most virulent female revolutionaries two especially are worthy of mention:

Rosa Luxemburg

Rosa Luxemburg (Polish, 1870?–1919) was a student of natural sciences and political economy. On leaving school she became involved in revolutionary politics, and by the age of 19 was already on the run from her home country. Her aims were not simply the restitution of Polish independence, but the far higher attainment of an international Socialism linked with the elimination of the Russian monarchy. By a marriage of convenience in 1898 she took German citizenship and, in that country, became involved with the Socialist Party. Soon, by her lucid definition of Marxist ideals, she became a member of their hierarchy and in close touch with the important revolutionary personalities of Europe, including Lenin, Trotsky and **Clara Zetkin** (German, 1857–1933). In 1905, when a Russian Revolution broke out and was crushed, Rosa Luxemburg openly admitted that bloodshed was inevitable in achieving her aims. She collided with the moderates of the party, at one time remarking that she and Clara Zetkin were 'the last of its men'. In 1914 she opposed war on the grounds that fighting fellow Socialists in other countries was abhorrent. When the Socialists supported the German Government in the war effort, Rosa Luxemburg and

Clara Zetkin formed the Spartacist League. Together, quite fearlessly, they spoke out – and were sent to prison. There Rosa Luxemburg wrote political tracts and articles which were smuggled out and distributed. The moment the Revolution broke out in Germany in November 1918, she was released and proceeded to virtually convert her Spartacists into the Communist Party, drafting its initial programme. On 15 January 1919, however, after the so-called 'Spartacist Rebellion' was suppressed, she was murdered by the anti-Communist Freikorps.

Clara Zetkin was luckier than Rosa Luxemburg in that she survived to implement some of the things for which they had struggled. She was one of the first students of the Leipzig Teachers' College for Women and married a Russian Socialist Revolutionary. A good organiser, she became the first editor of a Socialist women's paper called *Gleichheit* (Equality) and co-founder not only of the Spartacist League but, in 1907, of the International Socialist Women's Congress when many such women's organisations were blossoming. In 1915 she arranged the first international women's anti-war conference in Switzerland and for this was sent to gaol in Germany. But in 1919 she became an important member of the German Communist Party's Central Committee, after Rosa Luxemburg was murdered, and a member of the Reichstag.

Clara Zetkin

Eva Peron

Despite the fact that, from 1924, she spent more time in Russia than in Germany and was on the Presidium of the Executive Committee of the Third International, she remained a member of the Reichstag until 1932 when she presided over an opening session. She died as Hitler was coming to power.

As a contrast to the perils attending women's emancipation in eastern and central Europe, their attainment of democratic political recognition in the West was far less dangerous, even though its accomplishment was closely related to war and its aftermath (see section on the Fight for Equality). Invariably, those countries which granted women the vote admitted them to elected assemblies and Government posts either at once or not long afterwards, although sometimes the delay between admitting females by law and actually voting a woman into office was a long one. For example Australia waited nearly 41 years before voting in its first female Senator in 1943, and even in 1974 there was only one female Senator.

Below, by nationality, are a few of the world's 'notables' who either became first members of their country's Legislative Assembly or achieved ministerial rank, or are included because, although not 'firsts', they are of importance:

Argentina	**Eva Peron** (1919–52) was the wife and key personality to the coming to power of Juan Peron. Previously a small-time film star, her vivacious personality swayed the hearts of the working people. As President, he wooed the electorate with social benefits while she became Director of the Social Aid Foundation (a State charity for the poor) giving direction, also, to the Ministry of Health and that of Labour so gaining central power and with publicity, great popularity. Three years after she died Peron fell from power. However, in 1973 he was called back and took with him a new wife **Maria Peron**. He died in 1974, aged 78, but before doing so had delegated the Presidency to his wife. She therefore became, at 43, the world's first female President and the youngest Head of State in Latin America.
Australia	**Anabelle Rankin** was appointed High Commissioner to New Zealand in 1971, thus becoming the first woman of her country to head a mission abroad. **Ruth Dobson** became her country's first woman Ambassador in 1974 when she was appointed to Denmark.
Belgium	**Marguerite de Reimacker-Legot** became, in 1965, her country's first female Cabinet Minister.
Brazil	**Bertha Lutz** became a Member of Parliament in 1936. However, in a country where democracy cannot truly be said to have existed, her services in the official Federation for the Advancement of Women (with their high level of illiteracy) is of greater importance.

Britain

The Countess **Markiewicz** was the first woman to be elected to the House of Commons in 1918 but, as a Sinn Feiner, would not take her seat. Thus **Nancy Astor** (British, 1879–1964) (see section on Mistresses, Courtesans and Salonnières) became, in 1919, the first woman to enter the British Houses of Parliament and held her seat until 1945. Her special interests were women's rights, the retail trade, raising the school-leaving age and stricter control of intoxicating liquor. She was also a salonnière of note.

Margaret Bondfield (1873–1953), a good trade unionist, was the first Cabinet Minister for Labour from 1929 to 1931 when she was defeated in the election by **Irene Ward**. Irene Ward held the seat until 1945, then the Tynemouth seat from 1950 until her retirement in 1974, so sitting longer in the House than any other woman. Representing a tough mining industry, Irene Ward's maiden speech shocked many male MPs. Not having the 'church fête' image of most Conservative women MPs, she enjoyed heckling, and in 1968 was once ordered out of the House by the Speaker for making too robust a defence of free speech. She championed the cause of people living on small, fixed incomes.

Barbara Salt was the first woman to be appointed as a British Ambassador when she was appointed to Israel in 1962, but she did not take up the post. Before that she had been First Secretary in Moscow from 1951 to 1955 and a Counsellor at Washington from 1955 to 1957.

Canada

Agnes Macphail was the first female Member of Parliament in 1921 and **Cairine Wilson** the first female Senator in 1930. It is noteworthy that in 1972 there was still only one Canadian female MP.

China

Hsiang Ching Yu (1895–1928) was the first woman of importance in the Chinese Communist Party and was elected to the Central Committee in 1921, becoming head of the Women's Department in 1922. In 1924 she directed a strike of women workers at the Nanyang Tobacco Factory, Shanghai, but in 1927 joined the armed action against the Government. The following year she was caught, tortured and shot.

Chiang Ching, wife of President Mao Tse-Tung, has played an important part within the Central Cultural Revolutionary Group of the Communist Party hierarchy. In 1973 she was confirmed as one of the 18 senior leaders of the Central Committee.

Denmark

Nina Bang was the first woman in the world to become a full Cabinet Minister when she held the Portfolio of Education from 1924 to 1926.

Ecuador	**Isabel Robalino** was the first woman Senator of her country in 1969.
Finland	**Miina Sillanpää** was her country's first female Cabinet Minister in 1926. This country was the first in the world to have women Members of Parliament (19 in 1907).
France	**Françoise Giroud** was appointed Minister for Women's Affairs in 1974. When appointed she commented 'If discrimination against women did not exist, there would be no need for a junior ministry to deal with it.' About the same time **Annie Lesur** was appointed Minister for Education and **Hélène Dorlhac** Minister for Penal Affairs.
Germany	**Ruth Fischer** was one of the first women members of the 1919 Reichstag. A founder of the Communist Lenin Party she became an expert on Communist affairs and was anti-Stalin. She was detested by the Communists in power in East Germany. In that Reichstag, however, there were 41 women, among them those who had adopted a more moderate line – brilliant scholars and suffragists such as **Marie Baum**, **Gertrude Baumer** and **Marie-Elizabeth Löders**. **Annemarie Renger** became, in 1972, the first female Speaker of the Bundestag, after an election that had left only 29 women Deputies (the lowest number since 1949). Meanwhile **Margarette Hutten** was appointed as the first female Ambassador, heading the Embassy in El Salvador.
Grenada	**Hilda Bynoe** became Governor in 1968 after working as a Medical Officer of Public Health in Trinidad and Tobago.
Guinea	**Jeanne Lisse** became a Permanent Delegate at the United Nations and, on 15 November 1972, made history by presiding over the Security Council.
Hungary	**Ilona Burka**, at the age of 20 in 1973, was the youngest MP in a House of 352 in which one in every four members was a woman, 21 of them under the age of 30.
India	**Annie Besant** (1847–1933) (see section on Religious and Social Reform) was elected first President of the National Congress in 1917, though she was by no means the first woman to be associated with that body since its formation in 1885. Though an elected assembly would not come until independence from the British in 1947, several were to play their part in achieving it. One was **Muthulakshimi Reddi** who was the first Indian woman to be nominated to a State Legislative Assembly and who, in 1930, by way of the All-India Women's Conference, pushed through the Child Marriage Restraint Act – after the Government had

sounded public opinion by referendum. Another, of greater note, was **Vijaya Pandit** who became India's first female Minister, for Local Government and Health, in 1937. A femininist and keen protagonist of Indian independence, she underwent a total of two and a half years' imprisonment by the British for her rebellious activities. After the granting of Independence in 1947 she began a series of appointments of rare distinction for any statesman: Ambassador to the USSR 1947–9; Head of the UN Delegation 1947–51; Ambassador to the USA and Mexico 1949–51; first female President of the UN General Assembly 1953; High Commissioner to the UK and Ireland 1954–61; Governor of Maharashtra 1962–4; Member of Lok Sabha 1964–8.

Indonesia
Julie Sullanti Sarosa was elected President of the UN World Health Assembly in 1973.

Malaya
Tan Sri Fatimah was her country's first female Minister, in 1973, with the Portfolio of Social Welfare.

New Zealand
Mabel Howard (1893–1972) was the first woman in the Commonwealth to hold full Cabinet status when she held the Portfolios of Health and Child Welfare in 1947. Although a kind and sympathetic person she was a dedicated enemy of injustice. New Zealand's first animal protection Act was her creation.

Norway
Kirsten Hansteen was the first female Cabinet Minister in 1945.

Pakistan
Begum Liaquat Ali Khan has been the most influential woman in the evolution of her country since its formation in 1947. As a Professor of Economics in her own right, she was also the wife of the Prime Minister and, prior to his assassination in 1947, his assistant in mobilising women. She formed a Women's National Guard, the Women's Reserve, the Women's Association, Pakistan Cottage Industries and many other organisations. In 1952 she led the Pakistan delegation to the UN and in 1954 became Ambassador to the Netherlands. In 1973 she became Governor of Sind, being the first woman to hold that post.

Papua and New Guinea
Josephine Abayah became the first, and only, female MP in 1972.

Philippines
Elisa Ochoa was the first woman to be elected to the Lower House of the Congress in 1941.

Poland
Irena Kosmowska (1879–1945) was one of the seven women of her country to become, jointly, the first female Ministers in the world when, upon the re-creation of the State in 1918, women were granted the vote and these seven were elected to the first Seym. She became Vice-Minister of Social Welfare. Always a

radical, she was imprisoned in 1930 for speaking against the Polish Government. During the Second World War the Germans deported her and, as a result of ill-treatment, she died.

Portugal **Maria Teresa Lobo**, as Under-Secretary for Health and Assistance in 1970, became her country's first female Minister.

Romania **Ana Pauker** (Russian), a ruthless Communist who played a leading part in the slender resistance to the Germans, was Romania's first female Cabinet Minister. On her own admission there were only 1000 members in the party before the Russians arrived in 1944. She came to power on a single-party election and received the Ministry of Foreign Affairs when her predecessor was removed on criminal charges. In 1949 she was made Deputy Premier but was herself ousted in 1952 by a counter-purge within the party.

South Africa **Mabel Malherbe** became the first elected Member of Parliament in 1933 (before that **Mrs Deneys Reitz** had been returned unopposed). However, women have not taken their opportunities for, up to 1973, the total of only nine white women had been elected to central government. Nevertheless, among the Bantu there is **Stella Sigean** who became Minister for Education in the Transkei and Queen **Modjadji** who ranks as head of tribe and, therefore, head of the Lebowa Legislative Assembly.

Sweden **Anna Wicksell** was the first female Member of Parliament in 1921.

USA **Jeanette Rankin** (1883–1973) was the first Congresswoman in 1917 and voted against the entry of the USA into the First World War, which cost her her seat at the next election. She did not return until 1940 and hers was the sole vote against entry into war in 1941. She maintained her opposition to war and, at the age of 87, led 5000 women of the so-called 'Jeannette Rankin Brigade' to Washington in protest against the Vietnam War.

Frances Perkins became the first American woman to attain Cabinet rank when she became President Roosevelt's Secretary for Labour in 1933 during the Great Financial Depression. As a pioneer for factory reform she had sat on many committees from 1923 to 1930, and helped push through the New Deal despite the opposition of politicians, businessmen and unions. **Perle Mesta** (1890?–1975) became the first female Ambassador (see section on Salonnières). **Margaret Chase Smith** is the longest-serving woman at the Capitol – a Congresswoman from 1940 to 1949 and a Senator from 1949.

Shirley Chisholm was the first Negro woman in Congress in 1968. She fights hard for equal rights for sex and race and serves on the Education and Labor Committee.

Eleanor Roosevelt (1884–1962) was the wife of President Roosevelt and interested him in the plight of the poor, inspiring him in his attempt to achieve political reform. Motivated by her high principles and need to be of service, she always supported her husband without in any way subjugating her own opinions. She travelled widely, wrote and broadcast. After her

Frances Perkins and
Shirley Chisholm

Eleanor Roosevelt
with *Jacqueline Cochran*

husband's death she was made the USA's Delegate to the UN and chaired the commission which drafted the Universal Declaration of Human Rights. She remained so absolutely independent of mind and fair that, at one time, her relations with Russian statesmen brought accusations of being a Communist. As a Democrat she supported Adlai Stevenson but not John Kennedy for President since the latter was a Roman Catholic – her opposition largely resulting from her dealings with Cardinal Spellman. She opposed Senator McCarthy and all he stood for and, although rare for her, she openly showed detestation of Richard Nixon and sounded warnings about the threat he posed. Her life was exemplary and it was not surprising she was voted, year after year, 'Most Admired Woman of the Year': it is doubtful if the USA has produced a greater one.

USSR

Ekaterina Furtseva was the first woman to reach the Presidium and did so from merit after long service in many exacting jobs (see section on Civil Administration).

Venezuela

Aura Celina Casanova was the first female Minister with the Portfolio for Development in 1969.
Ida Gramcko, a Licentiate in Philosophy, Professor of Aesthetics and a poet became Ambassador to the USSR in 1948. However, she is most celebrated for her literary attainments.

Zambia

Princess **Nakatindi** became the first woman to run in a Zambian General Election, the first as a member of the Government (1964) and the first to be a traditional ruler and MP in 1966. She has since led delegations to Britain and to the UN, and was Leader of the UNESCO Delegation in Tashkent in 1966.

The rank of Prime Minister has so far been achieved by four women, each attaining office either through compromise or a calamity. The world's first Prime Minister was **Sirimavo Bandaranaike** of Sri Lanka. A chief's daughter, she became the wife of Solomon Bandaranaike who formed the first Ceylon Government of the left in 1956. In the emotional backlash of his assassination in 1959, Sirimavo Bandaranaike was asked to form a Government even though she did not stand in the 1960 General Election: as a result she rather hurriedly had to be found a seat in the Senate. Her programme was one of continuing nationalisation at a time of great financial difficulty. When she had to turn to the Marxists for support in 1964, the electorate rejected her. She remained Leader of the Opposition until 1970 when she was returned to power at the head of a Coalition Government which included Communist support. Within a year there was trouble – an uprising instigated by extreme left-wing elements, probably aided by the North Korean Embassy staff, in which armed force had to be used. The country continues under an uneasy calm.

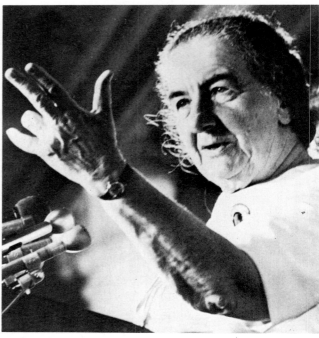

Indira Gandhi and *Golda Meir*

Indira Gandhi, like Sirimavo Bandaranaike, had a start in the political game because she was the daughter of India's first Prime Minister, Jawaharal Nehru. Yet all her life she has lived in the environment of the liberation of India and amid the growth of the new State. Educated in Switzerland and England, she began her work by way of the Indian Council for Child Welfare and inside the Congress Party, of which her husband was also a member. In 1959 she became Party President and revitalised it. Upon the death of her father, in 1964, she accepted her first Cabinet post of Minister of Information (although even then there had been a suggestion she might become Prime Minister instead). Upon the death of Prime Minister Shastri, in 1966, she took his place, for the party assumed that, by being linked with her late father's memory, she would bring in the votes. She was also a compromise candidate between the political factions which were squabbling in the aftermath of the 1965 war with Pakistan and the recurrent trouble over Kashmir. Her time in office has been difficult – fraught with endemic financial stringency, famines, floods and civil disturbances, and repeated confrontations with Pakistan, including the elimination of East Pakistan. Of prime importance was the struggle for leadership within the Congress Party itself when, from the outset, an attempt was made to oust her as Prime Minister. The party split into two factions though, in the 1971 elections, Indira Gandhi's Congress Party won with an overwhelming majority, so gaining a decisive victory for her. Although she was put into power by her party she has proved to be no political pawn, but a leader in her own right. When found guilty of electoral malpractices in 1975 she almost at once appealed for popular support, swept great numbers of opposing politicians into detention, censored the press and began rule as a dictator.

Unlike the previous two, the Prime Minister of Israel had no early political helping hand. One of **Golda Meir's** earliest memories was of narrowly escaping a charge by Cossack cavalry in Russia in the first years of the 20th century when the Jewish population was under persecution. She was born in Kiev in 1898 and went with her parents to the USA in 1906. She joined a radical intellectual circle, and her contact with Zionism led her to agree with those who yearned for a Jewish State. To the man who wanted to marry her she insisted that they live in Palestine, and, while for two years, he resisted the idea, she taught; at the same time she developed into a strong, lucid advocate of Labour Zionism and simultaneously carried on War Relief work. Marriage in 1917 allowed no slackening of these efforts with the result that home life took low priority. In any case, 1917 was the year of the Balfour Declaration when the dream of a Jewish National State became a probability.

In 1921 Golda Meir and her husband went to Palestine and, after a struggle, managed to gain admittance to the Merhavia kibbutz. In a communal environment where women were granted and exercised equal rights and toiled in the fields alongside the men for long hours, it was she who lasted the pace and began to take the lead in their administration. In 1924 her husband broke under the strain.

They moved to Jerusalem and lived in poverty for four years when their two children were born. At last Golda Meir returned to politics, and with a rush. Almost at once she became Secretary of the Women Workers' Council then, in 1932, representative of the Pioneer Women's Reorganisation in the USA. In 1934 she was back in Palestine and on the Committee of the Histradut (the General Federation of Labour) and thus among the top leaders of Zionism, with Ben Gurion, Sharett and Shazar. Her promotion was rapid and she eventually became Histradut's Chairman. However, in the process she found herself in the invidious position of having to argue against the workers in times of unemployment, in order to maintain sufficient funds to support the Zionist movement as a whole – and this when immigration was increasing because of German pressure against the Jews in Europe, and the Arabs were beginning their struggle to prevent Jewish dominance in Palestine.

During the Second World War Golda Meir walked a tightrope, trying to balance the needs of the Jews against the hostility of the Arabs and the demands of the British Mandatory Power whose support was essential for Jewish survival. She publicly objected to restrictions upon immigration, particularly in the light of what was going on in Europe, and aided Hagannah, the Secret Army, in its efforts to circumvent the British regulations. In 1946 the Jews began open resistance to the British, and the British retaliated by attempting to wipe out Hagannah and by arresting the Jewish political leaders – with the exception of Golda Meir who, therefore, moved into top place and led the Histradut and conducted negotiations with the British. In effect she controlled the struggle in both the political and military aspects and unflaggingly rallied her people as things got tougher. When, in 1947, the United Nations agreed that the British should withdraw and that Palestine should be partitioned, the Jews suddenly found themselves without a properly formed army surrounded by hostile Arabs. The British, meanwhile, refused them aid in their fight for survival. It was Golda Meir who went to the USA to raise $50 000 000 in two months and she, upon her return

in March 1948, who went to meet King Abdullah of Jordan in an effort
to avert war. Her dangerous journey, disguised as a man, was abortive
and war broke out in May. Once more they sent her to the USA to
raise more money. At the same time she was appointed Israel's first
Ambassador to Russia. In 1949 she returned to Israel to become Minister
of Labour in Ben Gurion's Government and thus head of the reconstruc-
tion of the new State. Ben Gurion once referred to her as 'The only man
in my office.'

As Labour Minister she demonstrated a tough determination tempered
with feminine gentleness, which so frequently helped her get her way.
In 1956 she changed portfolios to become Foreign Minister and almost
at once became engaged in the diplomacy related to the fresh outbreak
of fighting against Egypt in 1956; it was she who defended her country
in the United Nations. Later from her sprang the initiative to strengthen
practical ties with the new African States – bitterly resented by the Arabs
and the Russians, but conducive to enhanced Israeli security and influence.

Recurrent gall-bladder trouble hampered her work. In 1966 she
went into semi-retirement, although she continued to serve Israel either
on foreign missions including the UN, or as Head of the Mapai Section
of the ruling Labour Party. But in February 1969 Prime Minister
Eshkol died, and she succeeded him in office after a Government reorganisation in December. Since then she has led her country through a
delicate period, striving to reconcile the wishes of the arrogant hawks
with the doves who see Israel's future made safe by diplomacy.

After coping with the violence of the Yom Kippur War in October
1973, she finally lay down her task in 1974 after a turbulent crisis of
parties and personalities in the war's aftermath.

Golda Meir is unique in statecraft in that she competed against men on
men's ground, without having either connections of power to back her,
or by using sex to achieve her end as ruler of a country.

Are there in the world others of similar calibre to follow? Statistics of
several Western countries show a decline in female political representatives in their parliaments. They also show a preponderance of instances
where political parties choose women candidates for hopeless constituencies. But does the preference for male representation end there?
Are the arrivals of **Ella Grasso** (American) as Governor of Connecticut
in 1974, and thus the first *elected* female Governor in the U.S.A. and
Margaret Thatcher (British) as the first female leader of a major
political party in Britain, flashes in the pan? In the British General
Election of February 1974, the minority Liberal Party results showed
that in the six constituencies where their woman candidate followed a
previous Liberal woman candidate, she polled an average of 23·8 per
cent of the votes (total average of the party was 27 per cent). However,
in the nine places where a Liberal woman followed a Liberal man, she
only polled an average of 20·9 per cent. Can it be that the electorate
prefer men to represent them? If so, the future of women in government might, in the first instance, depend upon a country's (approximate)
52 per cent of women's votes, upon women's faith in the ability of their
own sex and in their own political education.

WOMEN RULERS OF THE WORLD AND THEIR YEARS IN POWER

COUNTRY	NAME	REIGN
ANTIOCH	Princess Constance (joint ruler)	1131–63
ARGENTINA	Maria Peron (President)	1974–
LESSER ARMENIA	Queen Zabel	1219–26
CAMBODIA	Queen Kossamak (joint ruler)	1955–60
CENTRAL AFRICAN REPUBLIC	P.M. Elizabeth Domitien	1975–
CHINA	Empress Wu Chao (Emperor)	655–705
	Empress Tsu-hsi	1875–89
	Empress Tsu-hsi	1898–1908
DENMARK	Queen Margaret	1387–1412
	Queen Margarethe II	1972–
EGYPT	Queen Hatshepsut	1501–1498 BC
	Queen Eje	1351–1350 BC
	Queen Arsinoe II (joint ruler)	279–270 BC
	Queen Berenice	81–80 BC
	Queen Cleopatra VII	51–30 BC
ETHIOPIA	Empress Waizero	1916–30
GREAT BRITAIN	Queen Jane (Lady Jane Grey)	1553–for nine days
	Queen Mary I	1553–58
	Queen Elizabeth I	1558–1603
	Queen Mary II (joint ruler)	1689–1702
	Queen Anne	1702–14
	Queen Victoria	1837–1901
	Queen Elizabeth II	1952–
SCOTLAND	Queen Mary Stuart (executed)	1542–67
HUNGARY	Queen Mary	1382–87
	Queen Elizabeth	1439–40
	Queen Maria Theresa	1740–80
INDIA	P.M. Indira Gandhi	1966–
ISRAEL AND JUDAH	Queen Athaliah	842–837 BC
	P.M. Golda Meir	1969–74
ITALY	Queen Theodelinda	1590
	Queen Joanna I	1343–81
	Queen Marie	1377–1402
	Queen Joanna II	1414–35
JAPAN	Empress Suiko Tenno	593–628
	Empress Kogyoku	645
	Empress Jito	686–97
	Empress Gemmyo	703–24?
	Empress Koken (abdicated)	749–58
	Empress Shotuku (Koken restored under new name)	764–70

COUNTRY	NAME	REIGN
MADAGASCAR	Queen Ranavalona I	1828–61
	Queen Rasoaherina	1863–68
	Queen Ranavalona II	1868–83
	Queen Ranavalona III (deposed)	1883–96
NETHERLANDS	Queen Wilhelmina (abdicated)	1890–1948
	Queen Juliana	1948–
NORWAY	Queen Margaret	1387–1412
POLAND	Queen Hedwige	1384–99
PORTUGAL	Queen Maria I	1777–1816
	Queen Maria II	1826–28
	Queen Maria II	1834–53
ROMAN EMPIRE (BYZANTIUM)	Empress (sometime as 'Emperor') Irene	797–802
	Empress Theodora (joint ruler)	1055–56
RUSSIA	Queen Tamara	1184–1212
	Empress Catherine I	1725–7
	Empress Anna Ivanovna	1730–40
	Empress Elizabeth Petrovna	1741–62
	Empress Catherine II (the Great)	1762–96
SPAIN	Queen Dona Urraca	1109–26
	Queen Juana I	1274–1307
	Queen Juana II	1328–49
	Queen Dona Blanca	1425–41
	Queen Isabel I (joint ruler)	1474–1504
	Queen Catalina de Albret	1481–1512
	Queen Isabel II	1833–68
SRI LANKA (CEYLON)	Queen Anula	47–42 BC
	Queen Sivali	35
	Queen Lilavati	1197–1200
	Queen Kalyanavati	1202–8
	Queen Lilavati (restored)	1209–10
	Queen Lilavati (restored)	1211–12
	P.M. Sirimavo Bandaranaike	1960–5
	P.M. Sirimavo Bandaranaike (re-elected)	1970–
SWEDEN	Queen Christina (abdicated)	1632–54
	Queen Ulrica Eleonora (abdicated)	1718–20
TONGA	Queen Salote Tubou	1918–65
USA (HAWAII)	Queen Liliuokalani	1891–3

5

AT WAR

" Shall we join the gentlemen ? "

Osbert Lancaster.

In war women more generally play the non-combatant roles. Although the earliest cave-drawings do not always identify sex, nor the Middle Eastern records of Hittite and Assyrian days clarify if women were or were not involved in combat, it is unlikely that women, with their weaker physique, were of any fighting significance in a time when the manual weapons were axes, spears, swords and bows – all of which wholly depended upon main force for their effect. Amazon fighting women seem to have been but a figment of Greek mythological imagination for, as Greek knowledge of the surrounding lands encompassed farther horizons so the supposed Amazon territory moved just beyond those limits. And although much later the 16th-century Francisco de Orellana claimed to have been attacked by fighting women when he was exploring the Marañón River in South America, later called the River Amazon, this name could more likely have come from the Indian *amassona* (boat-destroyer) used by them to describe its tidal bore.

There is no doubt, however, about the existence and the havoc caused under the leadership of **Boudicca** (English, 1st century AD) in the year 60 when she led a rebellion against the occupying Romans, whose administration and heavy taxation had become harsh and unbearable. When her husband Pragutagus had died the year before he had left half of his kingdom in Norfolk to her and her daughters and half to Nero, thereby hoping to avoid further confiscations. But the Romans seized it all by force, lashing Boudicca and raping the two princesses – from which one can surmise she had not docilely submitted to the annexation. The following year when the main Roman Army, under the Governor, Suetonius Paulinus, was away in Wales crushing the Anglesey Druids, a general rising of thousands from different tribes was secretly planned under the war leadership of Boudicca to capture the three Romanised cities of Colchester, London and St Albans. All three fell to them within two weeks; the inhabitants suffering awful atrocities and bestialities. Suetonius Paulinus meanwhile had returned with a depleted army of 10 000 disciplined men to meet the much larger but disorderly British force that was drunk with victory and plunder. The British were slaughtered and Boudicca died shortly after the battle, but although her tribe, the Iceni, were severely punished, the more important outcome of the uprising was the replacement of Suetonius Paulinus and the beginning of a more lenient Roman administration.

It is unfortunate that the first printed edition of Tacitus' narrative describing these events had a printer's error – Boudicca became Boadicea.

More passively linked to war by working at defence, the heart of the subject, was **Eudocia** (Greek, d 460) who was originally called Athenais but renamed at her baptism just before her marriage to the Eastern Roman Emperor, Theodosius II, in 421. In 438 like many good Roman Christians, she went on a pilgrimage to Jerusalem, returning there for good in 443, where she spent the rest of her life rebuilding the fortifications in a most formidable style. She also built churches and these two interests were reflected in her poetry which was either about religious matters or past Roman military campaigns.

Aethelflaed (English, d 918), who was the daughter of Alfred the Great and became ruler of the Mercians, demonstrated her understanding of both defence and attack. She co-operated with her brother, Edward the Elder, to resist Danish invaders by supplementing his fortified enclosures with her own fortresses. From 910 to 915 she built ten fortresses and restored Chester's defences. The following year she ordered an expedition as a 'show of strength' into Wales, and records suggest that she arranged a temporary alliance between the Picts, Scots, Britons and Anglo-Danish Northumbrians. In 917, in a joint attack with her brother against Danish positions, she captured Derby and 12 months later, Leicester. She died in June before their campaign was finished but had achieved enough to ensure her brother being accepted as lord over all Danes and Englishmen south of the Humber and becoming the most powerful ruler in Britain.

It might be argued that because of her royal blood, Aethelflaed enjoyed a privileged position which made her, a woman, more acceptable as a military leader, but about 500 years later, in the village of Domrémy in France, a peasant girl was born who did not have this advantage and yet achieved a war leadership which was to inspire her countrymen and be the decisive factor in the revival of her country. She was **Jeanne d'Arc** (French, *c* 1412–31), a pious, hard-working child who helped her mother about the house or took her turn to lead the village cattle out to pasture.

A present-day theory is that she was suffering from an abnormality in the region of the left temporo-sphenoidal lobe of her brain caused by bovine tuberculosis, and that her death would have been early whichever path in life she had taken, for, when aged about $12\frac{1}{2}$ years, she started to see and hear visions of saints (always coming from her right) and to smell agreeable odours. These manifestations occurred two or three times a

Boudicca and *Jeanne d'Arc*

week, but by the time she was 18 years they happened two or three times a day. This in no way detracts from her courage during her short life.

The throne of France was being disputed between the English King Henry VI (whose armies were spread over the northern part of the French kingdom), and its Dauphin, Charles. The latter's case seemed hopeless because, although his father had died five years before, in 1422, he could not strengthen his claim by actually being crowned, for the simple reason that Reims, the traditional place for the coronation, was in enemy-held territory. Jeanne d'Arc's 'voices' told her to go to Vaucouleurs, the nearest garrison friendly to the Dauphin. This she did but it was not until the following year, in February 1429, that her request for an audience with the Dauphin at Chinon was granted. Entering his presence she immediately identified him, although he had hidden himself among courtiers, and told him she would make war against the English and have him crowned at Reims.

A long interrogation of her, plus the news of the grave situation at Orléans, which was being besieged by the English, decided the Dauphin. Equipped with a military household she set out for that city where she joined battle and, due to her tenacity, ousted the English. In June the two armies met at Patay and the English were routed. By this time the French soldiers had such faith in her that they thought her unbeatable, and from then on her mere presence seemed to assure success; she was utterly fearless in battle, frequently standing at the head of her followers in full view of the enemy, and it was she who ordered and personally supervised the battle tactics and she who now insisted that the army, with the Dauphin, make all haste to Reims where he was consecrated on 17 July 1429.

From then on the fortunes of war worked less to her advantage and in September, unable to overcome the defences of Paris, she was compelled to withdraw. At last, on 23 May 1430, after a winter of fluctuating achievements, she was captured at Compiègne by the Burgundians (allies of the English) and eventually brought to a famous trial at Rouen on 70 charges in which the aims of her interrogators were to destroy her faith and her claim to divine guidance. Her habit of wearing men's attire was most offensive to the Church; but most irksome of all was her reluctance to recognise the Church itself since she preferred to put God first. Towards the end, under dreadful pressure, she recanted, but finally returned to her original beliefs. She was handed over to the English who burnt her at the stake on 30 May 1431.

The code of chivalry by which military society was governed during the Middle Ages severely limited women's part in world affairs just as it sought to limit the scope of war for the benefit of a privileged minority of aristocrats. Evidence of combatant females is sparse until the 17th century, but there must have been innumerable occasions upon which they took up arms. By Tudor times they were already beginning to agitate for better education and to become deeply involved in religious strife as the Wars of Religion swept Europe.

Militant women appeared in the British Civil War of the 1640s. There were 'Maiden Troops' in London and Norwich, although few of their sex were for the war, and in 1643 many demonstrated against the Parliament with cries of 'Peace!'. In fact the major feminine contribution to this war, as to so many others, was in support of their fighting husbands, and their involuntary involvement in sieges and clandestine warfare. It is a little later in the century that records of fighting women become more profuse. There was, for example, **Kit Cavanagh** (English, 1667–1739) who, disguised as a man, joined the British Army in 1693 in search of the husband who had deserted her. She has been described as having 'as much sex in her as you would find in a class devoted to the higher mathematics' – so perhaps her husband's flight is explained. At Landen she fought and was wounded. Then, in 1694, she was captured by the French but later exchanged, to re-enlist in the army. She joined the 2nd Royal North British Dragoons (Scots Greys) and in years to come was to see action during the War of the Spanish Succession at Namur, Nijmegen, Venlo, Bonn, Schellenberg (where she was wounded in the hip), Blenheim and Ramillies, where she was seriously wounded in the head. At this point the surgeons discovered her sex and she was removed from the fighting ranks to become an officer's cook. This was also an opportunity for her to remarry her husband whom she had met again in 1704. Nevertheless she continued to go into battle (now dressed as a woman) and at Malplaquet was hit in the stays when searching among the casualties for her dead husband. Her end came from natural causes, but she was buried with military honours.

Another martial woman in search of a lost husband was **Hannah Snell** (British, 1723–92) who joined Frazer's Marines (taking the name James Grey) and found herself embarked for the attack upon Pondicherry in 1748. She received 11 leg wounds and 1 in the groin but, in order to conceal her sex from the surgeons, did not disclose the groin wound and

Hannah Duston in action

extracted the ball herself, despite terrible pain. Later she saw service on the man-of-war *Eltham* and once received 12 lashes and four hours' solitude at the masthead for a minor misdemeanour. There is no record if she found her husband. There is record, however, in the form of a print, of **Ann Mills** (British, 18th century) who saw action in the frigate *Maidstone* in 1740: she is shown sword in one hand and a Frenchman's head in the other. Another gory souvenir, ten in fact, were taken by a North American colonist **Hannah Duston** (American, 1657–1736?) after she and other women had been captured by Red Indians. Knowing that when they reached their destination they were going to be stripped, beaten and then have to run the gauntlet between the whole army of Indians, Hannah Duston, aided by a lad previously captured, massacred the band (consisting of two braves, three squaws and seven children), killing nine herself and returning home with their scalps to prove the deed. A reward of £25 was paid to her.

Indian tribal warfare also produced **Nancy Ward** (American, 1738–1822), a Delaware, but of the Cherokee tribe, who took command when her husband was killed in a skirmish with Creeks and routed the enemy. In recognition she was made 'Beloved Woman' of the tribe, headed the Women's Council and sat on the Council of Chiefs. In 1760 she married a white man and subsequently used her influence to keep peace with the whites – but to minor effect since she put the Cherokees' interest first every time.

The clandestine part played by women in war is illustrated by the exploit of **Flora Macdonald** (British, 1722–90) when, in 1746, she helped Prince Charles Edward to escape from Scotland after his defeat at Culloden. He took refuge in the same house in the Hebrides where she was staying and her aid was sought. She journeyed to Skye, taking with her a party including 'an Irish spinning maid' – Charles in disguise. He got away safely but a boatman's idle talk led to her arrest and imprisonment in the Tower of London. She was freed after the Act of Indemnity in 1747.

Whether or not they actually fought, most women who went to war went either as army camp-followers or among ships' companies, to be near their husbands. The term 'show a leg' is of naval derivation from the time when the women in British ships, who were allowed to remain longer in bed, exposed their legs as identity of their sex. The camp-followers in the 7th Pennsylvania Regiment during the American War of Independence – the first people's war – were called the 'company of women soldiers' and were joined in 1776 by **Mary McCauley** (Molly Pitcher) (American, 1754–1832) to be near her husband. She helped cook and care for the wounded, but at Fort Clinton, in October 1777, she laid and fired a cannon at the British, then escaped. At the Battle of Monmouth in 1778 she again served a gun in the crisis of the fighting, giving priority to this rather than to her wounded husband.

The widening scope of war in connection with people's revolutions increasingly involved women in combat. The knitting women in attendance at the French guillotining of reactionary elements where ghoulishly symbolic. In the French Army, among several others, was **Angélique Brulon** (French, 1772–1859) who fought as an infantry sous-lieutenant and was awarded the Legion of Honour. There was also **Thérèse Figuer** (French) who, as a dragoon on active service from 1798 to 1812, had four horses killed under her – and survived to the ripe age of 87. Also there were women in the ranks of their enemies, like **Mary Anne Talbot** (British, 1778–1808) who, seduced by a British Army Captain when she was 14, served disguised as a footboy and drummer. She saw army service at Santo Domingo in the Caribbean and at Valenciennes in France, where her Captain was killed. She then deserted and became a seaman, enduring wounds and imprisonment as, in the meantime, she was captured and recaptured by the British and French. Her identity was revealed in 1796 when she was seized by a press-gang in London and so her fighting career ended. There was also **Augusta Krüger** (German) who became a subaltern in the 'secret' Prussian Army a year after it rose against the French in 1813. She was decorated with the Iron Cross and the Russian Order of St George, and as a true daughter of the Regiment, married a brother officer to produce a family from which, in due course, a grandson was to join the same 9th Regiment in 1869.

Among the most successful clandestine women warriors of all time was **Harriet Tubman** (American, *c* 1820–1913) an escaped slave who, in 1849, was brought north from Maryland by the so-called 'Underground Railroad', run by United States Abolitionists. The following year she

Harriet Tubman

herself began as a guide for the Underground and in the next ten years was to make perhaps 19 journeys to and from the Southern States to bring out over 300 slaves – in later days to Canada to defeat the Fugitive Slave Law. The measure of her success is that she was never caught, an immunity made possible by her meticulous planning, total avoidance of old routes and application of strict discipline among her followers – at pistol point if necessary. John Brown called her 'General Tubman'. During the Civil War she acted as a spy for the Union forces and took part in raids upon the Confederacy. Her only failure was that she was unable to get the US Government to grant her a pension after the Civil War. In her retirement she established a Home of Rest and then lived to the age of 93.

There were many women in arms during the American Civil War, among them:

Mary Dennis, a 6 ft 2 in (185 cm) officer in the Minnesota Regiment.

Anny Lillybridge from Detroit who joined the 21st Regiment to be near her lover.

Loreta Velasquez (Spanish, 1842?–97) married to a US Army officer, who joined the Confederate forces in 1861, fought at First Bull Run and then took up espionage. However, she had little talent in this field because she was arrested by her own side as a Federal spy. Having talked her way out of that she joined the 21st Louisiana Regiment and became engaged in guerrilla warfare before she was wounded and, at last, compelled to confess her sex.

Of equal, if not greater influence, among the women of the American Civil War were those who operated less belligerently behind the lines. Celebrated among those on the Federal side was **Anna Carroll** (American, 1815–93) who has been called 'a great unrecognised member of Lincoln's Cabinet'. Her claims as a military genius are not substantiated, but as a propagandist in the Union cause she was undoubtedly of great effect in writing evocative pamphlets in the President's support. As in past wars, women were to the forefront in caring for the wounded and many voluntary hospital units which sprang into being at the outset of war were gradually absorbed, on both sides, into organised units. Celebrated among the first hospital-founders was **Sally Tompkins** (see section on Science and Medicine) who, from her own large fortune, equipped and ran a hospital for the Confederates.

A turning-point in women's capability to carry arms came with the invention, during the 19th century, of much lighter weight, more easily manipulated fire-arms. At the time when revolution was common and women staking their claims for greater independence, a hardy fighter at the barricades was **Louise Michel** (French, 1830–1905), a trained school-teacher who was forbidden to teach in a State school because she refused to take the oath of loyalty to Napoleon III. Her chance to rebel openly came during the Siege of Paris by the Prussians in 1870. At first she worked for the wounded but as a member of the Commune was to the forefront in the National Guard. She became known as 'The Red Virgin of Montmartre' and was one of the last defenders before the Government troops overcame this early Communist uprising. After trial she was deported to New Caledonia where she remained until 1880. Returning to France she travelled the country preaching revolution and was once imprisoned for three years for mob incitement, but she continued lecturing for the 'cause' up to her death.

In 1892 the French crushed the only authenticated **Amazon Army** – the fighting women of the kingdom of Dahomey in West Africa. These women had been formed into an army by King Agadja in the early 18th century and trained into a serious fighting force by King Gezo in the early 19th. When the explorer Sir Richard Burton visited them in 1863 he described them in his typical facetious manner '. . . They were mostly elderly and all of them hideous. The officers were decidedly chosen for the size of their bottoms. . . . They manœuvre with the precision of a flock of sheep. . . .' But he knew that neighbouring kingdoms had reason to fear them for, although they were not voluntary soldiers, they numbered about 2500 (and were all official wives of the King), of which about 1700 were the actual fighting force. They carried muskets, blunderbusses, duck-guns, enormous knives and bows and arrows, and their method of warfare was surprise.

Amazon Women of Dahomey

When still a few days' march from the town or village to be attacked they lit no fires and observed silence. Avoiding trodden paths they made their own way through the bush and (barefoot) through the thorny acacia defences, noiselessly surrounding the objective by night to attack in mass just before dawn. They killed only in self-defence as their aim was to capture slaves to sell and victims for their King's human sacrifices. The latter took an annual toll of about 500 people, but when a king died an extra 500 were sacrificed to accompany him on his way. It was for these reasons the French, who were established on the coast of West Africa, conquered the people of Dahomey and made it a French protectorate.

Far better equipped and of great skill in battle were the women of eastern Europe and Turkey who became embroiled as combatants in the Balkan Wars of the early 20th century. They fought ferociously in the ranks alongside the men. The Turkish female snipers who took toll of British soldiers during the fighting at Gallipoli in 1915 were treated with respect by their opponents – on the rare occasions they got sight of them. Likewise the Russian women's 'Battalion of Death', was not to be despised. **Flora Sandes** (British) was to fight in the trenches with the Serbian Army and suffer the full rigours of the retreat in 1915. She was promoted from the ranks and wounded in hand-to-hand conflict in 1916.

Although in the First World War the majority of women took non-aggressive roles, some were to be shot by their enemies for the parts they played. Nurse **Edith Cavell** (British, 1865–1915) helped to smuggle some 200 soldiers to safety from Belgium. An incompetent organisation led to her subsequent discovery by the Germans which was followed by a charge of aiding enemy soldiers to escape and she with a colleague, **Louise Thuliez** (Belgian), faced a German firing-squad. Female agents were also shot, probably the most glamorised – and undeservedly so – was **Margaretha Zelle** (1876–1917), who called herself Mata Hari (Eye of the Day in Malay) and was neither very clever nor so beautiful as is sometimes supposed. She had developed Hindu-style strip dancing stopping short of exposing a pair of rather flat breasts. After being recruited for espionage by the French she also chose to work for the German Naval Attaché in Madrid. A French military court on 24–25 July 1917 had little difficulty in unveiling her treachery and had her shot by a firing-squad. It was in this war that an entirely new kind of fighting woman appeared. Princess **Eugenie Shakhovskaya** (Russian) had gained her pilot's certificate in Germany in August 1911. With special permission from the Tsar (at her request) she began operations as a reconnaissance pilot at the front in November 1914 (about the only military use there was for aircraft at that time). Not only was she probably the first female military pilot in the world, but she also survived and during the Revolution so managed to ingratiate herself with the Bolsheviks that she became, not only a member of the Secret Police (the Cheka) and no doubt in the hunt for members of her own aristocracy, but also the chief executioner at Kiev.

Modern women continue to fight for the cause in which they believe, and a typical successor to Louise Michel was **Caridad Mercader** (Spanish), a middle-class mother of five, who embraced Communism in the early

1930s and acted as a courier between Paris and Belgium (women are favoured as couriers since men are less likely to search them thoroughly). She was in Barcelona at the outbreak of the Spanish Civil War and, putting herself in charge of the Union of Communist Women, led the rebellion which prevented General Franco's Nationalists from taking over the city. Later she was wounded on her way to the front. On her recovery she was sent to Mexico as head of a delegation to recruit support for the Republicans and there she laid the foundations for the plot to assassinate Leon Trotsky – a task carried out by her son, Ramon, in 1940.

Communist revolution, with its deeper involvement of women in intensified strife, brought more women much closer to combat. There was **Li Chen** (Chinese), who was a local Communist Party Secretary in 1927 and thus heavily involved in the war which began against the Government in the same year. She retreated before the tide which ran against Mao Tse-Tung's first campaigns and stayed with the celebrated Long March of 6000 miles in 13 months to Shensi. She took part in many actions – even when pregnant – and became China's first female Major-General.

During the Second World War most of the major combatant Powers, with the significant exception of Germany, raised considerable uniformed women's services, but for the most part these services were involved in administration or defence (such as anti-aircraft gun sites) and, therefore,

T. Tasheva and *N. Meklin* Russian pilots of a women's bomber regiment in 1945

in no greater danger than many civilians. In Russia, however, there was an élite of the women who fought alongside the men; there were the female pilots of whom **Lydia Livak** (Russian, d 1943) was the top scorer with 12 victories before she was killed serving in a mixed Guards air unit.

In the Soviet Air Force's 122nd Air Group, comprised of fighters and bombers, there was a special all-female unit, the 586th Fighter Air Regiment, which was commanded by Major **Tamara Aleksandrovna**. It flew 4419 sorties, took part in 125 combats and destroyed 38 enemy aircraft. Typical of the bomber pilots was **Polina Gelman** who flew 18 sorties and was decorated five times. Thirty Russian airwomen received the Gold Star of a Hero of the Soviet Union. The following table shows still more clearly the deep involvement of Soviet women in the defence of their country against the German invasion:

Those decorated	over 100 000
Those with Hero of the Soviet Union	86
Those with all three classes of the Order of Glory	4

By comparison British women, who won numerous decorations, have been awarded, all told:

George Cross	4
George Medal	50

Clandestine warfare involved most women, particularly in the countries invaded by the Axis Powers. Their most extensive participation was, as before, in occupied eastern and south-eastern Europe where they joined in all aspects of the struggle and suffered tremendously. In Yugoslavia of over 100 000 women in the guerrilla army 25 000 were killed and 40 000 wounded in company with the men. Female agents were frequently employed as couriers, radio operators and organisers, besides the conventional nursing and administrative services. Many women spent the entire war face to face with the enemy, sharing time between their normal duties and those of Resistance. In Belgium there was **Marie-Louise Henin** (Belgian, 1898–1944) who graduated as a Doctor of Medicine and then practised as a dental surgeon. She helped to produce a clandestine newspaper and guided escapes and agents until she was caught. She was taken to Germany and beheaded. Also very active in the clandestine Press, intercepting information over the air and writing articles by night, was **Germaine Devalet** (Belgian, 1898–1945), who never failed to give hospitality to a fellow citizen being pursued by the Gestapo. She was arrested in 1943 and slowly died in the notorious Ravensbrück Concentration Camp. And there was **Marguerite Bervoets** (Belgian, 1914–44), a graduate in Literature, Philosophy and Law who was a Professor at the Ecole Normale, Tournai. She was co-foundress of a Resistance group and acted as guide, courier and spy until she was caught in 1942. She also was taken to Germany, where she, too, was beheaded.

Of those who survived there was **Pearl Witherington** who ran a highly successful sabotage circuit in Indre in 1944 and **Christine Granville** (Polish, 1915–52) (Countess Skarbek) who was, perhaps, the best of all the female agents in France. Before the war she was judged 'Miss Poland': in the course of it she showed no fear and, by exercising great caution with strict security, never caused anybody to be caught.

She made three clandestine journeys to Poland and carried out several minor Balkans missions before being sent to southern France in 1944. Of her successes here, one was to talk a German garrison of Polish troops located on the Italian frontier into surrendering, and another time she bluffed the Gestapo into releasing two of her captured comrades just three hours before they were to be shot. Although she survived the war this over-modest holder of the George Medal met a violent death. She was murdered by an Irishman in London in 1952.

There were also, of course, the women who operated the escape lines for Allied servicemen. Of these maybe the most outstanding was the wife of a Belgian. She was **Anne Brusselmans** (British) who operated from Brussels for four years and was responsible for transferring some 180 British and American airmen to safety. Her flat was searched three times by the Gestapo but by quick-wittedness, an iron nerve – and a little bit of luck – she survived. In the end she was the sole survivor of her group: the rest were either dead or in captivity. And all this time she ran a home and brought up two children.

Women, with their less violently aggressive natures, have always received and cared for the broken human flotsam thrown up and left by war – or mourned without even that comfort. These experiences of centuries, together with women's greater participation in government, must surely be the way to world peace – not by aping men with their use of modern, light and now manageable, deadly weapons.

Christine Granville

AS EDUCATIONALISTS

Some privileged women have received a formal education since its inception, though it has varied according to the country and the times. In the early Aryan community of ancient India, education was secular, progressive and open to women, as well as men, of all castes. However, by the time of the birth of Christ the growing rigidity of the caste system and the vogue for child marriages almost eliminated women from the opportunities of education. The teaching of the Vedic religious scriptures passed entirely into the hands of the Brahmin males and so Vedic education was prohibited to women until, by medieval times, the Brahmin caste alone received any sort of education.

While China had educational institutions going back to 2000 BC, education in ancient China was linked to Government service from which, it appears, women were usually excluded although, in the Later Han Dynasty a woman called **Pan Chao** (Chinese, *c* 45–*c* 115) had a reputation as a scholar and was commissioned by the Emperor to complete the history of the Former Han Dynasty. This she did, with some helpers, by completing the tables and treatise on astronomy. She was a respected teacher at court and wrote verse, but her best-known work is *Lessons for Women* written in AD 106.

China's educational progress was greatly hampered by the use of a classical style of writing which was quite unlike the spoken tongue. It was not until the 20th century AD that the printing of books in *pai-hua* (plain talk), instead of the classical style, enabled pupils to comprehend the sense as soon as they understood the words. Only then could missionary schools establish a firm foundation for modern education and become the pioneers of widespread Chinese female education.

The Japanese improved their education by sending students to study in ancient China and, by the 7th century AD, had their own official colleges for sons of the aristocracy. There were also private and family schools, and the Heian court ladies produced great literature (see **Murasaki Shikibu** in section on Literature and Journalism). These ladies of the Heian court also firmly discarded the Chinese classical style writing, then used in Japan, and developed a Japanese phonetic script which was adopted and may account for the earlier advance in Japanese education.

Greece was the cradle of education in the Western world – but for males. Athenian girls lived physically and mentally within the bounds of their homes and, while the Spartan females led a less secluded life, their primary role was to give birth and rear perfect physical specimens. To this end they were trained to do physical exercises, learn the importance of ante-natal care and become skilled nurses to their children and warrior menfolk.

Christianity was at first adopted mainly by the poor and illiterate, but by the 2nd century AD educated people started to embrace the faith. This meant they either trained their children to be pious Christians – with no education – or sent them to the Greco-Roman schools with their non-Christian culture. Most compromised. For example, the future Bishop of Ptolemais, Synesiu of Cyrene, was taught under the female **Hypatia** (Greek, d 415) who was said to have occupied the Chair of Platonic Philosophy at Alexandria, the most famous centre of education then, and to have lectured on Plato and Aristotle. Although her philosophy seems to have been Alexandrian Neoplatonism, her works are lost and records give several titles of mathematical and astronomical interests. A friendship between this pagan teacher and her Christian pupil is shown in his later letters to her. She was murdered by a Christian mob.

Under the invasion of the barbarians, Roman schools were destroyed and intellectual darkness settled over Europe until a gradual reawakening of culture emanated from the expanding Christian Church as it attracted and trained monks and nuns. An early woman educator was **Hilda of Whitby** (English, 614–80) who founded and built Whitby Abbey in 657 – a double abbey for men and women – and for 30 years taught theology, medicine, grammar, music and all the known arts. Bede wrote: 'five bishops were taken from her monastery', and it was she who saw the potential and took into her abbey the illiterate herdsman Caedmon who became the earliest English Christian poet. Monastic teaching was limited but cathedral schools, the forerunner of the modern English grammar school, slowly started to appear in England and France in the 6th century. In England these blossomed and multiplied into colleges, independent schools and schools attached to guilds, hospitals, chantries, etc. By pre-Reformation times there was in England 1 grammar school to every 5625 people; in 1864, it was only 1 grammar school to every 23750 people. These schools were for boys only but some girls received an education; sometimes nunneries took girl pupils of good birth as a source of income; a few little girls might have attended the cathedral song schools, where they were taught to read and write; but most of higher birth were educated in their own homes.

The term 'governess' meant, in Chaucer's time, a moral protector and guardian rather than a teacher (see his *The Doctor's Tale*). There were women teachers outside the nunneries, as is illustrated by the Abbot of Rievaulx Abbey in Yorkshire in the 12th century when he warned solitary women, for spiritual reasons, against running schools. Centuries later in England women ran 'dame schools' in the villages, teaching the basis of education to the poorer classes, sometimes for a fee and sometimes aided by charity. There was neither inspection nor check on these women's qualifications or suitability, but they could not have been more brutal than the average schoolmaster who, if need be, beat the knowledge into his pupils; nevertheless in 'The School-Mistress', a poem by William Shenstone in 1742, it says:

> A matron, whom we school-mistress name,
> Who boasts unruly brats with birch to tame.

In England, before the 19th century the majority of women had no education. This also appears to be true of most European Catholic-dominated countries which, from the 16th century, had excellently run Jesuit schools – for boys – (Italy was an exception in so far as its universities accepted suitably qualified women as students and teachers), and in those areas of Calvinist religion which from the 16th century had Calvinist Schools – but, again, for boys only.

The first country in which a lasting educational system for both sexes appeared was Germany in the 16th century – even if the Lutheran aim had been solely to teach them to read the Bible. Also the setting up of the first printing-press in Mainz, Germany, in 1456, with presses appearing all over Europe by the end of that century, paved the way for mass education. Few women stood out as educationalists during these formative centuries, and those who did usually taught theology. But **Herrade of Landsberg** (German, d 1195), Abbess of Hohenburg, was also a teacher of sciences, medicine, the entire Trivium and Quadrivium and wrote an encylopædia (324 parchment pages with 636 coloured drawings) of Bible stories, plants and their uses.

A few European females received and gave instruction in specialised subjects of education. For example there was a co-educational medical school in Salerno, famous throughout the 11th and 12th centuries, whose most important teachers were women, **Trotula** being the most noted (see section on Science and Medicine).

Queen Hedvige (Polish, 1373–99) with agreement from the Pope, opened a Faculty of Theology at Cracow Academy in 1397, giving her personal jewels for the Academy's restoration. (When her coffin was opened in 1949 her sceptre and orb were found to be made of wood and her crown of gilded leather.) In Britain **Mary of Chatillon** (British, *c* 1300), widow of the Earl of Pembroke, founded Pembroke College, Cambridge in 1347. For a time the governess (in the modern sense of the word) to Princess Joanna, daughter of Edward III, she devoted her entire life to learning and education. However, it was in Italy in the 14th and 15th centuries that women made their greatest impression. For example, in 1390 **Dorothea Bocchi** (Italian, d 1436) was appointed Professor of Medicine and Moral Philosophy at Bologna University and taught there for 40 years, while at Padua **Laura Cereta Serina** (Italian) became a

Professor of Philosophy. And the first woman's teaching Order in the Catholic Church was begun by **Angela Merici** (Italian, 1474–1540) at Desenzano in 1494 when she collected a small group of girls as teachers of Catechism to village children. But not until 1535 did she fulfill her dream of founding what became known as the 'Order of Ursulines' with its aim of educating girls through individual attention, gentleness and persuasion without force. Soon she had recruited 60 members: today the Order is world-wide and famous. In fact Italy was the only country which, in the 15th century, allowed women to matriculate, with the result that they began to take an ever-increasing part in the world's affairs. **Beatrix Galindo** (Italian, 1473–1535) graduated in Italy but then became a Professor of Latin and Philosophy at Salamanca University in Spain and also founded a hospital in Madrid.

Each century produced its crop of particularly brilliant women who managed to make good use of their influence and talents. There was **Margaret Beaufort** (English, 1443–1509), the mother of Henry VII, who began the Lady Margaret professorships of Divinity at Oxford and Cambridge in 1502 and founded Christ's College and St John's College at Cambridge while, in her own right, she translated several religious books and was a valuable patron to the printers William Caxton and Wynkyn de Worde. **Aloysia Sigea** (Spanish) taught Latin, Greek, Hebrew, Syriac and Arabic at the Portuguese court. **Marie de Coste**

Margaret Beaufort

Blanche (French) taught mathematics and physics in Paris and in 1566 published a work called *The Nature of the Sun and Earth*.

It was the 17th century, however, which produced one of the most outstanding of all educated women who had the drive to propagate her views widely. She was **Anna Maria van Schürman** (Flemish, 1607–78), a prolific linguist who learnt Latin at the age of seven and three years later could translate it freely. In a short time she acquired command of Dutch, German, French, Greek, Hebrew, Samarian, Arabic, Chaldaic, Syriac, Ethiopian, Turkish and Persian, besides a working knowledge of English, Spanish and Italian – despite some initial obstruction by her mother, whose thoughts were conventional and who wished to confine her daughter's activities to needlework. Inevitably Anna Maria van Schürman began to develop ideas of her own. At Utrecht University, where she was accorded special facilities, she graduated in law and began to teach history and philosophy. She also dabbled quite seriously in medicine (unsuccessfully seeking a cure for blindness) and worked in hospitals. The best scholars of the day came to her for advice on all manner of matters. Moreover, in addition to working on her main subjects and indulging in a strong religious bent at a time of deep religious schism, she developed a wide variety of artistic activities. Her delicate engraving with diamond upon glass is renowned, but she was also an expert sculptress, carver in wood and ivory and modeller in wax. As a painter she commanded not only respect but a useful fee too: one portrait by her was valued at 1000 florins.

Anna Maria van Schürman acquired a widespread reputation. In addition to scholars, royalty asked to consult her and tried to confer honours upon her. She was extremely modest, however, and often went out of her way to avoid the outward tokens of adulation. Similarly she was reluctant to publish her writings and so it was not until 1636 that her first poem appeared in print. Thereafter a number of her works were published, including *Apology for the Female Sex*, in response, it seems, to a physician's paper entitled *Advantages of the Female Sex* which he dedicated to her. She was an early, influential supporter of women's rights.

Later she lived simply in Cologne and there in 1664 met Jean de Labadie, a Jesuit who had been converted to Protestantism and who had founded a break-away religious sect. Anna Maria van Schürman (who never married because, it has been suggested, men might have been frightened of her) became fascinated by Labadie and his ideas. He favoured a contemplative approach to religion as a means to acquiring perfection of character and as purification of the Lutheran Church: in 1670 he was excommunicated. She became his principal helper and in 1673 published her last work, *Eucleria*, in his support. After he died in 1674 she took the lead in spreading his ideas in Holland. But she died in 1678, having used up all her money in service to the poor: Labadism became extinct about 1750.

The schooling of the under-privileged – particularly girls – universally left everything to be desired. Remedies were piecemeal and meagre. **Ann Radcliffe**, Lady Mowlson (English, d *c* 1661), widow of a Lord Mayor of London, founded in 1643 the first scholarship at Harvard University in the American colonies: it was after her that, in 1879, Radcliffe College was named – the first centre for instruction of women

Anna Maria van Schürman

by the Harvard Faculty. The Marquise de Maintenon, **Françoise d'Aubigné** (French, 1635–1719) sponsored a home for poor girls at Rueil in 1681 and in 1686 managed to achieve, with the assistance of her husband Louis XIV, the founding of the Catholic Institution for poor girls at Saint-Cyr. In Russia the University of Moscow and the Academy of Arts at St Petersburg were founded during the reign of Empress **Elizabeth Petrovna**, (Russian, 1709–62), while it was **Catherine II** (German, 1729–96) who issued the first Russian Education Act in 1786 which required a two-year course for minor schools in every district and a five-year course in major schools in every provincial town. The system was State controlled, free, co-educational and, for political reasons, slow in actuation. Nevertheless, by the end of the 18th century 254 towns had new schools though it was the boys much more than the girls who benefited.

At the beginning of the 19th century women in several countries, acting independently, started solo efforts for mass education; these solos soon joined into choruses.

The leading French woman educationalist was **Henriette Campan** (French, 1753–1822) who, in 1794, opened a *pension* at Saint-Germain-en-Laye and soon had 20 pupils – one of them the daughter of the US Ambassador, James Monroe, who later became President of America.

A year later Henriette Campan moved to the rue de l'Unité, calling her *pension* 'Institution Nationale de Saint-Germain'. In 1798 Napoleon sent his sister Caroline to her school, thereby establishing it as the most exclusive in France. The number of pupils swelled to 100, their uniform was black with a white close-fitting collar and a sash coloured according to their class from green for beginners, through violet, orange, etc., to white for seniors. Classes began at 10 am for writing, grammar, history and geography in the morning, followed by drawing; also singing, dancing or the playing of a musical instrument. Her own daughters had to make their own clothes and learn household accounting also. People who were the most distinguished in their profession or art taught at her school and the concerts and prize-giving fêtes were attended by the society of the day. This was the first secular school in France to give girls a broad education.

In 1805 Henriette Campan's plans for a school or schools under the patronage of the Emperor first started to be discussed. These schools were to be for the daughters of modest families, but when the first 'Maison Impériale Napoléon' was established in 1807 with Henriette as Superintendante (having already given up her *pension* at Saint-Germain) of the 300 girl pupils most were from high-ranking Army, Navy and Diplomatic families – modest families not being interested even in free education for their daughters. A second Maison for another 300 girls was established in 1809. The older pupils in these schools learned English, Italian and German, and the high standard from Saint-Germain was maintained.

Henriette Campan published a number of books on education: her *De l'Education*, published in 1824, is the most important.

The principal 'Maison d'Education' is now at Saint-Denis, where 400 girls are educated. In the junior school, 'Maison des Loges', the 600 pupils still wear coloured sashes.

Young ladies' boarding-school in the 18th century and, right, *Henriette Campan*

However, she was not the only educationalist stirring in France at that time, for in 1801 Saint **Madeleine Barat** (French, 1779–1865) founded the Society of the Sacred Heart and opened its first convent. Its educational objectives were clear and its methods always open to improvements so that, by her death, the Order had spread to 11 countries while still keeping its uniformity and aims.

Among the first parochial schools in the USA was one opened by **Elizabeth Seton** (American, 1774–1821) in Baltimore in 1809, later taking in a few young women under her care. She has been called the first American Catholic sister-school nun but is not as important as **Emma Willard** (American, 1787–1870). She was born in Connecticut, became a teacher at 16 and the principal of a girls' academy at 20. When she was 27 she opened her own boarding-school. In 1819 she submitted to the New York State Legislature her 'Plan for Improving Female Education' which appealed for State aid in founding schools for girls and for equal educational opportunities. It was rejected. Between 1845 and 1847 she travelled 8000 miles within the US counselling in education and in 1854 was one of the two representatives of the US at the World's Educational Convention in London. She wrote several textbooks, widely used, and going into many editions, and a volume of poetry; 'Rocked in the Cradle of the Deep' is one of the poems. The first known woman to introduce physical exercises into an American girls' school curriculum was **Catharine Beecher** (American, 1800–78) who founded the Hartford Female Seminary in 1827. She included hygiene and 'callisthenics' (Greek – beautiful strength) in order to promote graceful movements – no apparatus being used.

A courageous pioneer in the education of US Negro girls was **Prudence Crandall** (American, 1803–90) who, in 1833, admitted a negro girl to her private academy, then considered one of the best in Connecticut. Because of her action she lost her white patrons and when she opened a school for 'young ladies and little misses of colour' she was socially ostracised, persecuted and town meetings were held to break up the school. The State Legislature passed the notorious 'Black Law' refusing permission for anybody to set up a school for non-resident negroes without the consent of the local authorities. Prudence Crandall, refusing to comply with this law, was arrested, tried and convicted, but a Court of Appeal reversed the decision on a technicality. The local opposition redoubled and in September 1834, she had to close her school and leave the district.

Mary Lyon (American, 1797–1849) was a pioneer for higher education for women in America. She started teaching at 17 but, at the same time, continued her own education, using her teaching salary to pay her way. In 1836, with financial backing, she founded Mount Holyoke Female Seminary which opened the following year with herself as Principal. This first step into higher education for women was an important one because it set an example.

The first woman to spread the Froebel kindergarten teaching theory to another country was **Bertha von Marenholtz-Bülow** (German, d 1893) who was largely responsible for bringing it to the notice of educators in England, France, Italy and the Netherlands, and who, in 1860, managed to persuade the Prussian Government to remove their ban on Froebel's methods, besides clarifying them.

The first kindergarten in England opened in London in 1851 under the supervision of **Bertha Ronge** and her sister **Johann** (German), both pupils of Froebel. In India Froebel's principles were introduced in 1891 by **Pundita Ramabai** (Indian) but its greatest success came in America. There the first kindergarten was started by **Elizabeth Peabody** (American, 1804–94) in 1860. Seven years later she travelled to Europe to study Froebel's methods at first hand and on her return to the US spread his theory by lectures, training classes, contributions to magazines and in the *Kindergarten Messenger* which she edited.

Even as primary and secondary education for women was being placed upon its feet, **Elizabeth Blackwell** was exploring the possibilities of large-scale higher education (see section on Science and Medicine). She founded the first women's Medical College of New York in 1868 while, in 1898, **Ellen Mussey** (American, 1850–1936) who was herself a lawyer, founded the Washington College of Law and **Annie Meyer** (American) established Barnard College, the Women's Department of Columbia University – a somewhat surprising venture since she was strongly against women's suffrage! Nor had religious teaching been forgotten, for in 1838 **Rebecca Gratz** (American, 1781–1896) founded a Hebrew Sunday School in Philadelphia – the first of its kind in the USA. Almost simultaneously **Sarah Hale** (American, 1788–1879) an intrepid feminist and Editor of the magazine *Female* brought pressure to bear in order that Vassar Female College, founded at Poughkeepsie in 1861, should be renamed Vassar College in 1867. It became co-educational in 1970. What was to become the largest independent college for women in the USA – Smith College at Northampton, Mass. – was founded by **Sophia Smith** (American, 1796–1870). She chose the site and the first trustees and financed it out of money she left in her will. The college was opened five years after her death. Likewise Leland Stanford Junior University in California was brought about by a woman's endowment, and determination – that of **Jane Stanford** (American, 1828–1903), to the sum of $11 000 000. The idea was her husband's, but it was she who forced it through against all kinds of opposition and she who, at the same time, generated antagonism within the college by her dictatorial methods.

A much more directly personal attack upon educational methods was made by the women of Europe throughout the 19th century. Following in the footsteps of the great social reformer **Elizabeth Fry** (British, 1780–1845) (see section on Religious and Social Reformers) came a bevy of women dedicated to the raising of educational standards. **Mary Carpenter** (British, 1807–77) was the most significant of English women concerned with the needs of deprived children. The daughter of a Unitarian minister who was taught by her father, she first worked as a governess and then, in 1829 with her mother, opened a small girls' school in Bristol. The needs of the deprived appalled her and led her to study conditions in India, with the aid of a rich Boston philanthropist, Joseph Tuckerman. She was to visit India four times in her lifetime, but it was in England that her greatest work was accomplished and here that her compassion was zealously converted into constructive acts. In 1846 she opened a 'ragged' school in the slums of Bristol with emphasis on play as a means to learning. She also stressed: mutual confidence between teacher and pupil; no corporal punishment or holding up to ridicule, but discipline to be maintained by firmness and kindness; teachers to become acquainted with parents and homes of pupils; warm and airy classrooms; teaching of a trade as well as formal education; visits to museums and exhibitions. Result – '. . . from one to two hundred of the most destitute and neglected children of this large city are seen coming voluntarily and regularly to school'.

Mary Carpenter

It worked well except for the most delinquent, the poorest, and those with the worst home influence and environmentally affected. For these she started the Red Lodge Reform School for girls in 1854 and, in 1857, a school at Kingswood, near Bristol: both cottage-home communities in rural surroundings. Mary Carpenter emphasised the importance of love, faith and obedience – in that order – and paid great attention to after-care, maintaining contact and interest after placing the child with a suitable employer.

Many of her proposals were incorporated into the 1861 and 1866 Amendments to the Industrial Act of 1857. In 1876, she succeeded in persuading the Government to authorise school-boards to establish day-feeding industrial schools. It was she who, virtually, created the present English structure of child care for deprived and delinquent children.

In 1870 she established a National Indian Association to propagate information about India. Yet her work took her much farther afield apart from her journeys there, for in 1873 she went to America and Canada and, later, to France. In all three countries she studied the prison systems and pointed out, with all the force of Elizabeth Fry, the defects that she found. And throughout her life there came from her pen a flood of books and pamphlets designed to reform education from primary to higher levels.

A vital central location for the growth of women's education during the latter half of the 19th century was Zürich in Switzerland. The University had been founded in 1833, the Federal Institute of Technology in 1835, along with many other cultural institutions to match Swiss constitutional reforms which gave the people of Zürich the right to propose legislation in 1865. An atmosphere of liberalisation grew and people from other countries, who felt oppressed, flocked in. Notably there were Russian radical political refugees of both sexes. In 1872–3, the year in which higher courses of lectures for women were first organised in Moscow University, 140 Russian women enrolled for the course at Zürich University. They enhanced their education but at the same time created a hot-bed of revolution (see the sections on Politics and Statecraft, Reform, Science and Medicine, and on Crime for many instances of Zürich-based initiatives).

Institutions and educationalists of important international repute and influence quite naturally were in a minority. For the most part each country found its own reformers who developed the systems that were currently in use.

In Germany **Emilie Wüstenfeld** opened the first women's Oberlyceum in Hamburg in 1851.

In Britain **Frances Buss** (British, 1827–94) founded the North London Collegiate School for Girls in 1850, the forerunner of all the high schools for girls' secondary education in England, where the evolution of women's education typifies the pattern elsewhere. Frances Buss had attended a series of 'Lectures to Ladies' which had been given by a committee of professors from King's College, London at the instigation of **Mary Maurice** (British), a helper at the Governesses' Benevolent Institution. The lectures had been such a success with 200 attending and crowding out the rooms in the first year that, in 1848, it was decided to create what became known as 'Queen's College'. Diplomas were given to the students, who spread about the land, raising the status of women educationalists from that of lowly governess (the only respectable occupation open to impoverished gentlewomen who were lucky if they received £25 a year on which to live and dress). In 1854 Cheltenham Ladies' College, which had been founded in 1850, was put on its feet by **Dorothea Beale** (British, 1831–1906): she introduced science to the curriculum and, as the school flourished, began to take in boarders in 1864. (From 60 pupils in 1854 it rose to 500 by 1894 and 1000 in 1906.) At the same time another step forward had been taken: Frances Buss and **Emily Davies** (British, 1830–1921), the secretary, organiser

The gymnasium of the North London Collegiate School for Girls

and tactical arbiter of a committee dedicated to securing women's admission to universities, had managed in 1863 to persuade Cambridge Senate to allow an experimental plan whereby 91 girls could take the Local Cambridge Examination. (In 1865 Cambridge formally agreed that future local examinations should be open to girls.) Aided by Dorothea Beale they gave evidence before the Schools Enquiry Commission (1864–8) and eventually, in 1870, the Commission insisted upon the need for the qualification of higher education for teachers.

In the meantime **Anne Clough** (British, 1820–92) had begun putting the ideas of university lectures into practice by forming the North of England Council and arranging for a young don to give an experimental lecture on Astronomy in four different towns in turn. Five hundred and fifty women attended and thus encouraged the formation of what became known as the 'University Extension Scheme', centred in Cambridge in 1870. There, in a small house provided by Henry Sidgwick, five students began to study under Anne Clough. Though it was not yet part of the University it was the beginning of Newnham College that became fully established in 1875. From then on British universities increasingly opened their doors to women when it was seen that educated women's mental capacity was quite the equal of men's. Also working closely with this group was **Barbara Bodichon** (British,

1827–91). With Emily Davies she established Hitchin and then Girton College and unstintingly supported various schemes, both financially and with her time. Simultaneously, **Emily Shirreff** (British, 1814–97) a founder of Girton who was a member of its Executive Committee, also founded, in 1871, the National Union for Improving the Education of Women of All Classes, the aim being to provide proper schools and trained teachers for girls' secondary education. From this grew the Girls' Public Day School (1872) and, in 1877, incorporating the Teachers' Training and Registration Society, a teachers' training college called the Maria Grey Training College.

Numerous streams of initiative in Europe and the USA gradually joined into a river of progress throughout the world. Of those who concentrated their attention upon educating women there was:

Joan Bethune (British) who founded the first women's college in British India (Calcutta) in 1849.

Isabelle Gatti de Gamond (Belgian) who founded the first secondary school for girls in Belgium in 1864.

Anna Leonowens (British, 1834–1914) who became the Governess to King Mongkut's children at the Siamese Court between 1862 and 1867. Upon her experiences the film, *Anna and the King of Siam* was tenuously based.

Georgina Archer (British) who inaugurated the first university lectures for girls in Germany when she started the Victoria-Lyceum in Berlin in 1868.

Helene Lange (German, 1848–1930), **Franziska Tiburtius** (German, 1843–1927), and **Minna Cauer** (German, 1842–1922) (leader of the Academic Union) who started in 1889 the first German establishment to prepare women for university study. This was in the presence of the **Crown Princess Victoria** who was, herself, an exponent of education for women. The establishment was called the 'Realkurse' and it mostly prepared girls for Swiss universities as the German universities were still not open to women. In 1893 Helene Lange converted the Realkurse to that of gymnasium grade but by then Frau **Kettler** had already advertised 'the first girls' gymnasium' to bring girls up to standard to enter German universities; thereby putting more pressure on the universities to open their doors to women. This happened gradually and grudgingly but it was as well they did for, by 1917, 52 per cent of the undergraduates in Heidelberg (to take one example) were women and not only needed to be self-supporting but also to help rebuild Germany, because German women outnumbered men by 2 500 000 after the massacre of the First World War.

Marguerite Bourgeoys (Canadian) who widened the system of feminine education established by Ursuline nuns in Quebec in 1642 by opening the 'Congrégation de Notre-Dame' in 1858 as the first of several such schools to come. In 1789 it had been noted by a Bishop that literate Canadian women exceeded literate men and thereafter Canada's women maintained a good record, even though there was strong resistance to them as teachers and in the professions. Yet the first women were not admitted to the Quebec College of Surgeons until 1930, and it was 1914 before a woman received a law degree from McGill University and 1941 before a woman practised at the Canadian Bar.

Ibu Dewi Sartika (Indonesian, 1884–1942) who pioneered the first girls' school in Indonesia at Bandung on 16 January 1904. This was a domestic science school but also taught the girls to read and write. Similar schools spread into West Java and Central Sumatra with pupils setting up schools once their own education was finished.

Concordia Löfving (Swedish) introduced Swedish drill into England in 1878 and the first English women's college to train physical education teachers was founded in 1885 by **Martina Österberg** (Swedish): but they were just two among several Swedish women who played educational roles.

Quite apart from the efforts of the feminists to acquire a fair share of the educational facilities of their day there were the attempts by specific women to improve education in its widest aspects for both males and females. Frequently their efforts were inspired by a desire to help the disabled or the deprived and helpless through improved teaching methods.

Harriet Rogers (American, 1834–1919), the first Principal of the Clarke Institute for Deaf Mutes, which was established in 1867 in Northampton, Mass., rejected the finger alphabet method of teaching deaf mutes, hitherto used in America, and introduced the German oral method whereby the children were taught to speak and lip read. And a colleague, **Caroline Yale** (American, 1848–1933) (who collaborated with Alexander Bell in experiments to invent the first telephone) also became Principal as part of 63 years' service with the Institution and added athletic and manual training to the curriculum.

Anne Sullivan (American, 1867–1936), herself partially blind, was initially responsible, through intelligent application and loving sympathy, to educate and give speech to the blind, deaf mute **Helen Keller** (American, 1880–1968), and then was her constant companion throughout the years in which Helen became an exceptionally proficient educator herself and the author of ten books – mostly of a biographical nature. Helen Keller became a graduate of Radcliffe College in 1904.

Alice Salomon (German, 1872–1948) started the first German school for social work by giving regular courses for social workers in 1899. Later she became the school's President which, in 1932, was named after her. She was also the President of the federation of German schools of social work, her ideas and influence spreading beyond Germany. In 1937 she was exiled by the Nazis and spent the rest of her life in America.

Nadezhda Krupskaya (Russian, 1869–1939), the wife of the Bolshevik leader, Lenin, was an educationalist before she became a revolutionary. As a graduate from the Woman's College at St Petersburg she was one of a quite large élite of higher educated Russian women of whom there were already 2000 of university standard by 1881. When Lenin came to power in 1917 she was made Vice-Commissar of Education

Nadezhda Krupskaya with her husband Lenin

and, with the same earnest drive that had characterised her support for her husband, formulated the Communist Party's plan for mass education – perhaps the most important aspect of the effort to modernise the failing State and raise the bulk of the people from its current level of ignorance.

Perhaps the most significant among modern women educationalists, however, was **Maria Montessori** (Italian, 1870–1952) who was started on her life work through being put into contact with defective children. The daughter of a soldier, she was strictly disciplined as a child but, though exhibiting no pronounced scholastic ambition, developed a strong aptitude for leadership. A fierce ambition came later, although teaching was the one avenue of approach she rejected. Instead she opted for medicine and thereby drew upon herself, as the first Italian woman to qualify under modern rules as a doctor, the customary marks of disapproval from men. However, she had a quite unquenchable determination to succeed. Of her student days she once said that she thought she could have done anything. Once during a blizzard she was the only student to force her way through to attend lectures. At the same time she developed into a staunch feminist with a quite remarkable grasp of almost any subject and immense powers of delivery when addressing an audience.

She became Assistant Doctor at the Psychiatric Clinic in the University of Rome and thus into contact with mentally deficient adults and children. In 1899 she expressed the view that these children were entitled to education and this led to her appointment as Director of a State orthophrenic school. Gradually she began to obtain hitherto unsuspected results: these children began to read and write and achieve successes in examinations. In 1906 she was given the opportunity to work with normal children, the inhabitants of a block of flats who needed care while their parents were at work. She already knew that in other countries pupils were reduced to immobility in the classroom. She reversed this, and designed teaching aids aimed to allow the child to find out for itself. This did not mean that the child was allowed to do exactly as it pleased: indeed she noticed that children spontaneously learnt and rejected play methods in favour of work. The outcome of her experiment in the Casa dei Bambini won local and then world-wide recognition: disorderly children of lowly standing came to read, write and count before the age of six – and liked the experience.

Maria Montessori became renowned as her ideas spread. Her lectures were listened to by people from all over the world and her disciples disseminated the movement throughout Europe and to the USA where she herself went in 1914. Meanwhile she was writing prolifically and

Maria Montessori

developing fresh ideas to cope with the demands of older children. Sometimes her methods diverged from the original concepts and led the movement into disrepute. In America one of her students, **Helen Parkhurst** (American), founder of the Dalton School in New York, later became Director of the Montessori Schools in the USA, though her approach did not always keep in line with Maria Montessori's evolving concepts in Europe. Maria Montessori who became Italy's Inspector of Schools in 1922, lectured ceaselessly, and constantly sophisticated her methods to keep pace with new discoveries and social changes. Much of her last ten years was spent in the Indian sub-continent. Here, even as an enemy alien in time of war, she was given special freedom to continue her work, and after the war she went back to Italy to re-establish the Montessori organisation which had been suppressed by the Fascists. She travelled and worked almost ceaselessly until her death at the age of 81.

The children of today have benefited enormously from the courageous pioneering work of the women educationalists of the 19th and early 20th centuries. Progress is now made on a broad front and the place of the few pioneers has been taken by a host of trained teachers. Experimental work continues within the framework laid down by the original innovators.

Grace Owen (British) and **Margaret McMillan** (British, 1860–1931), for example, pioneered the idea of growth (physically, mentally and socially) of the young in play groups under the supervision of a qualified teacher. Margaret McMillan held the view that only trained and qualified people should work in nursery schools and set up training centres in Manchester, London and Deptford for three-year courses. These centres supplied nursery teachers to the entire British Commonwealth as well as the early US nursery schools.

And **Leila Rendel** (Swedish) who started in 1917 the first English co-educational boarding-school for working-class children, began in 1925 to take children from emotionally inadequate homes – those whose parents' death, etc. or the child's illegitimacy had deprived them of a loving family environment. By 1934 local authorities were sending disturbed children from broken homes to her, and so her school became one of the first schools to be recognised by the British Board of Education under the Act of 1921 as a place for maladjusted children. This was followed in 1956 by a 'family group' home for children needing more individual attention.

Innovations in educational methods have found women to the forefront. **Mary Field** (British, 1876–1968), a teacher by training, began directing documentary films in 1926 and in 1944 became the Executive Officer of the Children's Film Foundation which had as its aim the making of children's films on a non-profit-making basis. She also wrote children's educational books and from 1959 until 1963 advised television companies on children's programmes.

The list of teachers and teachers' instructors is endless and growing, the following being merely a random sample:

Brenda Jubin	American	First woman resident Dean of Yale University, 1970.

Elsa Tabernig de Pucciarelli	Argentinian	Professor of French Literature at the University of Tucuman (1937–47); Head of Institute of Foreign Languages at La Plata from 1960 as well as General Director of Arts Education for Buenos Aires (1963–8).
Barbara Drysdale	British	Pioneered the Mulberry Bush School, a therapeutic community for psychopathic children.
Margaret Graham and Mary Stewart	British	Pioneered women's higher education in East Africa and were instrumental in having Makerere University start admitting women in 1945.
Janet Grieve	British	Founded at Lendrick Muir the only Scottish school for maladjusted teenagers with a high intelligence.
Christine Sandford (1893–1975)	British	Started a school in Addis Ababa. Now called The Sandford School it numbers 800 boys and girls of 40 different nationalities.
Alice Sette	French	First woman Rector of a university in France in 1973.
Parvin Birjandi	Iranian	First Dean of Women at the University of Teheran, 1958.
Halide Edib Adivar (1883–1964)	Turkish	Supervised girls' education in Syria in days of the Ottoman Empire, fought as a Sergeant Major in the War of Independence and became the first woman Professor in the University of Istanbul.
Bayan Vedida Pars	Turkish	In 1957 first woman President of the Turkish National Educational Association and one-time Head of the Gazi Institute in Ankara, the leading Turkish teachers' training school.

There remains ample scope for more feminine achievements in education as shown in the latest world illiteracy figure of 33 per cent. To increase understanding of this figure consider a large underdeveloped country – India, where 58·6 per cent of all males and 86·8 per cent of all females, over 15 years of age, are illiterate.

Before achieving anything one must first learn how.

7

IN THE STRUGGLE FOR EQUALITY AND SUFFRAGE

„Divorçons!"

The first known group of women to fight for equality took their stand in Roman times in 43 BC. There was a civil war going on between Antony, Octavian and Lepidus, on the one side, and Brutus and Cassius on the other; funds were short so Antony's side proposed to tax the properties of 1400 rich women – women already deprived of their menfolk through a conflict not of their choosing. The women appealed to Octavian's sister and then to Antony's mother but without success. As females had no representation in the Government there seemed only one course left – an immediate and probably the first-ever female political march to the Forum to state their case, put forward by a well-chosen spokeswoman, **Hortensia** (Roman), the daughter of an advocate and orator. Hortensia did her job so well that, although the Triumvirs were angered at the women's audacity, they were also shamed into reducing the number to be taxed from 1400 to 400 – with equal taxation for 400 rich men. It was a long time, however, before women were to make a prolonged and consistent bid for equality by right of law.

The timing of many nations' steps towards equal status for the female half of their populace has frequently been closely related to those countries' struggle for survival. **Three prerequisites initiated the greatest number of advances towards equality – a major revolution, a modern full-scale war or the demands of pioneering in an undeveloped country, when female collaboration was vital to the men.** For many centuries, therefore, women's calls for equality came as lone voices in a wilderness.

An outstanding medieval advocate for women's emancipation was **Christine de Pisan** (see section on Literature and Journalism), a writer well known in educated circles, who advocated women's clubs (or unions) to protect women's interests and stated that women should educate themselves, and also train in law in order to manage their own estates. She was too far ahead of her time.

Probably the first major female written petition to any Government was in England in 1649, towards the end of the Civil War, when a request with 10000 signatures was put before Parliament. Although primarily a Leveller petition, it particularly emphasised that women should have an equal share and interest in the Commonwealth and reminded Parliament that it was a Scotswoman who started the overthrow of the Episcopal Tyranny in Scotland. It continued: '. . . Have we not an equal interest with the men of this nation in those liberties and securities contained in the Petition of Right, and the other good laws of the land?' The reply was that '. . . the matter was of higher concernment than they understood', and they were told 'to look after their own business and meddle with their housewifery'. These women had not asked for the vote, just the right to petition and voice their opinions.

A prominent writer **Mary Montagu** (English, 1689–1762) also pleaded for equality, though she disguised a belief in feminine emancipation until her later days, when she finally made it clear that '. . . Nature has not placed us in an inferior Rank to Men . . . where we see no distinction of capacity.' (See also section on Literature and Journalism.) A more militant attitude was taken by **Olympe de Gouges** (French, 1748–93) in her work *Declaration of the Rights of Women* published about 1791, the year in which her compatriot **Rose Lacombe** (French, 1765–*c* 1796) founded a society for women supporting the Revolution and Republican ideas.

The recognised pioneer of the suffrage movement in England was **Mary Wollstonecraft** (British, 1759–97) though her book, *A Vindication of the Rights of Women*, written and published by herself in 1792, was little noticed at the time. Only later did it become the text of the English suffrage movement. Nor was a tirade for women's emancipation, poured out by **Mary Radcliffe** (British) in her book *The Female Advocate, or an attempt to recover the rights of women from male usurpation*, any more successful in 1799. The approach had to be more subtle, and grown from the roots.

The first German woman to write a book for the equality of women, **Amalia Holst** (German), in 1802 hit on the right method. It was called *Ueber die Bestimmung des Weibes zur höhern Geistesbildung*, and advocated that women should be allowed educational opportunities to study without restraint. This, she believed, was the keystone to female equality. But these were theories.

A practical fighter for the Infants Custody Bill in England was **Caroline Norton** (British, 1808–77) who married George Norton in 1827, a parasite who depended upon his wife's income and political connections for his own advancement. In 1836 George Norton sued Lord Melbourne, the Prime Minister, for seducing his wife after she had sought Melbourne's aid in having her husband made a judge, but the action went against Norton, who thereupon did all in his power to see

Caroline Norton

that the existing marriage laws were fully implemented to his wife's disadvantage. Caroline Norton discovered that any money or property she possessed at, or acquired during, her marriage was her husband's, and after the break-up of the marriage every penny she earned to keep herself could, by law, be taken from her by her husband; by law she could neither enter into contracts in her own right nor sue anybody – no matter how much they maligned her. Finally, by law, her husband could take her children from her and never allow her access to them. That really started her into action. In 1837 she met and collaborated with Mr Talfourd, a Member of Parliament who had already decided to introduce an Infants Custody Bill. Together they decided policy for pursuing the Bill further and, by 1838, it reached the House of Lords – where it hung in the balance. Caroline Norton wrote a pamphlet, *A Plain Letter to the Lord Chancellor*, in which she set forth a strong and well-argued case for the Bill. Fearing it would carry less weight if it came from a woman, she had it printed privately under the name Pierce Stevenson, and delivered to every MP and Peer. Favourable reaction carried the Bill which was passed in 1839, and laid down that a judge might make an order allowing a mother, against whom adultery was not proved, to have custody of her children under seven years and, for older children, access at stated times. (This Act was amended in 1925 to give full, equal guardianship.) Then, in 1855, George Norton stopped her allowance, and again she took up the cudgels on behalf of a Marriage and Divorce Act. When it was passed in 1857, despite 29 speeches of characteristic length by Mr Gladstone in opposition to one clause alone, it could be claimed that Caroline Norton was chiefly responsible. Her pamphlets and work behind the scenes in support of amendments to protect the deserted wife from her husband's claim to her earnings; to make possible the payment of a separate maintenance allowance through a trustee; to allow a separated wife or divorcee to inherit or bequeath property acquired after her separation (she still had no claim on any property from or before her marriage); to give the power to sue or be sued and to enter into contracts in her own right, were of fundamental importance. Divorced people might now legally remarry and, if the court so decided, the 'injured' wife might have custody of the children and payment of maintenance. Even so, things were not yet equal: only men could sue for divorce on grounds of adultery. There was a happier side to Caroline Norton. All her life she wrote articles, books, poetry and songs – many of them of such merit that she was compared with the élite in their field. Her four novels reflected her earlier experiences. In the final two years of her life she did at last enter into a happy marriage.

The literary advocates of women's equality were important:

Fredrika Bremer (Swedish, 1801–65) argued the case for women's emancipation in *Hertha* and *Fader och dotter* published in the 1850s.

Camilla Collett (Norwegian, 1813–95), wrote novels advocating women's rights. And **Olive Schreiner** (South African, 1855–1920) saw her *Woman and Labour* in 1911 become a textbook of the Women's movement. (See also section on Literature.)

It was in New Zealand, however, where the breakthrough towards women's electoral rights came. **Mary Müller** (British, 1820–1902), had arrived in that budding country in 1850 and married Dr Müller, later to be Resident Magistrate for the district of Wairau. Mary Müller had been well aware of the inequality of the English laws towards women and, in New Zealand, held many conversations with influential law-making men, suggesting the vote for women. Some listeners were polite, but most were shocked – including her husband.

Through a relative who owned the *Nelson Examiner*, then possibly the country's most influential newspaper, she gained space in this and other newspapers for anonymous articles championing her ideas. In 1869, under the name 'Femina', she issued a pamphlet, *An Appeal to the Men of New Zealand*, asking for the vote for women. The men were not yet ready to be appealed to, so she achieved the first step towards equality by working for, and seeing passed, the Married Women's Property Act in 1884. However, the anonymity necessary to guard against her husband's disapproval compelled her to give up.

Into her place stepped **Katharine Sheppard** (New Zealander, 1848–1934), a woman of great charm but also inflexible determination and sound administrative ability. When the New Zealand Branch of the Women's Christian Temperance Union (WCTU) was started in 1885 by **Mary Leavitt** (American, 1830–1912), during a world-wide campaign, Katharine Sheppard was appointed Superintendent of the Franchise Department and organised area franchise departments throughout New Zealand. In 1888, when the Parliamentary programme for the coming session included a new Electoral Act, Katharine Sheppard drew up and submitted a petition from the WCTU asking for women to be included. For the next few years the debate and struggle for women's vote ebbed and flowed within the House of Representatives, with the WCTU pressure group nudging the MPs along. A petition containing 10085 women's signatures was collected in 1891 from the WCTU's areas and sent to both the House of Representatives and the Legislative Council. More delays provoked a telegram from Katharine Sheppard to the Council reminding them of the 10000 women, but at the Second Reading the Bill was rejected. A fresh petition, this time containing 20274 signatures, was presented in 1892. Now, it must be remembered this was organised by a temperance body; therefore other temperance organisations wanted women to have the vote and the liquor trade did not. A counter-petition, with organisers paying canvassers a rate per 100 signatures, was submitted. By the end of the year, despite further readings of the Bill, there was still no vote for women, though the Lower House was now in favour. Before the 1893 Parliamentary Session the WCTU worked feverishly, visiting remote areas, holding meetings and collecting women's signatures until yet another petition, signed by a third of the women of New Zealand (31872 signatures, then the most

Katharine Sheppard

signatures to be presented to any Parliament in Australasia) was submitted. On 8 September, by a majority of two votes, the Bill passed the Third, and last, Reading of the Upper House. There still remained the need for the Governor's signature. The opposition sent him a petition and Katharine Sheppard wrote to him 'on behalf of 31 000 women'.

On 19 September 1893, the following telegram was forwarded to Katharine Sheppard:

> 'The Electoral Bill assented to by his Excellency the Governor at a quarter to twelve this day.'

The women of New Zealand had won the vote, though this was only a beginning.

South Australia, in 1894, then Western Australia, in 1899, followed suit and by 1902 all Australian women had the vote. They were followed by Finland in 1906 and Norway in 1913.

BRITAIN

The bitterest struggle by women for the right to vote took place in Britain, their efforts combining from a variety of different sources. When the first women's employment bureau in Britain was established in 1857, one of the persons behind it was **Barbara Bodichon** (British, 1827–91) who had previously campaigned for the Married Women's Property Bill (which was negated by the Marriage and Divorce Bill) and had also worked for the founding of Girton College (see section on Education). In 1857 she helped set up an important English suffrage publication, *The Englishwomen's Journal*, which became the voice of suffrage aspirations and achievements and, in 1865, successfully campaigned for John Stuart Mill, a known supporter of women's suffrage, when he stood for Parliament. However, the most persistent advocate and leader of the Suffrage movement in Britain was **Millicent Fawcett** (British, 1847–1929) who, with Barbara Bodichon and four other women, formed the first Woman's Suffrage Committee in 1866. They collected signatures for a petition; committees were formed in Manchester and Edinburgh and by May 1867, when the Reform Bill came up, the first petition to Parliament for Woman's Suffrage was presented. So came about the first Parliamentary debate on woman's suffrage and the first open public meeting to agitate for the vote, held in the Free Trade Hall, Manchester, in 1868. Millicent Fawcett gave her own first public speech in London that same year, and by so doing she, with a friend, brought forth the comment in Parliament that 'two ladies, wives of members of this house, who have disgraced themselves by speaking in public . . .'. The admonition in no way deterred her from travelling the country, speaking at public meetings.

An ardent opponent of the Suffrage Bill was William Gladstone (who had been opposed to many aspects of the Marriage and Divorce Bill). After the Bill was carried to its Second Reading by 124 to 91, in 1870, it was he who produced so much opposition during the Committee Stage that the Second Reading failed by 106 votes. The battle, however, simmered on with women making steady gains in a number of ways besides improving their education. For example a deputation of women nail- and chain-makers, escorted by Millicent Fawcett, went to the Home Office in 1887 to put to the Home Secretary a case for keeping their jobs and won their point.

Carrie Catt (seated, centre) with
Millicent Fawcett (seated, right)

From now to 1914 Millicent Fawcett organised meetings and marches
and spoke on behalf of woman's suffrage. Petitions were drawn up and
the Bill came before the House almost annually. But no party would
commit itself and in Parliament the Suffrage Bills on the Order Paper
were consistently talked out: it became a sort of junior-school-type,
Parliamentary joke to do so. At the same time there were numerous
women's societies brought into existence, often in disagreement with
each other. The birth of a combined society took place in 1897 when 2
London and 18 provincial suffrage societies amalgamated, under Millicent Fawcett as President, into the National Union of Women Suffrage
Societies (NUWSS), a well-organised constitutional body composed of
members who were not militant extremists. They did not attack, but
aimed to convert, public opinion: always Millicent Fawcett presented
balanced and succinct arguments and achieved a rapid growth in membership. Its Secretary was **Helen Blackburn** (British, 1842–1903)
who also edited *The Englishwoman's Review* from 1881 to 1890. She
was among the first to recognise the significance of women in industry
and published *The Condition of Working Women* (1896) and *Women
under the Factory Acts* (1903).

The most militant of suffragettes was **Emmeline (Emily) Pankhurst** (British, 1858–1928). Let down first by the Liberals and then by
the Labour Party, both of which she had supported in turn, she was
already politically disillusioned by 1903 when she and her daughter
Christabel Pankhurst (British, 1882–1960) formed the non-party
Women's Social and Political Union (WSPU) in Manchester – mostly
from mill girls – and became engaged in the first act of physical aggres-
sion in the struggle for the vote at the hands of Liberal Party supporters
during a meeting in Manchester in 1905. Sir Edward Grey had ex-
pounded on the intentions of the Government about to be formed and
at question time Christabel Pankhurst and **Annie Kenney** (British,
1879–1953) asked what its intentions were over votes for women. Grey
ignored them (he had answered all other questions but thought this one
not 'a fitting subject'). The women unfurled banners and asked again.
They were seized, kicked down the gallery stairs, then thrown bodily

from the hall suffering physical injury. Outside they held a protest meeting, were arrested for obstruction and, upon refusal to pay their fine, sent to prison, the first of many prison sentences to be served by suffragettes in England. This episode was given world-wide newspaper coverage: it also provoked a wave of bitter violence from the frustrated WSPU Party whose motto became 'Deeds not Words'. In 1906 they moved to London and started a deliberate policy of sensationalism. They chained themselves to the railings of the Prime Minister's residence, harangued the terrace of Parliament from the river, broke windows – and one woman, **Emily Davidson** (British) threw herself in front of the King's racehorse in the 1913 Derby and was killed. Women in prison went on hunger strike and were forcibly fed. Mr Asquith parried and procrastinated about the Bill throughout, while, in 1913, his Government passed the so-called 'Cat and Mouse' Act – officially called the Prisoners (Temporary Discharge for Ill-Health) Act. Imprisoned suffragettes who went on hunger strike would be released when in danger of death but, as soon as they were strong enough, would be re-arrested to continue their sentence. This frequent and repetitive starving to near death permanently undermined the health of more than one woman. On the other hand the depredations of the militants turned many previously sympathetic people against the women – among those who changed being Winston Churchill.

Emily Davidson throws herself under the King's horse in the 1913 Derby

The First World War started in 1914 at a time when the NUWSS, under Millicent Fawcett's leadership, had a constitution of 411 self-supporting societies and was still growing rapidly. This organisation was turned to help the war effort; women were needed and proved their worth. Emily Pankhurst rallied thousands of munitions workers but her WSPU faded away, while Millicent Fawcett kept a small suffrage department of the NUWSS running. Thus, in January 1917, when a Government Report recommended enfranchisement for women householders and wives of householders if over 30 or 35 years, the NUWSS was ready to report its support if the age of 30 years was agreed. The greater number of English adults were now women, as a result of the carnage of the war, and the first suffrage demonstration since the outbreak of the war was arranged for women war workers from 70 different trade unions representing over 2 000 000 women. The NUWSS had its way because it carried popular opinion with it and so the Representation of the Peoples Act was passed, the Royal Assent being given on 6 February 1918. The shortest Statute of Parliament – just 27 words, making women eligible to stand for Parliament – came into force the same year.

THE USA

In the USA the women's vote was won more easily, but still by diverse means. Linking the US women's rights movement to the anti-slavery campaign were **Sarah** (American, 1792–1873) and **Angelina Grimké** (American, 1805–79) (see also under section on Religion and Social Reform), and taking a literary step towards the feminist movement was **Margaret Fuller** (American, 1810–50) in 1845 with her book *Woman in the Nineteenth Century*. However, the first outstanding leader of the US women's rights movement was **Elizabeth Stanton** (American, 1815–1902) who, as a girl in her father's (a judge) office, had seen at first hand the effects of the discriminatory laws, and also the condition of slaves. She was determined to prove women's capability and independence and declined to swear obedience at her wedding. By 1845 she was circulating petitions to secure Married Women's Property Rights law in New York, and the same year she and another pioneer for women's equality, **Lucretia Mott** (American, 1793–1880) (see also section on Religion and Social Reform) organised the first women's rights convention in the US, at Seneca Falls, N.Y. A Woman's Bill of Rights, drawn up by Elizabeth Stanton, was adopted, and demanded equality for women in State, Church, Law and Society. A resolution (without Lucretia Mott's approval) in favour of women's suffrage introduced the first organised demand for a vote for women in the US.

In 1850 Elizabeth Stanton met **Susan Anthony** (American, 1820–1906) (see also section on Religion and Social Reform) and for the next 40 years, while the former did the writing and the latter the business management, they worked together, publishing from 1868 to 1870 *The Revolution*, a New York women's rights weekly and, with **Matilda Gage** (American, 1826–98), the first three volumes of the six-volume (1881–1922) *The History of Woman Suffrage*. In 1872 Susan Anthony, by actually casting a vote, claimed rights as a person and a citizen. Arrest, trial and conviction followed, but although she refused to pay the fine the authorities declined to gaol her.

In 1869 the National Women's Suffrage Association had been formed with Elizabeth Stanton as President and Susan Anthony as Chairman of the Executive Council, its aim to obtain an Amendment to the Federal Constitution, giving women the vote. For the next 50 years the Association held an Annual National Convention and sent delegations to the committees of every Congress pleading their aim. In 1890 the Association amalgamated with the American Suffrage Association which had been organised by **Lucy Stone** (American, 1818–93) and her group, in 1869, forming together the new National American Woman Suffrage

Association, which continued pressure on the States and gradually gained women a State vote, so increasing the number of Members of Congress who had depended upon women's votes to win their seats.

When Elizabeth Stanton and Susan Anthony died, **Anna Shaw** (American, 1847–1919) and **Carrie Catt** (American, 1859–1947) took over. Anna Shaw caused friction but Carrie Catt, a woman of immensely wide outlook and systematic powers of persuasion, reorganised the Association on political district lines during 1905 to 1915, trained women for direct political action and co-ordinated their efforts. As in Britain the part played by US women in the First World War did much to break down the opposition to their suffrage; but it was not until after the British, German and Russian example and the association was 2000000 strong that Congress, after bitter opposition in the Senate, submitted the Nineteenth Amendment to the State legislature in June 1919. It was ratified in August 1920 and owed much to Carrie Catt's statesmanship. The first President of the International Woman Suffrage Alliance was Carrie Catt from 1902, when she founded it, until 1923. In between 1911 and 1912 she made a feminist voyage round the world, making contact with the main organisations. Strongly opposed to war she formed an alliance in 1925 of 11 national women's organisations into the National Committee on the Cause and Cure of War to pressurise the US Government into participation in a world organisation for peace. After the Second World War, she pinned her hopes on the United Nations, and used her influence to get qualified women placed on crucial commissions. A creation of great importance was her non-party League of Women Voters, founded in 1920 from the then 2000000 strong National American Women Suffrage Association. Today it is organised into more than 1200 local leagues, nation-wide with a head-quarters in Washington, D.C., and has as its aim the study of national and local issues with a view to producing objective information from which people can formulate their own opinions. It concentrates upon clearly defined projects – anything from a study of China, through the Tennessee Valley Authority to local housing issues and environmental problems. It publishes biographical reports upon political candidates for office and indirectly exerts much educated liberal influence upon the electorate as a whole. It does not blatantly pressurise, but tries to guide in a purposeful manner as its founder did.

GERMANY

The leader of the German women's struggle for equality was **Luise Otto-Peter** (German, 1819–95), a writer of revolutionary lyrics and publisher of the first German sociological novel (in 1842). Her main interest was the lot of the working woman. Writing in liberal papers she stated that it was not only women's right, but their duty to partici-pate in affairs of the State. She managed to persuade a Board that was studying the status of labour, to include women workers in their considerations. In 1849 she founded a paper advocating equality for women but in 1852 it was suppressed by the Monarchist group. In 1865 the Association for Women's Education was founded with Luise Otto-Peter as its President, but she was acting now less as a militant and more as an administrator, forming branches in other cities and calling the first German woman's convention – a great success with women from all over Germany attending. The Association became the nucleus of the women's movement when it merged into the larger National Association of German Women with its aim to support women's right to work. By 1877 there were 11 000 members enabling the lobbying of Government to begin in earnest. Petitions were sent to the Reichstag to employ women in the postal services (1867), to use more women teachers in the lower school and to train them (1872) and for the rights of married women and guardianship (1877). These petitions were of little immediate avail, but they made German women aware of their status and paved the way for still greater feminist activity in the 1890s, including a demand for the vote.

An important German woman's paper was *The Woman's Advocate*, edited by the Jewess **Jenny Hirsch** (German, 1829–1902), an able, self-made woman, who was Secretary to the Lette Society for 17 years and translated John Stuart Mill's *Subjection of Women* into German in 1870, which had quite a wide circulation. **Alice Salomon** (German, 1872–1948), one of the first women PhDs from the University of Berlin in 1906 (see also in section on Education) wrote a thesis analysing the inequality of pay between men and women doing equivalent work, and also wrote on the position of women and children in industry, and on public health. However, the first German women's organisation with a clearly stated political aim was the German Association for Woman Suffrage, founded in 1902, with **Anita Augspurg** (German, 1857–1943) as President. The same year it was represented at a seven-nation delegation in Washington to plan the launching of a world-wide suffrage association. Two years later, under the direction of Susan Anthony, there congregated in Berlin what was said to be the largest gathering of women in the world's history at the founding of the International Woman Suffrage Alliance. The German association changed its name to Union for Woman Suffrage and started branches throughout Germany. Characteristically these split into two factions but still managed to keep pressure on the Government during the First World War, in which German women, too, proved their worth to their country. On 12 November 1918, the day after the Armistice, universal suffrage was proclaimed on the wings of the Revolution.

FRANCE

Women's part in French political matters had always been strong (see sections on Statecraft and on Courtesans,) but perhaps the first French suffragist to obtain a nomination to the Legislative Assembly of the Seine was **Jeanne Deroin** (French) in 1849. She demanded universal suffrage and got 15 votes. Two years later she went to prison for six months for taking part in the creation of working women's associations, but she also wrote a paper, *L'Opinion des Femmes*, in which she campaigned for higher education and entry into the Faculties, and achieved her aim in 1863. The foundation of the Association for Women's Rights in France took place in 1870 under **Maria Deraismes** (French) (helped by Léon Richer), its aim being the complete emancipation of women; but with social and civil equality put before political equality it was not therefore revolutionary. A more militant line was taken by 'La Ligue pour les Droits des Femmes', founded in 1879 by **Aubertine Audert** (French), a Socialist who later went to prison for refusing to pay taxes. She became isolated and was not taken very seriously, whereas La Ligue became Suffrage des Femmes in 1883 and, working quietly and democratically under **Maria Veroné** (French), made an impact. Nevertheless, progress towards suffrage in France was very slow. Successive attempts to push an Act into law failed, mostly by being rejected in the Upper House. Not until 1944, in the aftermath of the German Occupation, was the vote granted as one of several measures designed to re-establish political stability.

CANADA

The pioneer for women's equality in Canada was **Emily Stowe** (Canadian, 1831–1903) of Toronto who graduated from the New York Women's Medical School in 1868 and thus became the first Canadian woman doctor. It was she who caused Toronto University to open its doors to women in 1886, and she, too, who fought to secure factory and health laws and the Married Women's Property Act. In 1876 she launched the Toronto Literary Club – an unlikely name for an organisation which aimed for women's suffrage.

The vote was first granted in the Province of Manitoba in 1916 after years of work by **Lillian Thomas**, **Mary Crawford** and **Nellie McClung**. And the last Canadian province to give women the vote was Quebec in 1940 after campaigns carried on for over two decades by **Idola St-Jean**, **Thérèse Casgrain**, **Flora Martel** and others. Besides their annual petitions to their Government they petitioned King George V in 1936 and also broadcast their views over the radio.

A law-court fight was necessary to gain women the right to sit in the Senate. In 1927 five Alberta women, **Henrietta Edwards**, **Emily Murphy**, **Nellie McClung**, **Louise McKinney** and **Irene Parlby** required an interpretation of the word 'person' from the 1867 Act stating 'any qualified person could be summoned to the House'. On 24 April 1928, the court decided that a woman was not a 'person'. The five women appealed to the Judicial Committee of the Privy Council – and won.

BELGIUM

Marie Popelin (1846–1913) was the leading woman for equality (see also section on Law). After being refused the oath of barrister in 1888,

Marie Popelin

only because she was a woman, she worked as a law consultant and then became the driving force behind the first Belgian feminist organisation, the Belgium League of Women's Rights, founded in 1892. As its President she organised an International Feminist Congress at Brussels in 1897, and in 1905 became President of the Council of Belgian Women at its foundation. This council represented most of the feminine movements in Belgium and on behalf of it she attended international conferences. As well as for equality she also worked for world peace.

INDIA AND PAKISTAN

The founder of the Women's Indian Association, in 1917, was Mrs **Cousins** (British), whose aim was equal political status for women. It sent a deputation, headed by **Sarojini Naidu** (Indian, 1879–1949), to the Secretary of State for India, but to no avail. Gradually, however, women's organisations and political groups joined in the struggle and in 1926 women were allowed to vote and be elected in the Provincial Legislatures. The Women's Indian Association put forward candidates and Dr **Muthulakshmi** (Indian) became the first woman to be elected to an Indian Legislative Council. The reservation of seats was then introduced and gradually increased in men's favour until the ratio was seven to one against women. Women fought for direct election on a non-communal basis, without reservation of seats, but knew there was no prospect until they first gained independence from British rule; so for this they also campaigned. They won a complete franchise when they voted in their first General Elections in 1952–3, five years after Independence and the partition of India into India and Pakistan.

The problems of Muslim women are greater than those of most other religious bodies. One of the pioneers for emancipation in Pakistan (at that time part of the Dominion of India) was Begum **Jahanara Shah Nawaz** (Pakistani), who was one of the three women delegates at the second and third London Round Table Conferences on India (in the 1930s) to represent women's point of view on Home Rule. Like the Indians the Pakistani women won the right to vote shortly after Partition, but its implementation has regularly been circumscribed in a country where 'democracy' is in difficulty.

TURKEY

The pioneer for the emancipation of women was the author **Halide Edib Adivar** (1883–1964) (see also section on Education). She was actively engaged in literary, political and social movements in Turkey and in her early novels, such as *Handan* in 1912, studied the problems confronting educated Turkish women. The vote was eventually conceded by Ataturk in 1933 as political sop; women were discouraged from taking part in politics.

INDONESIA

Here, recent pioneers for equality were **Maria Ullfah Santoso**, **Mrs Harahap** (Professor of Law in the University of Djakarta), **Roesial Sarjona** and **Nani Soewondo** (author of *Legal and Social Status of Women*), who studied and worked to help formulate the draft Marriage Law Bill in 1952 in Indonesia. The Muslims found it unacceptable, as they did the more progressive draft put forward in 1958 by Mrs **Soemario** and which advocated monogamous marriage. Even so, the male-orientated Muslim religion is beginning to be stirred by women's petticoats, and the inclusion of the first women members of the Muslim courts, which apply the Islamic laws, has been achieved by women's organisations.

COMMUNIST COUNTRIES

Women gained a measure of equality wherever the Communists came to power since, particularly in China, the promise of equality was bait to attract the support of the downtrodden women – Chinese women had previously been forced to watch, helpless, when unwanted new-born girl babies were literally thrown out to die because of their lack of potential work strength.

DATES WHEN VARIOUS NATIONS GAVE VOTES TO WOMEN

Australia	1902	Italy	1945
Austria	1918	Japan	1945
Belgium	1919	Jordan	1973
Brazil	1932	New Zealand	1893
Bulgaria	1947	Norway	1913
Canada	1918	Pakistan	1926★
China	1947	Philippines	1937
Denmark	1915	Poland	1918
Finland	1906	South Africa	1930
France	1944	Spain	1931
German Federal Republic	1918	Sweden	1919
Great Britain	1919	Switzerland	1971
Holland	1919	Thailand	1932
India	1926★	Turkey	1933
Indonesia	1955	USA	1920
Iran	1963	USSR	1917
Ireland	1919	Yugoslavia	1945
Israel	1948		

★ *Provincial vote*

Women get the vote in Britain

8

MISTRESSES, COURTESANS AND SALONNIÈRES

Even a short study of history will bring to light records of marriages arranged for political reasons, often when the couple were children of a very young age. It is not surprising, therefore, that upon reaching maturity they often looked elsewhere for an additional relationship, and it was an accepted practice that many male rulers had their mistresses or concubines. These women were either an integral part of the royal household or were established in dwellings befitting their rank. If an arranged marriage brought forth no heir then a mistress's child sometimes contended for the throne. One of the frequent penalties imposed by monarchs taking mistresses was the problem of recognition of their offspring. For example, the legitimised children of **Catherine Swynford** (English, 1350–1403) by John of Gaunt were soon a factor in the factional struggle of the Wars of the Roses, though their progeny by marriage eventually brought the unification of the rival Houses of York and Lancaster. Mistresses were not always mere toys of pleasure but intelligent, educated women of good family who manipulated the political scene, advised on State matters and, occasionally, dominated the ruler himself.

Courtesans, or prostitutes, had an opportunity of gaining importance in history if they raised their status above that of casual acquaintance and became either wives, mistresses or salonnières. Salonnières – women who made their homes the meeting-place of the intellectuals of the day – may have been mistresses or courtesans as well, though many were neither of these things but highly intellectual women of strong personality who encouraged stimulating discussion and the arts and were, of course, rich enough to indulge in this productive entertaining. It can be seen, therefore, that although very different in some aspects, the élite of mistresses, courtesans and salonnières did have a common role – that of imposing their characters and intellects, mostly by indirect means, upon the current critical situations and great men of their acquaintances.

The first of the élite courtesans to make a deep impression upon history was **Theodora** (*c* 500–48), who seems to have been born in the circus at Constantinople. By all accounts she trod the stage when a child and quickly graduated to prostitution, serving men of the highest grade. Her profession took her to North Africa but eventually brought her back to Constantinople where the Emperor's son, Justinian, who was 20 years her senior, fell in love with her. To enable Justinian to marry her, a law forbidding Senators to marry actresses had to be repealed in 523. There were historical reasons for the law in the first place, no doubt, but this amendment was really productive. For Theodora completely abandoned her old profession and, when she became Empress four years later, played an important role in helping to govern Byzantium. Not only did she institute hospitals on the model of Fabiola's (see section on Science and Medicine), but she opened homes to rehabilitate prostitutes whose case she understood only too well. Shrewd and positive in politics, she resisted rebellion at a time when her husband's resolve was in doubt and took a firm line in matters of religious controversy. She is, perhaps, the best example of a courtesan who raised herself to the heights of constitutional power.

Theodora

The first important salonnière, according to some authorities, was **Isabella d' Este** (Italian, 1474–1539), grand-daughter of King Ferrante of Naples – though it is most unlikely that she was the first woman to hold discussions on the arts and politics. Neither tall nor beautiful, she nevertheless had a splendid bearing linked to elegance, outstanding intelligence

Isabella d'Este

and a fine memory. At the age of 16 she was married to Francesco Gonzaga, the future Marquis of Mantua, a brave but stupid man who found it impossible to match his wife's versatility. Inevitably Isabella d'Este took a keen interest in affairs of State and attracted a following by the sheer brilliance of her personality: she dominated her contemporaries with '. . . an inventive art in arranging things to her own liking while capturing the consent of others', and drawing to her court such people as Leonardo da Vinci, Raphael, Titian and Baldassare Castiglione. She became famous as a conversationalist, for her appreciation of art and literature and for the instruction in manners which she spread as the Renaissance blossomed in her homeland. Indeed she was one of those who gave impetus to the Renaissance. This was a period of political turmoil in Italy compounded by pressure from France and the internal rivalries of the Italian despots. Isabella d'Este played a strong part in guiding Mantuan policy, when her husband was at home, and by running it as Regent when he was away. She formed uneasy alliances of convenience with the powerful Borgias and played one contender off against another. In 1509, when her husband was taken prisoner of war (while asleep), she began to govern in earnest and preserved Mantua from invasion. Unfortunately it did her little good in her husband's eyes: 'We are ashamed that it is our fate to have as wife a woman who is always ruled by her head', he is reported to have said when he returned in 1512. But in 1519 he died and his wife became Regent again, governing with the same success as before in her efforts to preserve something for her eldest son to rule when he came of age. The Mantuans said, 'She trusts no one and will know the motive of everyone', and admiringly followed her while the rest of Italy paid respect even when in opposition to her. She managed to have her second son made a Cardinal, survived with honour the ravaging of Rome by Lutherans in 1527 – and when the time came to withdraw from the government of Mantua as her eldest child took over, autocratically ruled the little State of Solarola, surrounded by the art collection and the clocks which she had assembled over the years, disseminating to the end the sort of civilisation in which she believed.

Isabella d'Este's sister-in-law, **Elisabetta Gonzaga** (Italian, 1471–1526), and wife of the Duke of Urbino, was at the same time stimulating debate and knowledge at Urbino with her literary salons. After **Lucrezia Borgia's** (Italian, 1480–1519) third husband became the Duke of Ferrara in 1505, she emulated Isabella d'Este by making the court of Ferrara a centre for poets, painters and philosophers. In her earlier life she had been dominated by her father and brother, so their infamous reputations rather undeservedly encompassed her. Other Italian Renaissance salonnières included **Vittoria Colonna** (1490–1547) who believed in the Platonic ideals of love and a life of intense spritual passion. Even in old age people found her fascinating, and it was then that she inspired Michelangelo's most passionate poetry. Of the courtesan salonnières there were **Imperia** (1481–1512) of Rome, who delicately gratified priests' spiritual, as well as their temporal, desires in her salon, and **Tullia d'Aragona** (*c* 1510–56) who could talk on any subject and sing airs and motets at sight. She was also the authoress of *On the Infinity of Perfect Love* – a subject about which she should have had at least a working knowledge. For a fee the salons of the courtesan élite were open to the public (some clients complained that conversation was as expensive as love) and attracted the greatest men of the age to discuss philosophy, listen to music or dance.

Throughout the existence of the French court there were courtesans connected with it, but **Diane de Poitiers** (French, 1499–1566) was the first to make an indelible mark and create a memorable style. As a lady-in-waiting at the court of Francis I she not only outshone the King's mistress, **Anne de Pisseleu** (French), but completely captivated his heir, Henry, who was 20 years her junior. As Henry's mistress she dominated the Queen, **Catherine de Médicis** (See section on Politics and Statecraft), though more out of selfishness than for reasons of State. As a salonnière she was in the mould of a d'Este rather than a d'Aragona, a beauty who augmented wit, intellect and good taste with sponsorship of literature, architecture and painting. A later salon which followed was presided over by a woman who had no taint of the courtesan. She was **Cathérine de Vivonne** (Italian, 1588–1665), who married the French Marquis de Rambouillet and came to live in Paris. At the Hôtel de Rambouillet, which she shaped and furnished to her special requirements,

The salon of
Cathérine de Vivonne

surrounding it with a garden of her own design, she entertained the cream of French society and letters and set standards of behaviour which transcended the rather lax manners permeating life in the capital. Her guests complied with her rules and were charmed – perhaps quelled – by superb surroundings and the high level of conversation she insisted upon. Literary works were read and undogmatically criticised so that rather pedantic personages only visited her rarely. There was a discipline in Cathérine de Vivonne's gatherings which was never again equalled, no matter how brilliant the later salons of France may have seemed.

The train of courtesans kept by Charles II of England probably achieved little in their day except trouble and rising costs – for an item of expense which almost invariably cropped up was the support of children who needed means to sustain them as well as titles. The King had at least 14 children by his mistresses while the Queen produced 6. **Barbara Villiers** (English, 1641–1709) interfered in the delicate Restoration politics; **Louise de Kéroualle** (French, 1649–1734) caused disquiet because of her French connections and Catholic religion and **Lucy Walter** (English, 1630?–58), who was one of his earlier loves, gave birth to James, Duke of Monmouth, who was to lead an unsuccessful rebellion against James II. Only **Nell Gwynn** (English, 1650–87) acquired sympathy in her day, but she was a professional, the daughter of a brothel-keeper who became an actress and made her way to the King's favour via the bedrooms of actors and the nobility. This good-natured, illiterate harlot was loyal to Charles throughout his life, and his death-bed wish for her to be provided for was honoured.

Like Charles, Louis XIV of France had his mistresses and also deflected their intervention in affairs of State. **Louise de la Vallière** (French, 1644–1710), the King's mistress from 1661, maintained supremacy until 1667 when **Françoise de Montespan** (French, 1641–1707) became co-favourite – a position Louise was compelled to accept until she admitted defeat by entering a convent in 1674 and turned to writing her memoirs. Françoise de Montespan held her status until 1679, despite her husband's objections at each confinement for the six children she bore the King and the hostility of the Queen who was treated with scant consideration. But Françoise de Montespan made mistakes which were out of character, judging by her brilliant wit in running a notable salon. She became associated with a plot to eliminate Louise de la Vallière (see section on Crime) and she allowed her children's governess, **Françoise de Maintenon** (French, 1635–1719), too much scope with the King. Françoise de Maintenon had been unhappily married to the writer Paul Scarron (who died in 1660) and was supreme in handling the King and his children by Françoise de Montespan. She not only ingratiated herself with the Queen, who welcomed her as the most cultured member of a conniving group, but also held the King in thrall by the brilliance of her conversation and a certain high moral tone. Moreover, the King married her secretly after the Queen died in 1683. Of all Louis's women Françoise de Maintenon was the most responsible, the one who took most interest in educational and religious matters and probably the only consort who even slightly influenced the Sun King's policies.

Françoise de Maintenon

The changes caused by the transfer of monarchies from rule by Divine

Right to Constitutional Rule had a profound effect upon the strategy of **Ehrengarde Kendal** (German, 1667–1743) and **Charlotte von Kilmannsegge** (German, 1675–1725) (nicknamed the 'Maypole' and the 'Elephant', for obvious physical reasons) who were joint mistresses in Britain of George of Hanover even before he became King George I of Britain in 1714. (George also had **Sophie von Platen** as his favourite mistress in Germany but kept his divorced wife locked up after a brief liaison on her part.) Ehrengarde Kendal exerted quite as much influence through Britain's first Prime Minister, Robert Walpole, as through the King and was avaricious in the extreme. She made use of inside information to buy and sell South Sea Stock and became heavily involved in the disposal of titles and public offices for personal profit. This unattractive character risked abuse whenever she ventured into the London streets.

The most celebrated 18th-century English women's salon acquired its name from a group of literary women nicknamed the 'Bluestockings'. It was founded by Mrs **Vesey** (English) as a discussion group to which learned men, particularly in literary art, were invited as speakers. It was later led by **Elizabeth Montagu** (British, 1720–1800) and gained a reputation for earnest pretension. The name was acquired, according to **Fanny Burney** (see section on Literature and Journalism), when Benjamin Stillingfleet was persuaded to attend '. . . even in his blue stockings' – his everyday blue worsted hose, because he had qualms about accepting the invitation without the correct evening dress to wear. The term 'Bluestocking' is still sometimes used to describe a female academic.

During the 18th century in France Louis XV assembled a most celebrated and influential band of mistresses and allowed them unusual power due to his political idleness and sexual bias. The number is uncountable though among the most distinguished were, in chronological order of service, **Louise** (French, 1710–51), **Pauline** (French, d 1741) and **Marie-Anne** (French, d 1744) **de Mailly-Neslé** – three sisters who, taking over from each other, held the status of favourite mistress from 1738 to 1744. The first two sided with those who wished to diminish Austrian influence and this caused French involvement in the War of the Austrian Succession. They were followed by the most powerful of all Louis's mistresses, **Jeanne Poisson** (French, 1721–64,) better known as **Madame de Pompadour**. Born in Paris of lower-middle-class parents she started her social ascent when her father, fleeing from debtors, went abroad for eight years and her mother found a rich protector. He gave Jeanne Poisson an expensive education and arranged her marriage to his nephew.

Now, as Madame Le Normant d'Etoile, she started to attract attention as an hostess. She could sing and act as well as a professional and knew how to hold attention with her sense of fun and animated conversation, debating intellectual matters with her guests who numbered Voltaire among other contemporary, leading writers. She also had an instinctive good taste for gracious living and held her own in the world of fashion.

In the spring of 1745 King Louis XV, attending one of his masked balls at Versailles, was much taken with this tall woman with her excellent figure, chestnut hair and most vivacious manner. During his absence on the Fontenoy campaign in the summer he created her Marquise de Pompadour, presenting her to the Queen upon his return and so

Madame de Pompadour

established her within the court as his mistress. She entered a court where the King never talked politics outside the Council Chambers, led daily hunting or hard galloping as his main relaxation and then conversed on the day's hunt while gambling during the evening, before indulging in love-making. The aristocrats resented her lowly background, especially the First Gentleman of the Bedchamber, the Duc de Richelieu, for she soon thought up new ideas for amusement and entertainment which had hitherto been solely his (repetitive) concern.

She introduced to the court a theatre in which amateur dramatics were performed to a professional standard – with herself always as leading lady. In five years this 'Théâtre des Petits Cabinets' staged 122 different plays, operas and ballets and started a vogue for privately owned small theatres on country estates. She also inspired the King with her enthusiasm for other arts and he enjoyed the diversion of sitting in her perfumed, flower-filled, hot-house of a room, crammed with furniture, pictures, *objets d'art*, plans, fabric patterns, embroidery, books and maps to discuss yet another beautiful house and landscaped garden being prepared for her on his land (all but one of which were to revert to him on her death – and most were wantonly destroyed during the Revolution). With her perfect taste she commissioned artists to make exquisite things and, understanding their problems, paid up promptly. She also took a personal interest in the Sèvres china factory. In all the arts, including literature, her influence and patronage was of importance. However, she dabbled very little in politics, restricting herself to internal affairs, such as appointments of Ministers.

After 1751 she ceased to be the King's mistress but remained a close friend and adviser. Her task in trying to please the seemingly tireless King, who was constantly looking for change and novelty, had not been an easy one and had entailed a régime of 18-hour days crammed with administrative and social duties, from being expected to look her most glamorous best for 8 am Mass, paying court to the Queen, receiving numberless callers and writing letters – sometimes 80 a day – for various projects and then presiding over a dinner-party of 18 until 2 or 3 am. It certainly shortened her life.

She died surrounded by works of art so numerous they would take eight months to sell. Yet, although she is supposed to have cost the notoriously mean King 36000000 livres, she died penniless and does not appear to have been acquisitive for her own selfish ownership but for the exhilaration of living in an atmosphere of artistic intensity and for the pleasure these projects gave her King.

She was followed as favourite mistress by an ex-shop assistant, **Marie Bécu** (French, 1743–93), who took the title Comtesse **Du Barry** despite the existence of a genuine Comtesse of that name – the wife of her lover. After a marriage of convenience to du Barry's brother, the now Madame du Barry was presented at court in 1769 and became the love-liest and last of the King's mistresses. She tried to emulate Madame de Pompadour as a patron of the arts, but, although she helped in the down-fall of the Duc de Choiseul in 1770, she did not have the same political influence in internal affairs as her predecessor. After Louis XVI came to the throne she was forced to live in retirement and only re-emerged in 1792, after the start of the Revolution, to make several trips to England taking financial aid from her own wealth for refugees. She should have stayed. On her return she was accused of being in league with the British and guillotined.

The dramatic, undisciplined, tumultuous, aspiring and idealistic times of the French Revolution are epitomised in the character of **Germaine de Staël** (Swiss, 1766–1817) who was born and lived most of her life in Paris. Her father, Jacques Necker, a very wealthy banker, was Louis XVI's Finance Minister during the early stages of the Revolution. She grew up in a household in which she was exposed to her mother's hysterical outbursts and her father's love of long philosophical discussions with men of learning. There was also, of course, the background of the very pulse beat of the political scene.

She was egotistical, undisciplined, sensuous, physically unattractive

Germaine de Staël
in conference

and a Protestant, but she was very rich and so was considered a matrimonial catch. After much financial haggling a marriage between her and the 37-year-old Swedish Ambassador, Eric-Magnus de Staël, took place when she was 20. She became the dominant partner as was later to be the case with her steady succession of lovers. When she turned her attention to the next, without accepting that the previous one could possibly have tired of her, she would only let go after violent hysterical storms with over-dramatised descriptions of how she was going to commit suicide. Benjamin Constant, who could outdo even Germaine de Staël in theatrical dramatisation, became her lover when she was 28 and introduced her to opium, to which she became addicted for the remainder of her life as it steadily took its toll.

As a salonnière whose home was constantly open to the literary and political figures of the day (irrespective of their political affiliation), she made it plain through her conversations and literary writings that she was in favour of the Revolution in theory and seemed to have favoured the Gironde Party (see section on Politics and Statecraft) when they were in power. She always maintained that it would be wrong for the Royalists to regain control as they would return for revenge, not as a moderate monarchy. On the other hand, with persuasion and argument, she worked hard to inject moderates as Ministers to outnumber the Jacobites with their Socialism and anarchy. However, neither side liked moderates: she had either to flee France or was exiled on more than one occasion.

After Napoleon took power in the *coup d'état* of September 1797, she was a constant thorn in his side with her verbal and written attacks on his authoritarianism. Even before they had met in December of that year, she had sent him emotional, unsolicited letters, some containing criticism of Josephine. Their meeting was a disaster. The remarks of her to Napoleon that 'Genius has no sex' and that, in intelligence, men and women are equals were, although the truth, provocative words for that time and might equally have helped or hindered female emancipation. Certainly Napoleon later collapsed women's hopes of equality being gained from the Revolution by setting out a new code of laws which set back their civil rights more than a century.

Germaine de Staël was a prolific writer but her many literary works are read today only by students. Her fiction was mediocre. Her theory on Romanticism, which was going through a time of vogue, was hers alone, believing as she did that it was Northern in origin and that 'Nordic' literature was of greater merit than Roman or Greek. Her importance lay in a realistic appraisal of political events and in her striving to formulate, to advocate, and to endeavour to bring into being the idea of true political freedom.

Orbiting round Germaine de Staël were the principal salonnières of the day.

There was **Rahel Levin** (German, 1771–1833), a woman denied rank, wealth or beauty but whose salon in Germany came into being and flourished by the sheer force of her personality and intellect. Men were the object of her concentrated efforts, for she considered most women stupid. Hence she became a recognised interpreter of Goethe, and a clearing-house for the latest ideas in science, art, philosophy and theology. When she met Germaine de Staël they seem merely to have come to an

Dolley Madison

understanding. As a close friend of Beethoven, she was one of those rare, privileged people for whom he would play his unpublished compositions. She has been called 'a miniature Renaissance of culture'. In Paris, **Jeanne Récamier** (French, 1777–1849), the wife of an aging banker, ran a successful international salon until Napoleon ostracised her. 'The Divine Juliette', as she was known, possessed a beauty and charm that was unmatched: not only men but also women fell at her feet. Unlike Germaine de Staël and Rahel Levin she did not possess the kind of intelligence that seeks to shine for itself, but that which seems to draw out the intelligence of others. Among her lovers were to be found Germaine de Staël's Benjamin Constant: the two women seem to have reached an amicable agreement over this conflict, for it was said that Jeanne Récamier brought the best out of Germaine de Staël! Chateaubriand was among the few men with whom she fell in love, and it is with his rise to become French Foreign Minister that she is closely associated. In due course it was he who presided over her salon, even after his many affairs with other women.

In the USA the ebullient **Dolley Madison** (American, 1768–1849) was the first salonnière in the White House since it was she, the young wife of James Madison, who dominated its social life after 1801 throughout the period of office held by President Jefferson and during the time her own husband was in power. She usually kept aside from the centre of politics, but when the British invaded Washington and burnt the White House in 1812 she was among the few who did not panic, and it was she who saved Stuart's portrait of Washington along with State papers. Above all she set high standards as a hostess and imparted a much-needed gaiety into proceedings, particularly during the Administration of her rather dry husband. She was friendly and sympathetic to all her guests who, throughout the 20 years following her husband's Presidency, often numbered 30 (many uninvited) and at times 100. Even in widowed old age and in much-reduced circumstances she was not forgotten: as President Polk passed among his guests at his final White House levee he had this 80-year-old lady on his arm.

There were no great salonnières in England at this time: even the courtesans of note turned to blackmail. **Mary Clarke** (British, 1776–1852), who became the mistress of the Duke of York, the Commander-in-Chief of the British Army, manipulated the sale of commissions at a cut rate and eventually caused such a scandal that, in 1809, the Duke was forced to resign. For a substantial reward she had willingly supplied the evidence to bring him down. In due course the Duke was reinstated, but in the meantime Mary Clarke had obtained a large sum, plus a pension of £400 per annum for suppression of her memoirs. Similarly **Harriette Wilson** (British, b. 1786) who, with her sisters, ran what amounted to a brothel for Government Ministers in Mayfair in the 1820s, later threatened some of her clients who included the Duke of Wellington, the Duke of Argyll, Lord Palmerston and Lord Castlereagh with publication. Some of them paid up – only to find they were included in her memoirs anyway, but Wellington coined the phrase 'Publish and be damned' by scrawling it across her demand before returning it.

The courtesans with the most effect were those who attached themselves to politicians and statesmen: royalty was no longer important except as a provider of security, prestige and comfort. Although Ministers frequently had their courtesans, a protective system was established for these liaisons because, as arranged marriages decreased, extra-marital relationships became less socially acceptable. The first practical commercial shorthand was introduced in 1837 by Isaac Pitman and the first typewriter in 1868 (see section on Commerce and Agriculture). These tools in the hands of women produced, in due course, the modern female shorthand typist and secretary. The latter, almost inevitably, became the confidante of men in management and government, tending to create a new style of mistress. The subject has become too hackneyed to need elucidation. One supreme example will be mentioned, that of **Frances Stephenson** (British, d 1973) who became governess to David Lloyd George's children, then his mistress, next his secretary (in which role she came close to the Government of Great Britain both during and after the First World War) and finally her lover's wife after the first Lady Lloyd George died. It is a classic example of its kind: the secret was known by many people as well as the Lloyd George family, but it was not allowed to become public property until she divulged it in her autobiography long after Lloyd George died.

One of the most orthodox of highly influential political salons of the period after the First World War was run by **Nancy Astor** (see section on Politics and Statecraft) at Cliveden, England. Backed by a rich husband and her own influence as an MP, she brought together the best political brains of her day – sometimes at a dinner-table so crowded that it was difficult to raise a fork to the mouth. It must be added that the same people met in a great many salons in Britain, some of which catered more for literature and art. A more original salon was that run by **Margaret Morris** (British) in the Club she formed to teach dancing (see section on

Margaret Morris dancing at the age of 65

Stage and Screen). In the 1920s over tea, coffee and lemonade, she brought together people of such diverse interests as Eugene Goossens, Constant Lambert, Epstein, Picasso, Augustus John and George Bernard Shaw. And of course there were the enormous and typically American parties, run by **Perle Mesta** (1890?–1975) who became celebrated as the model for the lady Ambassador in *Call me Madam* – the hostess with the mostest of them all. In due course she did, indeed, become an Ambassador – for Luxembourg from 1949 to 1953. **Jacqueline Kennedy** attempted to bring back to the White House the semblance of culture in a salon, but the death of her husband cut that short. There seems less time for civilised conversation adjacent to Government than there used to be.

Exchanges of ideas, whether political, philosophical or of the arts, now take place between a far wider range of educated people who are more likely to be drinking instant coffee from mugs rather than sipping champagne from glasses, and who can listen to music, via stereo, which surpasses anything many wealthy salonnières provided in the past. With mass education and communication and the gradual redistribution of wealth, it seems that the days of the old-style salonnières are diminished.

And yet there was **Marie Budberg** (Russian, 1892–1974), an aristocrat, the mistress of five languages, who became what has been described as 'the centre of London's intellectual, artistic and social life' for four decades. In the early days of the Revolution, when survival was at a premium, she alternately had an affair with Robert Bruce Lockhart (and thus became involved with espionage) and lived with Maxim Gorky in a colony of starving Russian artists and writers in St Petersburg. From 1921 to 1933 she moved about Europe with Gorky but in 1933 settled in London (when he returned to Russia) and there, as H. G. Wells's mistress, began a new career as translator, adviser to theatre, film and television directors, costume-designer and author in her own right with 30 books eventually to her credit. Hard drinking and informal, yet of a commanding personality, she attracted a wide range of the most distinguished people of her day, from artistic celebrities to the doyen of the Diplomatic Corps. She turned her home into something, in 20th-century guise, like the salons of the 18th and 19th centuries.

Prostitutes there will always be: but when bewailing today's permissive society it is worth remembering that in Renaissance Italy common prostitutes stood naked at their windows to attract clients! It is also becoming less and less socially acceptable for men in public political office to have extra-marital relationships – as some have found to their cost.

9

AS RELIGIOUS
AND SOCIAL REFORMERS

Apart from the initial desire to propagate their beliefs, some religious Orders concentrated on tending the sick (these are in the section dealing with Science and Medicine), while others were teaching Orders (to be found in the section on Education). Many religious bodies, in common with social reformers, were concerned for the well-being of their fellow men in society and these will be found in this section, as will those Orders whose aims were solely to spread their beliefs, thus limiting the good they achieved.

Priestesses abound throughout history from pagan times to the present day, but their social impact was usually minimal and local. The ancient pagan festival of Thesmorphoria, celebrated solely by women, took place in many parts of the Greek world before Christian times and was basically a fertility rite, both for the participants and their crops. To take part a woman had to be freeborn, observe chastity for nine days and forego certain foods during this time.

The first recorded Christian deaconess is mentioned in the New Testament (Romans 16:1) as of the church at Cenchraea with the noble Roman ladies **Marcella**, **Paula** and **Eustochium** living in a religious retreat at Bethlehem *c* 386. Thus, from the earliest Christian times, women's Orders were established and shortly began to acquire a social impulse since they tended to make attempts at improving living conditions in addition to teaching piety. The first recorded female social reformer, the Empress **Theodora** (*c* 500–48) of Byzantium, who had turned from prostitution to devout Christianity, opened a home to rehabilitate prostitutes as one of her many good deeds (see section on Mistresses, Courtesans and Salonnières). Naturally the most progress in reform was generated by the enlightened people who, in the West, held power at least until the 17th century, a power that almost invariably implied the inclusion of royal patronage and the involvement of an established church. For example, each of four English abbesses, St **Etheldrida** (*c* 660), St **Mildred** (*c* 650), St **Hilda of Whitby** (614–80) and St **Walpurga** (754?–80) were of royal blood. Hilda exercised the greatest influence of them all, training churchmen, bishops and missionaries at her monastery and spreading her teaching throughout the north and east of England. Walpurga, after the death of her brother, ruled over the only double monastery in Germany in the 8th century, though until his death he ruled the monks and she the nuns.

Later many Orders were started at the initiative of single, dedicated women who were not necessarily of the royal blood. **Clara** of Assisi (Italian, 1194–1253) founded the Poor Clares after she had run away from an arranged marriage and gave her vows to Francis of Assisi in 1212. Her Order required complete poverty, both individual and communal, and a penitential prayer life, which she believed would revitalise the Church and the community at large. The Order was reformed by **Colette Boillet** (French, 1381–1447) who thought the earlier Poor Clares' régime insufficiently severe. In 1402 she had become a recluse, but four years later the anti-Pope Benedict XIII took her into the Poor Clares and in 1408 put her in charge of a moribund convent at Besançon which she ran in accordance with her ideals. Initially there was opposition but eventually the Order spread, under the name of the Colettine Poor Clares.

Mythology played its part, of course. The founder of the Brigittine Order, **Birgitta Persson** (Swedish, 1303–73) was said to have had visions, as did the Patron Saint of Italy, **Caterina Benincasa** (1347–80) whose aim it was to secure peace within the Church and throughout Italy, while at the same time waging war against the Muslims. She achieved neither of these aims.

In line with the religious practices of the day female religious Orders turned the minds of their members to lofty philosophies or reorganisation. One of the most remarkable documents of medieval religious perception was written, or dictated, by the anchoress, **Julian** of Norwich (English 1342–after 1416). In it she debated predestination, the foreknowledge of God and the existence of evil – and also revealed a strong and charming personality. The writings of **Teresa de Cepeda y Ahumada** (Spanish, 1515–83), the originator of the Carmelite Reform for both men and women, called for a return to austerity, complete separation from the world and more intense prayer and meditation. Her autobiography, *Life*, written under orders from the Church and not for general publication, is still widely known in Spain today.

Missionary work was nearly always dangerous and sometimes clandestine. **Luisa de Carvajal y Mendoza** (Spanish, 1568–1614), after hearing of the execution of the English Jesuit Henry Walpole in 1596, dedicated herself to furthering the Jesuit faith in England. She founded a college in Belgium for English Jesuits and settled in England in 1605, under the protection of the Spanish Ambassador, where she won converts. But she also made herself dangerously conspicuous by helping the

Gunpowder Plot prisoners, was arrested in 1608 and, but for the diplomatic intervention of her host, might not have been released.

An early disruptive religious influence in the USA was **Anne Hutchinson** (English, *c* 1591–1643). In 1634 she emigrated with her family to Boston where her nursing ability gained influence while simultaneously she started to hold meetings, protesting against the legality of the Massachusetts Puritans and attacking the authority of the clergy. Her actions split the Colony, with the Governor and Deputy-Governor taking opposite sides. At an election the Deputy-Governor ousted her supporter, the Governor, the issue hinging upon a threat to the State since some of Anne Hutchinson's followers refused to take up arms in its defence. She was tried for 'traducing the ministers', and banished. The Boston church excommunicated her. She established a settlement on Rhode Island in 1638, moved to what is now the Bronx and was killed by Indians. The people of Massachusetts considered that, in this particular incident, the Indians were tools in the hands of Divine Providence.

Every religion has its mavericks, some quietly beneficial and unrecognised, some extrovert and contentious. The largest Roman Catholic Congregation of women today, the Sisters of Charity, was founded in 1633 by St Vincent and **Louise de Marillac** (French, 1591–1660). Since St Vincent would not agree to these women being called nuns, they constituted, under Louise, the first unenclosed Roman Catholic religious group doing active work such as visiting and nursing the needy, feeding them and, later, teaching children. In a totally different manner a leading personality in 18th-century Britain's Methodist revolution, **Selina Hastings**, Countess of Huntingdon (British, 1707–91), devoted 50 years of her life and spent more than £100 000 (£1 000 000 or more by today's values) to promote Methodism. With the aim of evangelising the upper classes she used her drawing-room as a centre for prayer-meetings of the aristocracy, but with only modest results. She also built chapels in all the main spas and fashionable resorts of England and, later, in South Wales, a training college which gave three-year courses on theological instruction and practical evangelism. Additionally she gave financial help to the new Princeton University and Dartmouth College, New Hampshire, USA, as well as an orphange in Georgia. But when, in 1779, Selina Hastings opened a chapel in Clerkenwell, the local Anglican clergyman objected to this intrusion into his parish. After a prolonged lawsuit she had to re-register her chapels as Dissenting meeting-houses, causing all her Anglican chaplains to resign. Although sometimes ridiculed for her eccentricities, she did help persuade a section of the aristocracy to mend their quite disreputable ways and achieved some lasting stability in society. Her training college is now called Cheshunt College and, since 1905, has been situated in Cambridge.

The impact of the French Revolution was strongly felt in attacks upon social conscience among the relatively few members of the aristocracy and wealthier classes who happened to be thrown into contact with the misery that outraged the under-privileged. **Elizabeth Fry** (British, 1780–1845), a Quaker's daughter who was to marry a banker, was brought up with all the advantages of wealth as well as a sense of mission that was at first undefined. Seeking a task, in 1798 she began teaching poor

Elizabeth Fry and her followers in Newgate Prison

and uneducated children and, through visiting their homes, saw the primitive conditions in which they lived. Marriage in 1800 and ten confinements between 1801 and 1816 (plus another in 1822) curtailed her philanthropic activities until 1817, although she tried to do good whenever possible in the intervals between producing children. For example, she began preaching with persuasive effect (something in her delivery, charm and wholesomeness of manner, giving her an unusual hold over people), until, in 1811, she was appointed as an 'approved minister'. In 1813, at the instigation of Stephen Grellet, an itinerant American Quaker of French birth, she visited Newgate Prison and saw the quite appalling conditions in which the prisoners, particularly the women, were herded.

The year 1816 was crucial for Elizabeth Fry. Serious retrenchment brought about by her husband's difficulties in business led to the need to disperse most of the children among relatives. The relief was almost welcome to her. Capable though she was as a home nurse and a devoted mother, it was recognised that her children were out of hand: she did not manage them well; they were 'noisy brats', 'naughty and trying'. Indeed, Elizabeth Fry is an early example of a dynamic woman of ideas being forced to choose between the home and her ambitions. She chose ambition and in 1817 returned to Newgate Prison to tackle the problem of helping women prisoners and their children. Overcoming the Governor's objections and braving the terrors of caged and desperate prisoners, she arranged for a room in the prison to be set aside for a school and for the prisoners themselves to co-operate in running it under supervision by visiting 'ladies'. At the back of her mind was an attempt to prepare the prisoners for the day of their release, but the primary need was to inject order into chaos and raise the prisoners' self-respect. In less than a year she had triumphed. All who saw the change in atmosphere which followed her reforms were filled with admiration, this at a time when attempts were being made by men to alter the whole prison system through the Society for the Reformation of Prisoners' Discipline. Elizabeth Fry took the view that '. . . men are cleverer than women and yet I think the judgement of women equal to that of men in most if not all cases'. She had the prison Governor in her pocket, the approval of people who had seen her work; and almost overnight became 'fashionable'. In 1818 she was invited to give evidence before the House of Commons Committee on Prisons, the first woman to appear before any such committee – and with great effect.

Although there was always to be residual opposition to her aims by entrenched conservatives, her progress in reform was infectious and virtually irresistible. An opponent of capital punishment (about which there was little she could do), she did what was possible to alleviate the trials of those being transported to the colonies, visiting 106 ships between 1818 and 1843 and seeing about 12000 convicts on their way in better conditions than might otherwise have been the case. In addition in:

1820   she provided winter shelter for the homeless in a large, rented building.

1821   visited prisons in Scotland and northern England and wrote a report which attracted official enquiries from Italy, Denmark and Russia on the subject of institutional reform.

1827   visited and reported on the prisons in Ireland and extended her interest to improve the treatment of the mentally sick in the British hospital system.

1840 founded a home in which to train nurses – the Fry Nurses of whom a few went with Florence Nightingale to the Crimea (see section on Science and Medicine).

In 1829 the law to prohibit the practice of suttee in India was put through Parliament by Thomas Buxton as a result of her appeal, while between 1838 and 1843 she made official visits to the prisons of France, Switzerland, Germany, Belgium, Holland and Denmark in order to give her advice. It was to her satisfaction that, before she died, there was positive evidence of its acceptance.

Of the several liberalising causes for which women, particularly American women, felt themselves bound to enter battle during the 19th century, the abolition of slavery stood among the highest – and needless to say it was the same cast of dedicated women who fought hardest for emancipation of their sex. Their first leader was **Lucretia Mott** (American, 1793–1880), another Quaker, slightly built and of dynamic energy and purpose, whose flashing eyes and forked tongue often belied the gentleness which Quakers were meant to assume. Her religious bent was strong; she became a recognised minister in 1821 at the same time developing

Lucretia Mott

an individualistic approach to all subjects. In 1825 she acquired a convinced distaste for slavery, declining thereafter to use its products such as cotton, and going so far as to convince her husband, a cotton-dealer, to change his merchandise to wool. However, when the American Anti-Slavery League was formed in 1833 by William Garrison, and Lucretia Mott asked to join, she was rebuffed because women were excluded. The first task, therefore, was to form her own Philadelphia Female Anti-Slavery Society as a step to getting personally involved. After that progress was made and, in whatever capacity Lucretia Mott served, she proved the most forthright of the speakers and therefore a prime target for the movement's opponents. Meeting-places were burned, the Motts were ostracised, mobbed and stoned. Some of the male supporters were tarred and feathered. On one occasion she railed at a crowd who refused to tar her, claiming that she expected no courtesy at their hands on account of her sex. On a visit to London, England in 1840, she was, because she was a woman, refused admittance as a delegate to the World's Anti-Slavery Convention, though her personal press conferences and public meetings established her, nevertheless, as the 'Lioness of the Convention'. Back in the USA she and her husband, who never flinched from her cause, carried the fight to the legislative assemblies and to the President himself. At this time she also became involved with the leaders of the Women's Rights movement (see section on the Fight for Equality and Suffrage), though she was in opposition to those who demanded the women's vote, considering it of 'minor importance'. Her original thoughts and sceptical examination of each issue set her apart from the mob – even the leaders of the mob. Eventually her religious beliefs advanced to the point at which she admitted to a form of heresy, though firm in her belief in the doctrines 'preached by Jesus and by every child of God'. She flouted the law, too, when necessary, helping escaping slaves by using her house as refuge. And yet she was not deliberately divisive: for example, when the Equal Rights Association split, she mediated in an attempt to close the breach.

Two of Lucretia Mott's fellow Abolitionists were **Sarah** (American, 1792–1873) and **Angelina** (American, 1805–79) **Grimké**, both converts to the Society of Friends. In 1836 they moved to New York and continued to speak in halls and churches. But their brilliant talks to large mixed audiences had already provoked a letter from the General Association of Congregational Ministers of Massachusetts opposing women preachers and reformers. This prompted the Grimkés to join the pioneers in the Women's Rights movement and become largely responsible in 1838 for linking women's rights with anti-slavery – although they had little direct force in continuing the work after 1840, apart from writing propaganda.

It was the persistent reformers, both men and women, who finally brought about the abolition of slavery – women such as **Harriet Stowe** (American, 1811–96) whose famous book *Uncle Tom's Cabin* was published in 1852 and acted as the most persuasive of propaganda. She is described in more detail in the section on Literature and Journalism, but here it is appropriate to mention that not only was *Uncle Tom's Cabin* translated into 23 languages to become a minor cause of the American Civil War (making its author hated in the South), it was then followed

Harriet Stowe

in 1853 by *A Key to Uncle Tom's Cabin* which was an accumulation of documentary evidence justifying the original's accuracy.

Ex-slaves, too, played a militant role. The story of **Harriet Tubman's** (*c* 1820–1913) escape movement is told in the section on War. **Sojourner Truth** (American, *c* 1797–1883) provided another approach to the problem, that of a slave who was much abused by several masters and who, having won freedom in 1827, proceeded with the help of one Isaac Van Wagener and the Quakers to fight a successful court battle to recover her small son who had been sold illegally to the South. It was her belief that she held conversations with God and that God and the law were her guides. That being so she won a slander action in 1836 against whites (the first such action by any negro) who alleged she was involved with a notorious prophet called Robert Mathews. Illiterate though she was, Sojourner Truth travelled widely, lecturing on Abolition, braving mobs wherever she went throughout the 1840s and 1850s. But she was strongly opposed even to non-violent militancy and any question of revolution by the slaves, preferring that the law should prevail. During the Civil War she gathered food and clothing for negro volunteer regiments and became a 'counsellor' in connection with the resettlement of slaves after Emancipation.

In time with the thriving mood of liberalisation that blew through the USA, several vital American women turned to put the prisons and the mental institutions in order.

Abigail Gibbons (American, 1801–93), a disillusioned Quaker, became jointly interested in the early 1840s with anti-slavery, women's rights and prison reform, and in 1845 became the leader of the Female Department of the newly formed Prison Association of New York. This involved her in intensive welfare work for the inhabitants of slum dwellings, as well as prisoners, and led to work in hospitals during the Civil War with attempts to improve the condition of mental hospitals afterwards.

Dorothea Dix (American, 1802–87) tackled the problem of mental institute reform because of what she saw in 1841 when visiting a gaol in Massachusetts to teach a Sunday School class and discovered the insane incarcerated with criminals. For the next 18 months she visited every single place in Massachusetts where insane people were confined and, in 1843, sent a report to the State Legislature revealing the appalling conditions. Improvements followed but she started to travel farther afield until, by 1845, she had completed a 10000-mile journey visiting jails, almshouses and State prisons. She prompted special mental hospitals to be built in 15 States and in Canada, and the treatment of the insane to be improved throughout the USA – though Congress and the President were more dilatory than helpful. She fought vigorously and often vituperously for what she wanted and by the mid 1850s was exhausted. However, a tour in 1854 of mental homes throughout Europe, where she badgered officialdom with customary vigour, seems to have revived her. Yet, as the Superintendent of Army Nurses during the Civil War, she displayed less tact and administrative ability than was required and made many enemies, seeming somewhat confused in her aims when she laid it down that, 'All nurses are required to be plain looking women.'

Dorothea Dix

Nevertheless she achieved much for military nursing that might otherwise have gone unattended, while her work for the insane remained her memorial.

Ellen Johnson (American, 1829–99) first saw prisons while tracking down soldiers' relatives after the Civil War. This encouraged her to seek improvements in prisons and led her to found a women's reformatory at Sherborn in 1877. In 1884 she took over as Superintendent from Clara Barton (see section on Law and Civil Administration) and, by sound administration over the next 15 years inspired liberal practices and raised the establishment to a model institution of its kind.

Almost without exception the great reformers were inspired by some form of religious motivation. Although there was often unity of overall purpose in tackling the social horrors of the day, this sometimes led to important diversification among the religious bodies. For example in 1861 **Catherine Booth** (British, 1829–90) encouraged her husband, William, to leave the Methodist ministry and become an itinerant evangelist. Notwithstanding the births of eight children in quick succession, she had regularly carried on untiring social work and started preaching in 1860, after the birth of their fourth child, remaining an eloquent preacher until her death, even though she often went from sickbed to pulpit. She and her husband devised and created the Salvation Army which took its name in 1878, and from 1880 to 1884 she held a series of successful meetings in halls in London, becoming quite a famous orator. In 1855 she took part in a campaign which secured the passing of the Criminal Law Amendment Act, drawn up to protect young girls. It was Catherine Booth who implanted sex equality into the Salvation Army with a pamphlet entitled *Female Ministry*, which still has point today.

By 1890 the Salvation Army was established throughout most of Europe, in India, South Africa and South America. The Booths' eldest daughter, **Catherine**, started preaching in Paris in 1881 and was known as 'la Maréchale'. The seventh child, **Evangeline** (1865–1950) went to Canada in 1896 and, in 1904, took over command of the Salvation Army in the USA.

'The richest heiress in Europe' was the title given to **Angela Burdett-Coutts** (British, 1814–1906) when she unexpectedly inherited the vast Coutts fortune. Several men proposed marriage, but she preferred to spend her fortune unassisted and did it that way for about 40 years until aged 67, when she married a young man who helped spend her money. Her philanthropic schemes ranged from slum charities to protection for aborigines, from goats for farmers to homes for art students. She paid for a topographical survey of Jerusalem and provided lifeboats for Brittany, drinking-fountains for dogs and plants for Kew Gardens, endowed bishoprics to a total of $250000 in Adelaide, Cape Town and British Columbia, and built model dwellings in London's East End. She sent cotton-gins to Nigeria, donated bells to St Paul's Cathedral and built a church and three schools in Westminster. The peasants in Turkey received evidence of her generosity for which she was probably the first woman to receive the Order of Medjidie. In 1871 Queen Victoria bestowed a peerage on her, thus making her that rare example (until then) of a woman recipient of a peerage for service other than that of being mistress to a king.

The originator of Workhouse Reform in England was **Louisa Twining** (British, 1820–1911), who used to visit her old nurse in the parish of St Clement Danes and so made friends with the nurse's neighbours. The slum conditions shocked her but never so much as when, in 1853, one of these neighbours was admitted to the Strand Union Workhouse and she was able to see that there were no washing arrangements, the linen was sometimes not changed for 16 weeks, the place stank and the food was nauseating. Children with infectious diseases shared a bed with accident cases and the sick were ill cared for, being nursed by fellow inmates who were incapable, epileptic, blind, half-witted and/or drunk, with no authority over their charges. Louisa Twining asked permission to come 'visiting' but was told 'unpaid and voluntary efforts were not sanctioned by the Poor Law Board'. She tackled the Board who were pleasant but it took a year of persuasion before permission was granted. Louisa Twining then formed a Workhouse Visiting Society that functioned countrywide, taking gifts to patients, questioning institutions, talking and writing of conditions. In 1875, after 20 years' persuasion and lobbying, the Poor Law Act was passed and Workhouse conditions improved.

Frequently a 19th-century woman's best chance of improving her position was by emigration to one of the developing colonial territories. However, British Colonial Governments only aided the passage of artisans. **Maria Rye** (British, 1829–1903) founded the Female Middle Class Emigration Society in 1862, the forerunner of seven similar associations whose purpose it was to find passages and employment for middle-class women – governesses mainly – who were over-subscribed and

Women immigrating

Josephine Butler

under-paid in Britain. She spent three years visiting New Zealand and Australia to see conditions first hand as the society began its work: as a result it expanded its activities to include a child emigration scheme for destitute children (4000 were helped to Canada alone by 1895) plus another scheme to help working-class emigrants. Eventually many thousands of women were helped to the colonies, a large number being among those who brought women's first political emancipation to New Zealand, Australia and Canada (see section on the Fight for Equality and Suffrage).

Towards the end of the 19th century nearly every major reform movement had women associated with it.

Frances Cobbe (British, 1822–1904) was probably the first active anti-vivisectionist but also wrote about 30 works on divorce, destitution and separation orders.

Josephine Butler (British, 1828–1906) had the courage in the face of prejudice to go to the aid of destitute women (many of whom were prostitutes). She visited workhouses and prisons and opened her home to them, also starting another place near by for those who were incurably ill. She formed working men's organisations to fight against the Contagious Diseases Acts of 1864, 1866 and 1869 which, on the pretext of controlling venereal diseases, made it law that any woman living in certain areas close to naval and military centres could be declared 'common prostitutes' by the police and compelled to undergo medical examination or be imprisoned. Men in the area were immune from these compulsory examinations. Intervening in an 1870 by-election at Colchester, she attacked the Government's candidate who supported the Act: indeed he wanted all soldiers' wives included. Subjected to mob violence, she persevered with her campaign and the candidate was defeated. A Royal Commission in 1871 heard Josephine Butler's evidence, found in her favour and in due course this led to the repeal of the Acts in 1886. Looking farther afield she proved that licensed brothels were markets for white-slave traffic and the sale of children for prostitution, and was successful in influencing a few European Governments against State-regulated brothels.

At the same time new religious movements were still being created. **Mary Eddy** (American, 1821–1910), a neurotic invalid, fell under the spell of Phineas Quimby, said to have made spectacular cures without medication (using a kind of Biblical faith-healing coupled with hypnosis). Be that as it may, Mary Eddy claimed in 1862 to have been cured by him. She borrowed his notes, lectured and wrote articles on his methods and, after his death, started to train successful healers. This was the beginning of what became known in 1876 as the Christian Science Association and in 1879 the Church of Christ (Scientist). Its mother church was dedicated in Boston in 1895. The movement prospered and enjoyed a rapid spread of practitioners and centres, though the new Church also had its ups and downs, its schisms and its lawsuits. Mary Eddy had written numerous articles for various publications in connection with faith-healing since 1862 and, in 1908, founded the *Christian Science Monitor* which became a US daily newspaper of influence. She created a doctrine and a Board of Directors who, they say, self-perpetuate their authority according to the Church Manual written by Mary Eddy which cannot be amended.

Mary Ward (British, 1851–1920) whose theory that 'Religion consists alone in the service of the people' (propounded in 1818 in her book *Robert Elsmere*) led her to advocate an ethical rather than supernatural Christianity and carry out her beliefs by working relentlessly for social settlements and children's play centres in London. Due to her an invalid children's school was founded in 1899 and in 1905 she was made responsible for the evening play centres set up by the London County Council.

Old religious organisations mixed in with the new. In India, in 1877, **Mary de Chappotin de Neuville** (French) founded the Franciscan Missionaries of Mary whose numbers rose to 10000 sisters – just one of thousands of Roman Catholic religious Orders in the world performing a variety of tasks. But on the same continent **Annie Besant** (British, 1847–1933), who had changed her Anglican beliefs to atheism in 1870, shifted much later to the Hindu religion. She was the first prominent woman in England to advocate birth control, not necessarily because she believed in the pamphlet on the subject by Charles Knowlton (which she and Charles Bradlaugh illegally circulated in England in 1876) but simply because she believed in freedom of expression. With Bradlaugh, she was found guilty of selling an indecent work (quite inoffensive by today's standards), convicted and sentenced to imprisonment and a heavy fine. On appeal they won on a technicality. Annie Besant was involved in all sorts of radical activity throughout the 1880s as a Fabian, union organiser, strike leader and as a member of the London School Board. In 1889, however, she adopted theosophy, the contentious creation of **Helena Blavatsky** (Russian, 1831–91) and thus a belief that India was the source of all wisdom in the past. As a leader of theosophy she moved to India and finally adopted the Hindu religion. Just before the First World War she founded the Central Hindu College at Benares and simultaneously became deeply involved in Indian nationalist politics, setting out her views in her own papers, *New India*. Her militancy led to imprisonment, but upon release she was elected President of the Indian National Congress in 1917. Yet this, like so much of her life, was a swiftly passing phase since she fell out with Gandhi and his policy of civil disobedience and passive resistance, arguing that it would only promote violence.

The most colourful reformer of all time, however, must surely have been **Carry Nation** (American, 1846–1911) whose role was quite literally that of a violent temperance advocate. Her first husband was an alcoholic whose habits launched her on her crusade in life – saloon-smashing. She was a formidable figure, nearly 6 ft (182 cm) tall, and she generally marched into a bar, alone or accompanied by a band of hymn-singing women, prayed, harangued or vilified the occupants, then proceeded to wreck the bar with a hatchet. This she called 'hatchetation of joints'. In retaliation she was clubbed, cut and shot at. Carry Nation's crusade rose to its peak of violence in the 1890s and was subsidised by her lecture and stage appearances and the sale of souvenir hatchets which, at one time, brought in $300 per week: they also helped to pay her

Carry Nation

numerous fines. Her first husband's other weaknesses made her anti-smoking, anti-foreign foods, anti-corsets, anti-skirts of improper length and anti-her day's equivalent of the pin-up picture. When she died the autobiography she left was like a bar she had visited – disorderly confusion.

More orderly in her intentions was **Octavia Hill** (British, 1838–1912), a disciple of John Ruskin whose home she often visited after he offered to teach her to draw. Housing projects were her main interest, the first in 1864 in Marylebone, for which Ruskin lent the money. As manager she did not employ the usual slum rent-collectors but a personal visitor instead. The scope of her work spread until, in 1884, she was appointed to manage property belonging to the Ecclesiastic Commissioners. Octavia Hill trained other women managers: her work became known abroad and this led to the founding of the Society of Women Housing Managers in England and similar societies in Europe and the USA. Seeing at first hand the cramped and grey life led by the poor people in slum dwellings, she worked for open spaces within towns, an approach which led to the creation of the National Trust (1895) of which she was one of the principal founders. As a diversion she also founded the first cadet corps for boys.

Like so many of the great reformers, **Jane Addams** (American, 1860–1935), a beautiful girl from a wealthy family, felt impelled to undertake her life's work by the sight of the impoverished majority of people – in her case viewed for the first time in England in 1884 and 1887. In 1889, with **Ellen Starr** (American, 1859–1940) she decided to make a fresh approach to welfare work through the foundation of a settlement at Hull House, Chicago (in the midst of an impoverished, multi-racial area) in which the aim was intended to be more beneficial to the over-privileged doers than to the under-privileged receivers. Hull House initiated a system that led to the establishment of clubs which promoted all kinds of group projects that embraced physical fitness, child care, the arts and home economy. Forty clubs helping over 2000 women a week were in operation by 1893, but by then their demands had increased so much that Jane Addams had to turn to charity to supplement her own limited financial resources. At fund-raising from the rich she proved equally successful, while contact with new-found areas of deprivation among the poor led her to instigate a wide range of proposals which led to Illinois' first Factory Inspection Act in 1893; to the first juvenile court in 1899; the first 'Mother' Pension Act; a law for an eight-hour working day for women; workmen's compensation and tenement housing regulations. She and her many 'over-privileged' disciples also used their influence (dangerously radical as it appeared to some of their kind) to help obtain justice for negroes, immigrants, women and children. From involvement in 1907 with the cause of women's suffrage, she plunged into politics in 1912 (having received the first female honorary degree at Yale in 1910) to second Theodore Roosevelt's nomination at the Progressive Party Convention – the Party having formulated many of its ideas at Hull House. All of this activity she publicised by books, articles and a whirlwind round of tours which strained her rather frail physique to the utmost but never reduced her enthusiasm or essential simplicity of approach to life's problems.

When the First World War began she addressed herself exclusively to the re-establishment of peace, organising and chairing the Woman's Peace Party of the USA in January 1915, chairing the International Congress of Women at The Hague later that year, and unsuccessfully trying to get President Wilson to mediate between the belligerents. After the war, when the chorus of disapproval which had been heaped upon her when the USA entered the conflict in 1917 died away, she became President of the Women's International League for Peace and Freedom and in this connection was associated with **Carrie Catt** (see section on the Fight for Equality and Suffrage). Inevitably she was depressed by the USA's withdrawal of support for the League of Nations, its drift into isolationism and tendency to conformity to the extent that in 1920 she was one of those who helped form the American Civil Liberties Union as an expression of independence of thought. Towards the end of her days, as her health declined and her hopes for the future lost some of their earlier optimism, she began to receive honours in boundless profusion, including the Nobel Peace Prize in 1931.

Among the many disciples of Jane Addams was **Emily Balch** (American, 1867–1961), a Quaker and economist. She carried out an intensive study of the homelands from which many Americans came and in 1910 published *Our Slavic Fellow Citizens*, which has been described as 'the most sympathetic and thoroughgoing study of Slavic immigrants ever made'. She also did much social work, including child welfare. In 1908–9 she was a member of the Massachusetts Commission on Industrial Relations; in 1913–14 was on their Commission on Immigration and from 1914 to 1917 on the Boston City Planning Board. After the First World War she was a delegate to the International Congress of Women at The Hague; then from 1919 to 1922, in Geneva, Secretary of the Women's International League for Peace and Freedom (and thus in close touch with Jane Addams), later becoming its Honorary International President. In 1946 it was her turn to become a winner of the Nobel Peace Prize – jointly with a man, however.

Another of Jane Addams's followers at Hull House was **Grace Abbott** (American, 1878–1939) who was Director of their Immigrants' Protective League. In both the *Chicago Evening Post* and the *Journal of Criminal Law and Criminology*, as well as in a book *The Immigrant and the Community*, it was she who exposed the exploitation of immigrants and she who, as Director of the Child-labour Division of the US Children's Bureau from 1917 to 1919, administered the first Federal child labour law. Later, as chief of the Bureau, she administered the Maternity and Infancy Act. In 1934 she became Professor of Public Welfare at the University of Chicago and wrote a number of papers, also the two-volume work *The Child and the State*. In 1935 and 1937 she was the US delegate to the International Labour Organisation.

Although Jane Addams had no equal in accomplishment of reform in her day, somebody akin to her in breadth of vision and personal industry was to be found in Britain. That was **Beatrice Webb** (British, 1858–1943) – although it must be noted that the vast majority of her work was done in close partnership with her husband Sidney. Closely engaged with radical bias upon local government work from 1891 onwards (the year before their marriage) they compiled vast and authoritive reports dealing with

Jane Addams and *Henrietta Szold*

labour conditions, trade unionism, local government, the poor laws and Socialism. Her home was a breeding-ground of social reform in the first part of the 20th century. But when, in 1929, Sidney was elevated to the peerage, after a few years on the Labour benches of the House of Commons and as a Minister, she refused to take his title.

While the Webbs had an international reputation (even though their work was mostly for Britain) the Jewish **Henrietta Szold** (American, 1860–1945) actually operated on a truly international scale. Yet her first efforts, in 1891, to Americanise Jewish immigrants by starting a night school for immigrant workers in Baltimore were strictly local although in 1888 she had been founder of the Jewish Publications Society of America, as its Editor General and as a translator of Jewish classics. In 1912, with 38 members, she founded Hadassah with the aim of fostering Jewish ideals through 'chapters' in the American Jewish communities and to sponsor health work in Palestine. Expanding its activity in 1918, Henrietta Szold, as President of Hadassah, organised a medical unit with staff and equipment for a nurses' school, clinics and hospitals which was sent to Palestine. This led to her being elected as the first woman on the World Zionist Executive and also as a member of the Palestine Jewish National Council in which she was responsible for health, education and social welfare. She established the Szold Foundation for child welfare and education which affected the lives of young Jews throughout America and Israel, and then, in 1933, became Director of Youth Aliyah, an organisation operating world-wide to rescue and resettle in Israel young Jewish victims of persecution. This organisation has rehabilitated over 100 000 children from 72 lands, including many from Nazi Germany, eastern Europe and Russia. Thousands of young people owe their lives to this outstanding Jewish woman.

Along with the growth of the budding Israeli State, even before it achieved independence in 1948, grew the largest Zionist organisation – Women's International Zionist Organisation (WIZO), which was founded in 1920 by **Rebecca Sieff** (British, d. 1966), **Vera Weizmann** (Russian, 1881–1966) and **Edith Eder** (Hungarian, d 1944). Its purpose was social work among the influx of immigrants from the many countries from which they came, its tentacles spreading through Palestine and outward to various Jewish women's associations in about 50 countries in an endeavour to help achieve unity. In Israel WIZO has 204 crèches, 2 baby homes, summer camps and clubs for 20000 children, 14 agricultural and vocational schools for 3580 youths and also trains women for employment and gives a legal advisory service.

The 20th century witnessed the merging of individual efforts by women in social reform into a pattern which covered practically every progressive activity. Countless women joined the myriad organisations that appeared once it became legal and easier in the atmosphere of liberalism created by the pioneers. Yet hard battles for recognition of fundamental needs such as population control remained necessary, as **Margaret Sanger** (American, 1883–1966) and **Marie Stopes** (British, 1880–1958) discovered when they began the birth-control movement and opened the first birth-control clinics (see section on Science and Medicine).

It was noteworthy that the trend of feminine leadership which began in the West was maintained when it came in contact with the East. For example, the founder of the Indian Red Cross, and its President from 1950, was **Rajkumari Amrit Kaur** (Indian, 1889–1964), an indefatigable organiser of social work. She had been a founder-member of the All-India Women's Conference in 1926 (the conference which under the leadership of **Muthalakshimi Reddi** (Indian) promoted the Sarda Act of 1930 which forbade child marriages), Minister of Health in the Indian Government from 1947 to 1957, founder of the All-India Institute of Medical Sciences, Vice-Chairman of the Board of Governors of the League of Red Cross Societies and Chairman of the Executive Committee of the St John's Ambulance Association. Recognition for her was world-wide: she was awarded the Count Bernadotte Gold Medal by the League of Red Cross Societies in 1957 and Gold Medals from National Red Cross Societies in 14 individual countries. In Rome, in 1961, she received the René Sand Memorial Award at the International Conference of Social Work and also several honorary degrees in America.

Religious reformers and workers abounded, as they had done for centuries. Some worked in traditional ways and others exploited the latest publicity methods. Of the latter **Aimée McPherson** (American, 1890–1944), the controversial founder of the International Church of the Foursquare Gospel, was pre-eminently bizarre and known (in the cricus context) by her detractors as 'the Barnum of religion'. She started her evangelical career as a missionary in China but returned to America after her first husband died. Physically attractive and also an immensely powerful preacher, she began revival services of Pentecostal origin in 1915 in Los Angeles. These were allied with spells of faith-healing that had a strong appeal to the gathering number of people who came to see and hear her speak. Aided by her equally dynamic mother, she used every sort of dramatic publicity that could be mustered, wrote and edited her own monthly magazine, dressed in pure white and claimed to be the first woman to make a radio broadcast. As her church grew in size and wealth from 1923 onwards – and dispensed to the poor large quantities of donated aid – it acquired its own radio station and developed a telephone network of counsellors who gave spiritual advice. There was something of an upset when she disappeared for a month, claiming she

Mother Teresa

had been kidnapped, because later it was discovered that she had spent the time in a secluded cottage with her radio operator. But her tumultuous life, its long series of lawsuits, scandals and rows did little to diminish the enthusiasm of the flock. Quite the reverse in fact: at her death it had grown to 22000 strong and by the late 1960s rose to about 80000. She herself suffered nervous breakdowns, brought about by a self-imposed régime of overwork, and died of an overdose of sleeping-powder.

More orthodox, and certainly of far greater benefit, has been the work of **Mother Teresa** (Yugoslav) who was the first winner in 1973 of the £34000 Templeton Prize for Religion – an annual award 'to stimulate the knowledge and love of God on the part of mankind everywhere' that is sponsored by a wealthy American businessman, directed by an Irish Methodist minister. The international panel of judges, numbering three Anglicans, a Jew, a Hindu, a Muslim, a Buddhist, a Roman Catholic and an American Presbyterian, made their choice by a large majority. She gave all the money to the Order she founded; the Missionaries of Charity. This had started by helping the destitute and dying of Calcutta and is now working throughout the world supported by lay people of all denominations.

Missionary zeal has, of course, stimulated all the great reformers, be they God-fearing or of atheistic persuasion. A classic, modern example of a female Christian missionary was personified by **Gladys Aylward** (British) who helped run the mission in Yangcheng, called the 'Inn of Eight Happinesses', as a means of taking Christianity to the Chinese. By example, extraordinary stoicism and bravery she won an astonishing influence over the local people and their ruler. On one occasion she confronted a prison riot and quelled it single-handed, later implementing much-needed reforms in the prison's administration. Having been appointed the area's official foot inspector to enforce the new law prohibiting the ancient and crippling custom of female foot-binding, she exploited the opportunity to spread the Gospel wider. When the Japanese invaded the area they beat her, causing internal injuries, but despite this she gathered over 100 orphans and led them for 12 days across wild, mountainous country to safety, begging food at the villages as she went.

Women who dominate the ecclesiastical hierarchy are rare, though there are signs that they are beginning to appear among the leaders.

The President of the Episcopal Church is **Cynthia Wedel** (American), who gained a PhD in psychology in 1957 and took up the appointment in 1969. She is also involved in the council dealing with the status of women in the Church and has written on this subject.

In a world where evolution is rapid, 'precedent' is not a valid argument against change and some religious sects already ordain women to their priesthood. These are few, but increasing. Most religions stress the mystical side of their teaching (prayer and meditation which shows the way to positive action for good) yet, because many religions insist that ministers or priests must be sexually male, their primary rule for choosing leaders in this mysticism is still strictly physical.

AT LAW AND IN CIVIL ADMINISTRATION

AS IT OUGHT TO BE. OR . THE LADIES TRYING A CONTEMPTIBLE SCOUNDREL for a "BREACH of PROMISE"

Women have rarely been left in much doubt as to their low standing in law and their presumed incompetence to hold office. Neatly contradicting each other, the Chinese were wont to say that women 'without ability' were normal, while Hindus dismissed them from positions of trust because of their 'infidelity, violence, deceit, envy, extreme avarice . . .' and, in fact, their 'total want of good qualities, with impurity'. Almost everywhere, except in the most outstanding cases prior to the late 19th century, women were relegated, by comparison with men, to an inferior position in law and were excluded from pleading in the courts: not until they had won recognition by the exploitation of improved education and political status were they admitted to public office. (See sections on the Fight for Equality and Suffrage, on Politics and Statecraft, and on Education.)

One of the first universities to foster female lawyers was that of Bologna. Between 1239 and 1249 **Bettisia Bozzidini** occupied the Juridical Chair while, a century later, **Novella Calderini**, the daughter of a Professor of Law, sometimes conducted her father's cases, appearing in court veiled so as to avoid deflecting the course of justice by her beauty. Is it possible that Shakespeare had her in mind when he created Portia?

There were numerous wives of estate-owners who, through temporary absence or death of their husbands, successfully tackled the task of administering estates themselves. But scope for administrative expertise in Government was limited by monarchal organisation of States up to the 18th century. Monarchal government, mainly implemented by men, was only slowly replaced by bureaucratic methods also administered by men. Therefore women were virtually excluded from participation in higher administration – as most of the sections in this book show. As colonists started to open up America one woman, however, had the opportunity to show what she could do. **Margaret Brent** (English, *c* 1601–*c* 1671) arrived in the country in 1638 and, by 1651, had become one of the largest landowners, besides a frequent attorney in court at Maryland. In 1647, as Governor Calvert lay dying, he named her sole executor to administer his estate saying 'Take all, pay all.'

Faced with a severe corn shortage, plus mutinous unpaid Virginian soldiers brought in by the late Governor to quell a riot, Margaret Brent found his personal estate inadequate to both import corn and pay the men off. Acting decisively she bought the corn and used tact and courage to maintain peace among the soldiers while she acquired the power of attorney held by the late Governor for his brother, Lord Baltimore, who was away in England. Lord Baltimore's Maryland property had been pledged by the late Governor, along with his own, to pay the soldiers. She sold as many head of Lord Baltimore's cattle as was necessary to raise the remaining sum needed and paid off the soldiers who quietly dispersed. When Lord Baltimore protested from England, the Assembly's reply in defence of Margaret Brent included the sentence '. . . it was better for the Collony's safety at that time in her hands then in any mans else in the whole Province . . .'. It must be added that when she tried to strengthen her bargaining position by obtaining two votes in the Assembly (one for herself as a freeholder – to which she would have been entitled had she been a man – and one as Calvert's representative) she failed on both counts.

The understanding of civil administration in Britain, America and elsewhere was helped along by the daughter of a rich Swiss merchant settled in London **Jane Marcet** (Swiss, 1769–1858). Her *Conversation* publications were designed as simple textbooks to enable more people to understand everyday matters. *Conversations on Chemistry intended more especially for the Female Sex* established her reputation in 1806 and, incidentally, sold 160000 copies in the USA alone. *Conversations on Political Economy*, her greatest success, in 1816, went to many editions and led the French economist, Say, to remark that she was 'superior even to men as a political economist'. In 1836 she produced *Willy's Holidays, or Conversations on different kinds of Government.* Her work inspired **Harriet Martineau** (British, 1802–76), the daughter of a wealthy manufacturer who, unusually for that time, provided his children with an education to give them security and independence. This daughter was a prolific writer of articles dealing with almost any subject from wages to divinity and political economy. Between 1832 and 1834 she wrote *Illustrations of Political Economy*, which ran into 25 volumes, and became so famous and lionised that even Cabinet Ministers accepted her criticisms of their methods. In effect, Carlyle allowed her to suggest and manage his first course of lectures. From 1833 to 1834 she had also written the ten-volume *Poor Laws and Paupers Illustrated*, and in 1834 published the five-volume *Illustrations of Taxation*. Travelling in the USA she became deeply involved in the abolition of slavery, which, at that time, was not decisively advocated. No doubt the quality of her work suffered from over-production, but its impact at the time was considerable.

Again it was in America that another administrator of note emerged. This was **Clara Barton** (American, 1821–1912), a little woman standing

Harriet Martineau

Clara Barton

just over 5 ft (152 cm) but full of drive, determination and nervous energy which helped her to overcome a childhood timidity. At 18 she began teaching and in 1852 very successfully founded at Bordentown one of the first public schools in the State of New Jersey. So successful was it that the authorities decided it warranted a man in charge, and appointed one over her. Clara Barton resigned and moved to Washington where she secured the position of clerk in the Patent Office, becoming, it is believed, the first regularly appointed female civil servant in America. Here, in the bastion of bureaucracy, the men resented female intrusion and she had to endure rudeness and antagonism – a situation which may have been further irritated by her efficiency which created notice among her superiors.

In her spare time she did charity work which included, at the beginning of the Civil War, befriending soldiers. It was then that she learned of the serious lack of first aid equipment on the battlefield. So, after advertising for supplies to be donated, she started off with friends and ladened mules towards the scenes of fighting, bypassing all official channels and, therefore, swiftly arriving on the scene with much-needed medical aid and comforts. Her practicality is illustrated by the story that at one place she found a surgeon who had only a 2 in stub of candle left for light and 1000 wounded and dying men to treat. He was handed four boxes of candles; she and her team immediately set to work giving first aid and providing soup and coffee for the men. She saw the necessity for running a quick-acting, efficient organisation – and determinedly kept it that way, maintaining complete independence from official channels, and therefore also from Dorothea Dix's division of nurses (see section on Religion and Social Reform).

In 1865, with President Lincoln's approval, she began collecting soldiers' records to trace missing men and at the same time started a small project for marking graves. When the Franco-Prussian War broke out in 1870 she happened to be in Europe recuperating from overwork. At once she associated herself with the International Red Cross to help victims of that war and distributed American funds for war victims in France. This led to a greater work – the commencement upon her return to America in 1873 of the formation of the American Red Cross and recognition of the Geneva Treaty by America. The latter she achieved in 1882 despite every sort of discouragement by the US Government, the former she launched in 1881 and became its President in 1904. In the years to come the organisation was to become involved in many wars in which Clara Barton supervised the frugal funds available and personally directed operations in the field. In her later years she proposed an amendment to the International Red Cross which opened the way for distribution of relief at times other than war – during calamities such as earthquakes and hurricanes.

When aged 77 this indomitable lady was riding mule-wagons under a tropical sun, taking aid to Cuban civilians and American soldiers during the Spanish American War. The song goes 'Old soldiers never die, they only fade away': at one time it looked as if she would do neither, for she remained youthful in looks, spritely and alert until she died, aged 91.

The strongest initial movement by women to enter the legal profession centred upon the USA, where **Arabella Mansfield** (American, 1846–

1911) became the first woman in the country to be admitted to practise in June 1869, in Iowa – though she abstained from actually practising, preferring to continue her profession as a brilliant teacher and academic. That same year **Myra Bradwell** (American, 1831–94) was refused permission to practise in Illinois and did not bother to reapply until 1890, even though that State opened its courts' doors to women in 1872. Instead, with her lawyer husband, she ran the influential *Chicago Legal News* and pitched in with the fighters for women's equality both in the courts and with other aspects of the growing Women's movement. Even after being allowed, by State law, to practise, the way could be far from easy. **Charlotte Ray** (American, 1850–1911), a negro teacher, began to study law in 1869 and was admitted to practise in 1872 – the first negro woman in the USA to do so. But her attempt to practise failed 'on account of prejudice'.

An outstanding example of the struggle demanded by women to win the right to practise law was that put up by **Belva Lockwood** (American, 1830–1917) on her way to becoming the first woman to plead before the Supreme Court. After many rebuffs she began to study law at the National University Law School, New Hampshire in 1869 and, in due course, passed her final examinations. However, the University, whose President happened to be Ulysses Grant, also the President of the USA, refused her degree. She wrote to him: '. . . If you are its [the University's] President I wish to say to you that I have been passed through the curriculum of study at that school and am entitled to and demand my Diploma. If you are not its President then I ask you to take your name from its papers and not hold out to the world what you are not.' Within 26 days she received her degree and filed and won her first case.

In the case of Charlotte von Corts against the Government for infringement of a patent, Belva Lockwood converted the case at issue into one for recognition of a woman's right to plead before the Supreme Court. In 1879, after a five-year struggle, she won that fight, creating

Belva Lockwood pleads before the Supreme Court of the USA

extensive comment, meanwhile, as she pedalled between office and courts on a tricycle with her red stockings showing. A dedicated feminist, for the remainder of her life she encouraged, advised and helped women from all over the country who wished to become attorneys-at-law and fought for women's equality and the vote. In 1884 she ran for the Presidency, without the same furore as accompanied Victoria Woodhull's efforts in 1872, and received 4149 votes from the all-male electorate. However, her most famous case came up in 1906 when she fought for, and won before the Supreme Court, a $5000000 reimbursement owed to the Cherokee Indians by the Government for land which it had bought but not paid for – to be settled with full interest.

Changes within the court system itself were being instigated by women. The first juvenile court in America was established in Chicago in 1899 and came into being mainly due to the efforts of Hull House which was started and administered by **Jane Addams** (see section on Religion and Social Reform). She, incidentally, also wrote an article, 'Ethical Survivals in Municipal Corruption', after a long struggle to defeat a notoriously corrupt alderman. It might make apt reading today.

American women had led the way in the profession of law. The following are a selection, mostly of 'firsts', from other countries:

Argentina	**Margarita Arguas** became a specialist and teacher in international law in 1926, taking a Professor's Chair in 1966. Her list of 'firsts' are impressive: First female judge of the National Civil Court of Appeal. First woman member of the Academy of Law and Social Sciences. First Woman President of the International Law Association. First woman member of the Argentine Supreme Court.
Belgium	The first woman to graduate as a Doctor of Law was **Marie Popelin** (1846–1913) in 1888 (see also sections on the Fight for Equality and Suffrage and on Clubs), but the Brussels Court of Appeal refused to allow her to take the lawyer's oath because 'the profession of a lawyer is a kind of public office which custom forbids women to occupy'. It was not until 1922 that **Marcelle Renson** and **Paule Lamy** became the first Belgium women to take the lawyer's oath. In 1930 the former became a barrister of the Court of Appeal and took part in The Hague Convention on the Unification of International Law. In 1947 some of the last barriers to women's participation in Belgian law fell when they were allowed to practise as solicitors – providing they had their husband's permission – and in 1953 **Marie Gevers** (who was the first woman member of the Royal Academy of French Language and Literature) became the first woman President of the Law School of Brussels University.
Britain	The first woman barrister, **Ivy Williams**, did not practise until 1921 and it was 1949 before the first British

women took silk to become King's Counsellors. They were **Rose Heilbron** and **Helena Normanton**. In 1956 Rose Heilbron became the first woman Recorder and before then had practised with great success – judges had been known to warn the jury against the blandishments of her charm! Recently she achieved the leadership of the Northern Circuit with authority over 300 barristers and has become the second woman High Court Judge, in the Family Division. The first woman Judge of the High Court was **Elizabeth Lane**. She became a barrister in 1940, Assistant Recorder of Birmingham in 1953, Recorder of Derby in 1961, a Judge of County Courts in 1962 and moved to the High Court in 1965, in the Family Division. Only 6 per cent of British barristers are women.

Rose Heilbron

China

An early woman judge in modern China was **Shi Liang** who took up her duties of Minister of Justice in 1957.

Denmark

Inger Paderson, a High Court Judge, was chosen as the first woman Judge of the European Court of Human Rights in 1971.

France

In 1888 France saw its first countrywoman graduate in law, **Jeanne Chauvin** (1862–1926). Mlle **Dilhan** became the first to be called to the Bar in 1903 and won three celebrated cases with such skill that she was sometimes rated the equal of Sir Patrick Hastings. During the First World War **Margueritte Isnard** became the only woman to act as defence counsel at courts martial at the front.

Germany
: **Gisela Niemeyer** became the first woman to be a Judge in the Supreme Court of Finances in the German Federal Republic, in 1973.

Ghana
: The first woman judge, **Annie Jiagge**, was called to the Bar of the Gold Coast in 1950, became a magistrate in 1955, a Judge of the Ghana Circuit Court in 1957, of the High Court in 1961, and the Court of Appeal in 1969. In 1961 she became Ghana's representative on the UN Commission on the Status of Women and its first African Chairman in 1968.

Holland
: The first woman judge was Miss **J H Kroesen** of the County Court, Amsterdam, in 1955.

India
: The first woman to graduate in law was **Cornelia Sorabji** in 1894 although she was not permitted to practise until 1923. It was not until 1916 that a second woman graduated, and even as late as 1956 there were only 78 women advocates out of 5755 in that country. It is, therefore, all the more to **Anna Chandy**'s credit that she has become the first woman Judge of a High Court, taking up the appointment in the State of Kerala.

Indonesia
: The first woman to graduate in law was **Ani Manoppo** who later became Dean of the Law Faculty of Medan in 1949. **Nani Soewondo** graduated in law in 1942 and throughout the Japanese occupation worked in the Department of Justice. Later she was on the Secretariat in negotiations with the Dutch Colonial Power.

Iran
: **Mehranguiz Manoochehrian**, who had already taken post-graduate courses in the juvenile courts of Europe and the USA, was Professor of Psychology and Philosophy at Teheran University from 1931 to 1954 and then practised as an attorney. All along, however, her main interests centred upon improving the lot of women and children of her country. There are few important Iranian women's organisations in which she did not play a leading part, and her *Criticism of the Constitutional, Civil and Criminal Law of Iran in regard to Women* took its inspiration from the Bill of Human Rights and was aimed against the crimes perpetrated upon children.

Japan
: **Jochiko Mibuchi**, a judge of the Tokyo District Court, became the first female head of Court when she was appointed head woman of the Niigata Court of Family Affairs in 1973.

Norway	The first counsellor at law was **Signe Ryssdal** in 1960, and the first Supreme Court Judge was **Ragnhild Selmer** in 1970.
Philippines	The first woman to practise law (in 1914), and who also became the first woman judge, was **Natividad Lopez**.
Poland	**Helena Wiewiorska** (1888–1967), became the first woman lawyer in 1925 (she studied at St Petersburg). Between the wars she was a founder of the Society of Women with Higher Legal Education and also took part in international lawyers' meetings and congresses. For her Resistance work during the German occupation she was imprisoned in 1940. Her health permanently suffered, yet she practised until 1956. **Marion Mushkat** became a Professor of International Law. Between 1944 and 1966 she was Vice-President of the Supreme Court and, coincident from 1946 to 1948, acted as an envoy at the UN while at the same time being War Crimes Mission Chief.
South Africa	The first woman judge was **Leonora Neethling** who took up her appointment in 1969.
Switzerland	The first woman to qualify as a lawyer was **Emilie Kempin-Spyri** (1853–1901) in 1887. In 1904 **Nelly Schreiber-Favre** became the first woman barrister, but it was 1972 before **Magrit Bigler-Enggenberger** became the first Judge of the Federal Court.
Tanzania	**Julia Manning** became the first African woman High Court Judge in East and Central Africa in 1973.
Trinidad	**Mona James** was called to the English Bar in 1939 and that same year became the first Trinidad-born woman barrister in her own country. There she practised and in 1968 became Registrar of the Supreme Court.
USA	**Charlotte Murphy** was, in 1973, the first woman appointed as a Trial Judge of the US Court of Claims. **Martha Griffiths**, who became a Judge in 1953, had in 1948 become a Member of the House of Representatives. Since 1953 she has been a Democratic Member of Congress (now in her eighth term) and was one of those who helped push through the Equal Rights for Women Amendment.
USSR	**Irina Yekaterina** became a member of the Supreme Court in 1951 and in 1957 a member of the Legal Collegium for Criminal Affairs.

As a postscript to this list, here is a rather different facet of woman's achievement in law: the world record for divorces by a woman is held by a barmaid in the USA, **Beverly Avery** who, in October 1957, obtained her sixteenth divorce from her fourteenth husband. Outside court she alleged that 5 of the 14 had broken her nose.

There is, quite naturally, a considerable overlapping between strict legal functions and those of civil administration. Many high administrators are essentially lawyers by training. Just a few of those qualified have been named above. But administrators must be drawn from all fields of endeavour and acquire their skills by experience rather more, perhaps, than from specific training courses. In Communist countries, where free choice between political parties of differing ideals is not allowed, the major way to reach governmental heights is by administrative posts within the narrow confines of the one party.

Ekaterina Furtseva (Russian, 1910–74), after a basic education and training in a trade school, became a weaver in a textile-mill and was an ardent enough Communist to be admitted to the Young Communist League at 14 instead of 17 years. At 20 she was a fully fledged member of the Communist Party where her ambitions and force – for there is no denying she was a forceful woman – plus her organising ability and oratory steadily took her up the party ladder. From 1937 to 1942 she went to university, qualifying as a chemical engineer. Returning to party work and becoming Secretary of the Frunze District Party Committee, she met Krushchev. It had been widely rumoured that they formed a liaison: certainly she followed in his star's trail as he rose to become eventually Leader of the Praesidium, of which in 1957 she became a Member – the first Soviet woman to do so.

Furtseva reached her pinnacle of power in the late 1950s to the early 1960s to become USSR Minister of Culture – a post which entailed travelling to Western countries. Western diplomats may remember, with wry humour, her propensity for taking over any parties given in her

Ekaterina Furtseva

honour and her forceful, biased and blind arguments that, although she admired Charles Dickens and approved of his 19th-century writings aimed at social reform, a Soviet writer's duty was to extol Russia because there was nothing in Russia to criticise. However, writers actually living in that Utopia, such as Boris Pasternak and Alexander Solzhenitsyn, and the artists who indulged in modern art 'which does not serve the people' also have reason to remember her – without humour. Lord Eccles, who had met her on several occasions, described her as 'beautiful and brutal'.

Her decline from political power started in 1960 and was due partly to Krushchev's policy of removing from the Praesidium anybody who had helped him establish power, and partly because although Communists profess complete equality for the sexes, the Moscow Party's Central Committee felt that a man, not Ekaterina Furtseva, should be their head, a position she had held since 1954. She ceased to be a Member of the Praesidium in 1961.

Another Russian administrator, **Mariya Kovrigina**, was a medical graduate from Sverdlosk and, as a party member since 1931, rose through the bureaucracy to become Minister of Health in 1954. It was she, between 1942 and 1959, who virtually reformed and centralised the Soviet Health Organisation.

A rising British woman civil servant, and typical of a new breed of dedicated female public servants, is **Elizabeth Llewellyn-Smith**, an Assistant Secretary who gained a Double First at Girton. She has helped draft four Bills, including the Monopolies and Mergers Act in 1965 and the European Communities Act in 1972. In the USA women civil servants are also to be found. **Helen Bentley** became Chairman of the Federal Maritime Commission (the Government's highest-ranking woman's appointment) and **Elizabeth Koontz** became the first negro director of the US Labor Department's Women's Bureau, as well as the first negro President of the National Education Association. On the other side of the Pacific, **Elizabeth Evatt** was appointed as the first woman member of the Australian Conciliation and Arbitration Commission in 1973, the same year that **Elizabeth Reid** was appointed to the Australian Prime Minister's personal staff as an adviser on women's issues.

In 1974 the tall, blonde 25-year-old **Florence Hugodot** became France's first female Sous-Préfet, in the Eastern Pyrenees Department. The French prefectoral system ensures that central Government policies are carried out in the provinces, no matter how remote. In the much more rarefied atmosphere of the European Commission hierarchy where women represent only a minor proportion of the civil servants, barely a handful have reached the upper echelons. An example of those making their way towards the top is **Lieselotte Klein**. One of her works is a thesis on public finance as an instrument of short-term economic policy in France and Germany. After three years' work in an economic institute she joined the Commission's Economic and Monetary Affairs Division in 1965 but in 1973 moved to become the first senior woman member of its Public Relations Department.

Offences against the law there have always been and always will be, but as the *Encyclopaedia Britannica* points out: 'The number of female offenders makes up only a fraction of that of male offenders. In the 1960s their ratio varied . . . between 1:4 (Belgium), 1:7 (Canada) and 1:9 (Denmark and Norway).' Those figures, with inevitable national irregularities, mark a common trend. Here, therefore, the destructive subject of women and crime is merely summarised. Celebrated and extreme cases are mentioned, none is extolled – not even when the dividing-line between crime and acts of violent revolution is indistinct, though it cannot be overlooked, however, that innumerable crimes have been committed directly or indirectly by women who occupied positions of political power. (For a few examples see the section on Politics and Statecraft.) A certain amount of local power must have shielded Countess **Erszebet Báthory** (Hungarian, 1560–1614) and enabled her to murder the greatest number of victims ascribed to any individual. The 610 young girls killed had lived around her castle. Having been found guilty she was walled up in her room until her death three and a half years later.

In England at the time of the Civil War **Molly Frith** (English, 1589–1663) was a notorious and versatile criminal. Her original skill was that of 'fencing' stolen goods and cutting purse-strings (pockets were not an integral part of garments until early the next century) which won her the nickname 'Moll Cutpurse'. Later she became a highwayman with a hatred for Parliamentarians and on one occasion wounded and robbed the Commander-in-Chief of the Parliamentary forces, General Fairfax, of 250 gold pieces even though he was guarded by armed servants and was no mean fighter himself. When captured she bargained for her re-

'Moll Cutpurse'

lease by returning compromising personal Fairfax property the family could not afford to lose. She then returned to work as a 'fence' and finally died of the dropsy – a rich woman. Less fortunate was **Joan Bracey** (English, 1640–85) who dressed up as a man, called herself 'John Phillips' and became part of the highway gang led by Ned Bracey. With them she took part in many successful hold-ups, but when in 1685 she tried to operate on her own, she was over-powered, tried and later hanged.

A series of poisonings of importance in French history, became notorious in the 1670s when they involved distinguished women. In 1676 **Marie de Brinvilliers** (French, 1630–76), the wife of an army officer, admitted under torture to poisoning her father in 1666 and her two brothers in 1670 with poisons supplied by her lover. It was a crime of revenge against her father's part in imprisoning him. The poisons were provided to the lover by the King's Apothecary and tested by her on hospital patients. In 1673 the crime came to light, but she escaped to England and was sentenced to death in her absence. Unwisely, she went to Liège, Belgium, in 1676 where she was arrested, returned to France, tortured and then executed.

In January 1680, **Catherine Monvoisin** (French, d 1680) was accused of providing love-potions and poisons to six important ladies at court. The poisons were supplied for the removal of unwanted husbands and rivals of their own sex. In addition, however, 'La Voisin', as Catherine Monvoisin was known, had held Black Masses and created a sinister web of witchery, the ramifications of which reached close to King Louis XIV. An investigation ordered by the King eventually involved 442 people, including his favourite mistress, **Françoise de Montespan** (see section on Mistresses and Courtesans). Accounts of the number arrested and punished vary, but eventually 36 people were condemned to death and over 30 either banished or sent to the galleys. La Voisin was executed by burning in February 1680. Although Françoise de Montespan had contact with La Voisin it is most unlikely that she was guilty, although she may well have used love-potions on the King. She was allowed to remain at court, but the King turned his attentions elsewhere.

Piracy saw its female participants and the two most famous women pirates **Mary Read** (English) and **Anne Bonny** (Irish), both disguised as men, quite by chance joined forces on the same sloop about 1719. Anne Bonny had entered piracy via marriage to a dull trading captain whom she deserted in favour of a privateer, Captain Rackham. She then conspired with Rackham to steal the sloop in which they carried out their marauding. Mary Read's previous career included being powder-monkey on a man-of-war, an infantry soldier, a cavalry trooper, then a seaman on board the trading-vessel bound for the West Indies where she joined Rackham's company.

Anne Bonny was a savage, avaricious and dominant partner of the Captain, always spurring him on to further exploits to assuage her greed. Mary Read was by no means the gentler sex, as was illustrated when she found herself attracted to a man she had captured. Hearing he had been goaded into a duel and deciding she was the more expert at handling arms, she deliberately picked a quarrel with the opponent, demanding a prior duel in which she safely dispatched the threat to her bewildered love's safety.

Mary Read and *Anne Bonny*

After many acts of piracy and bloody encounters on the high seas, a Government sloop captured the pirate vessel. Mary Read and Anne Bonny were two of the three pirates who fought it out on deck until captured, the remainder having retired below despite Anne Bonny's attempts with her pistol to flush them out into action. After a trial Rackham was hanged: his final farewell words of comfort from Anne Bonny being '. . . if you had fought like a man you need not have been hanged like a dog'. Both women pleaded pregnancy and were committed to prison until after their respective confinements. It is believed Anne Bonny eventually went free but Mary Read, who had been condemned to hang after giving birth, died of a fever in prison.

Women have managed to become involved, at some time or another, with every sort of crime. The earliest recorded version of one as leader of a gang of counterfeiters is of quite a well-to-do citizen **Mary Butterworth** (American, 1686–1775). She invented a way of producing bills of credit without using a copper plate and thus deprived the law of its chief source of evidence in cases of the kind. The first experiments, about 1716, led to mass-production in her kitchen and the employment of members of her family in specialised operations. Gradually, a large number of people in her home-town of Rehoboth, Mass., including the Town Clerk and Justice of the County Court, became involved with distribution of the output which eventually grew to include eight kinds of bill. Mary Butterworth dominated the gang and even when, at last, they were arrested under suspicion and interrogated in 1723, none admitted fully conclusive evidence so that, at the trial, all were acquitted.

Yet another who did not pay for her crime was the thief and plausible confidence trickster **Sarah Wilson** (British, b 1750). She was a village girl who used her position as servant to one of Queen Charlotte's maids of honour to steal from the Queen, in 1771, a gown, a diamond necklace and a miniature of Queen Charlotte. Caught and sentenced to death she was reprieved at the request of the Queen, her sentence being commuted to banishment as a convict to the American Colonies, where she was sold.

She escaped and, dressing herself up in her booty which she had somehow managed to keep hidden, passed herself off as the Marchionesse de Waldegrave, sister of Queen Charlotte (whose miniature she readily showed). So she travelled for 18 months, accepting top society's hospitality and promising Government posts or commissions in the army in return for fees – payable in advance. By keeping one step ahead of the authorities she avoided capture.

A more celebrated confidence trickster in connection with a valuable diamond necklace came to light in France in 1785. **Jeanne, Comtesse de La Motte** (French, 1756–91) tried to obtain the necklace valued at 1600000 livres for herself though, ostensibly, for Queen Marie-Antoinette. By forged letters in the Queen's name, Jeanne de La Motte persuaded Cardinal de Rohan to arrange the necklace's purchase by instalments and then removed and sold it in London. The intrigue was discovered and made public by Louis XVI. She escaped to England but the ensuing scandal denigrated Marie-Antoinette on the eve of the French Revolution. Napoleon, in fact, rated the scandal as a strong contributory cause of the Revolution in that the King's action in dealing with the high-level conspirators alienated the aristocracy just as the throne was coming under pressure for governmental reform (see section on Politics and Statecraft).

The two most famous political murders by women were committed under totally different circumstances, though both were conceived in a state of idealistic fervour.

Charlotte Corday (French, 1768–93), a pro-Girondin during the early days of the French Republic, saw in Jean Marat (a Deputy for Paris in the Convention and proprietor of an influential paper) a threat to the Revolution. Visiting his home on 13 July 1793, she gained access to his bathroom on the pretext that she had information about dissidents in

Charlotte Corday murdered Marat in his bath

Normandy, whereupon she stabbed him to death in his bath. Four days later she herself was guillotined for the crime, but, whereas she had hoped to undermine people's faith in the Convention she actually strengthened popular clamour against dissidents.

Sofia Perovskaya (Russian, 1853–81) was the inspiration of the Russian Populist Revolutionary 'Will of the People' organisation which determined to assassinate Tsar Alexander II (see also section on Politics and Statecraft). Well educated, calm and determined, it was she, a confined advocate of violence, who, on 1 March 1881, deployed a gang of bomb-throwers at a strategic point where the Tsar's carriage was due to pass and, when the announced route was changed, redeployed her forces on the instant. Yet once the attempt had succeeded she seemed to lose all will to live for she made no attempt to escape, was caught and went resolutely to the scaffold on 3 April.

Criminals who became legends, such as the 'Bandit Queen' of the South-west, **Belle Starr** (American, 1848–89), were not the glamorous figures some supposed. Belle Starr was an extremely plain, double-crossing, horse-thief of a woman who gave herself presence with her ornate pistols, clothing and saddlery. As a confederate of the Jesse James gang she came up before the 'hanging judge' Isaac Parker in 1883 on a minor charge and was indicted as 'the leader of a band of horse-thieves' – so there is a possibility she was the brains behind their organisation. Her legal knowledge was considerable and saved them from trial on more than one occasion. Her self-confidence was immense but it did not save her from being killed by a shot in the back – murdered, according to local rumour, by her son. The majority of her associates, including her son, died violently.

In a world which is supposed to be increasingly civilised, mass genocidal outbursts contradict the supposition. The magnitude of Russian victims during the Great Purge between 1936 and 1938 are estimated at about 10 000 000, and of Chinese victims under Mao Tse-Tung between 1949 and 1965 as about 26 500 000. It would be surprising if greater details are ever made known so, of the publicly recorded crimes against humanity, the worst and most prolific were perhaps those committed during the Second World War, in particular those connected with the genocide of the Jews by the Germans. A handful of depraved women as staff in the concentration and extermination camps were involved in this holocaust. Two are notorious – **Ilse Koch** (German) of Buchenwald and **Irma Grese** (German) of Auschwitz. They were tried and executed by order of International Courts run by the victorious Allied Powers.

The first woman to successfully hijack an aeroplane was **Leila Khaled** (Palestinian) who managed to take a TWA Boeing to Damascus in 1970 but later failed in an effort to repeat the performance with an Israeli airliner in 1972, during which attempt her companion was killed.

The countries which take the most emotional position over women's part in crime are sometimes said to be the Latin lands; though a degree of romanticism certainly touches the Americans over such gangsters' molls as **Catherine Kelly** (who 'pushed' Machine-Gun Kelly). There is something unique, however, about Italy's **Elena Pau**. In November

1970 she was given a two-month prison sentence for selling furniture placed under a sequestration order. Sentence could not be carried out because she was pregnant: moreover, by Italian law, imprisonment cannot be inflicted within six months of a confinement. Since then Elena has thwarted justice by becoming pregnant at every crucial moment in her fight for freedom. Baby ten was expected in 1973 – the third since sentence was passed. However, this is small beer compared with Meyrick Booth's observations in 1929, when he reported an instance in which an Italian girl, who had murdered her child in revolting circumstances, was acquitted and subsequently married the prosecuting officer.

Although an English judge in the late 18th century had remarked in court that he could not think '. . . why a woman should not be appointed to be a constable', the first semblance of a woman to be connected with the police force was in America in the form of prison matrons in New York City in 1845. In 1878, in Portland, Maine, the USA acquired its first officially paid 'police matron' to attend women prisoners – a practice which spread rapidly throughout the 1880s and was adopted in England in 1883.

The first woman to enter the Detective Bureau of a police force was **Marie Owen** (American) the wife of a Chicago patrolman, in 1893. However, it was only gradually that women acquired the power to deal effectively with social conditions and, in particular, prevalent threats to their sex. Drunken and sexual assaults were commonplace, but women's police patrols, backed by men, acted as an effective deterrent in all countries which adopted this system. It appears that the USA also led the world with its first regularly rated policewoman, **Alice Wells** (American) who, as the result of her petitioning, persuaded the Mayor of Los Angeles to appoint her to the job in September 1910. She actually acquired authority above that of the plainclothes men since she was consulted on the purpose and scope of woman police officers in general. From these small beginnings grew the women's police forces of the USA and many other parts of the world.

The first British policewomen were largely provided by private organisations in the early 1900s, though in 1908 the Home Office introduced 'police matrons' similar in function to those of the USA. The advent of war in 1914 accelerated the demand for women to work and the need to protect commuting female factory-workers. The Women Police Volunteers was formed in August 1914 by **Nina Boyle** and **Margaret Damer-Dawson**, the latter creating a small group of motoring ladies to meet refugee trains arriving from Belgium. With official aid and training from senior policemen these organisations grew and gradually official funds were made available for their maintenance when it was seen what a good job the women could do, particularly in clearing the streets of drunks. They became known as the 'Women's Police Service' and included many militant suffragettes who had records for assaulting the police and were inclined to tell the police how to do their job. Hence, when the Metropolitan Police Women Patrols were formed in 1918, those already in the WPS were rejected. After the war attempts were made to abolish this force but eventually they were retained on a reduced establishment. In the Second World War they again increased and have since maintained their position. For example, the operational head of Scotland Yard's Extradition Department, Detective Superintendent **Winifred Taylor**, recently led an armed raid for a man wanted in connection with a murder inquiry.

The example of the USA and Britain in recruiting women police was followed by most other countries in due course. Those in the British Dominions came into being during the First World War, but Germany had women police in Stuttgart as early as 1903, Finland and Sweden in 1907, Zürich in Switzerland in 1909, Norway in 1910 and Holland in 1911. But it was 1918 before Austria adopted women police and 1925 when Poland took the step. Their task in most countries retains the original nature – to deal with female criminals, juvenile deliquency and to act in the plainclothes role when the task is beyond men. They are kept busy.

Statistics show that women are the more law-abiding sex, and when they do break the law it is for a high proportion of petty crimes. However, this should not lead to complacency, for also taken into account must be the small rise in the trend of young female offenders indicted for crimes of violence. Policewomen play an invaluable, integral part in a country's police force, and according to **Shirley Becke** who has recently retired as Britain's most senior policewoman, after 33 years in the force, there is only one thing they cannot do, opt out of a situation; they cannot say 'Not me, I'm a woman.'

A Swedish policewoman in action against a bank robbery in Stockholm

AS SCIENTISTS AND IN MEDICINE

As human intellect evolved so did people's use and knowledge of medicine, and there is reason to believe that women's part in curing and attending the sick and injured, by acting as midwives to each other and caring for the incapacitated while the fit men went hunting, goes back to the beginning of that evolution. Superstitions and herbs were the forerunners of today's psychiatry and medicines, and although many 'cures' were useless, even harmful, there is also evidence that an impressive number of herbs and plants used by primitive peoples have proven beneficial, medicinal properties. So medicine was handed down as an art rather than a science. The first recorded applications of scientific methods, of systematic and unbiased observations, to medicine or anything else, are impossible to place but were definitely established by about 3000 BC, notably in India, China and the Middle East. It is fairly certain that women were involved in these intellectual pursuits for, in ancient India, women had equal educational opportunities, and it cannot be by chance that ancient goddesses were rated as healers of sickness or that priestesses practised medicine on their behalf. Perhaps the earliest known woman practitioner to be recorded by name was **Merit Ptah** (Egyptian, approximately 2700 BC), whose picture is in a tomb in the Valley of the Kings. Her son, a High Priest, described her as the 'Chief Physician'.

At Sais in Egypt, by about 500 BC, there was a fine medical school with a women's section dealing specifically with gynaecology and obstetrics, and here women were teachers as well as students. Egyptian knowledge was widespread and well advanced, above all to the Jews in Palestine and thence to Greece. When Corinth fell to the Romans in 146 BC the Greek medical women fetched by far the best price in the slave-market and were carried off to establish a medical tradition in Italy.

The most ancient record
of a woman doctor in Egypt

The first woman doctor of note was called **Cleopatra** (Roman, 2nd century AD) whose identity is obscure. She is of importance, however, because there are clues which trace back to her the treatise on gynaecology used extensively up to the 6th century and by midwives up to the 16th – despite the fact that various men who lived after her copied her writings without acknowledging their source. Approximately 100 years after Cleopatra there lived another distinguished medical woman, **Fabiola** (Roman, d 399). She had been converted to Christianity at 20, divorced her first husband, remarried and was widowed. She then turned her immense energy and riches to founding hospitals and raising the standard of nursing. Hers were by no means the first hospitals but may have been unique in their time by being both public and giving general treatment. Among her associates were at least 15 other rich, well-educated women, and they practised surgery as well as nursing. Fabiola was canonised after her death.

Women continued to practise medicine as the Pax Romana was replaced by the Dark Ages of destruction, and survived in the profession, more-over, despite the fact that religious orders fixed an ever firmer grip upon it, progressively relegating women to positions of obscurity. When people are sick and in peril, ecclesiastic faith is not always sufficient: confidence in secular competence is also demanded.

The most celebrated medical school, dating from the 10th century, was at Salerno and was both international and liberal, basing its methods upon pagan writings while respecting the Christian faith, enrolling men and women of all nations, including many Jews. The following century saw the most knowledgeable of all women physicians working there, the *Magistra medicinae* **Trotula Platearius** (Italian, 11th century), a leading gynaecologist and obstetrician who also made a special study of dermatology and epilepsy. In particular she was noted for a diagnostic method which depended upon skilful questioning allied to close observation and experience to recognise symptoms, since the rules of the Church forbade dissection and, therefore, precluded knowledge of pathology. Her fame rests upon her much-copied, celebrated book on obstetrics and gynaecology, but she was also something of a pioneer in nursing in that she demanded that the patient should be made comfortable. It seems that students thought her the most knowledgeable of their teachers because, when Rudolph Malecouronne, who later became the most important physician in western France, studied at Salerno between 1040 and 1056, a time when it is known that Trotula was a member of the Faculty, he wrote that there was only one teacher wise enough to answer his questions and that was a woman.

As the 11th century drew to its close, the First Crusade and thousands of unarmed pilgrims, followed by armies, travelled through Constantinople in 1096. There **Anna Comnena** (Byzantine, 1083–1148), the daughter of the ruler, Alexius, ran the hospital of 10000 beds which he had built. She was more than a brilliant physician for, besides being the author of a book on gout, she was also the historian of her father's reign. In fact Sarton lists her as one of the four great medical writers of the 12th century. After her brother succeeded to the throne in 1126 his wife, **Bertha Comnena** (Hungarian), built an even larger hospital to care for the pilgrims – the famous Pantocrator, or general hospital, which was divided into five departments, labour wards, accident.wards, etc., all headed by medical women with nurses of both sexes on the staff. The staff consisted of six surgeons, with consulting physicians doing weekly ward rounds, and its head for some time was **Edina Rittle** (English, 12th century) who came from the county of Essex. Further information about her is not known, though probably she arrived there as one of the pilgrims.

After the fall of Jerusalem to the Crusaders in 1099, the Order of the Knights of St John of Jerusalem was formed and one of its members of note was a 'fisicienne' named **Agnes** who cared for the Jerusalem sick. Women of this Order wore a uniform of a long black gown and cloak with the well-known shape of the white cross, about 9 in wide, appliquéd on the bodice of the dress and shoulder of the cloak. Undoubtedly the best nurses of the Middle Ages were those of the religious orders since they were well disciplined and of superior education. Thus the abbesses were often superior physicians, who were in constant touch with the subject as well as abreast of current knowledge, since the Church ran one of the best of rather poor international communication systems. Moreover, the members of religious orders, being celibate and, therefore, unburdened by constant child-bearing, could find time to give service and acquire practical knowledge.

Héloïse (French, 1101–64) was probably the most learned woman doctor in France in the 12th century. The story of the passionate

A lady physician
of the 15th century

love-affair between this brilliant 18-year-old student and her tutor, the
40-year-old nobleman, Abélard, is well known and apt to overshadow
the fact that, at the same time, Héloïse was undergoing the equivalent of
a graduate course in medicine, surgery, theology and philosophy. For
20 years after the couple's separation she, as a nun, taught and practised
medicine at the Hermitage of Paraclete. At about the same time the
Rhineland boasted an even more remarkable medical woman, the nun
Hildegard of Bingen (German, 1098–1179) whose *Liber Subtilitatum*
was considered by Reuss as the most scientifically valuable record of
medical knowledge and natural science in the Middle Ages. She also
wrote *De Simplicis Medicinae* and *Causae et Curae* which were, in originality, centuries ahead of their time. Even so it must be remembered
that in common with other medical practitioners of her day, her knowledge of the anatomy was, for religious reasons, still conjectural and far
from accurate.

The Renaissance, blossoming from Italy, where educated women of
ability tended to be treated by men as equals, worked a great resurgence
in scientific and medical subjects. The sudden thirst for knowledge,
stimulated by the introduction of printing, sharply improved the taste
for reasoning. When people began to realise the depths of ignorance
which prevailed, remedies were taken.

In England, in 1511, an Act was drawn up by Henry VIII (who experimented in pharmacy), his physician Linacre and Cardinal Wolsey which
decreed that all would-be physicians and surgeons, other than those
licensed by the Archbishop of Canterbury, had to pass an examination
in order to obtain, for a fee, a licence to practise. This Act was to work in
conjunction with the College of Physicians which they established. It

created a minimal standard for physicians. The graduating examination was no sinecure: some people took up to eight years of study before reaching the required standard, and any unqualified person found practising was punished. Of importance was the Act's application to both sexes – a study over seven dioceses has brought to light the original licences of 66 women and, of even greater importance, that the Statute was not repealed throughout the ensuing centuries. Yet, although English women continued to be entitled legally to a medical education and licence to practise, their gradual forfeiture of the ever-evolving comprehensive education and their consequent inability to pass examinations phased them out of competition with men. It was thus a short step for men to assume or claim that women were intellectually inferior and, by stages, establish a closed shop which extended its influence beyond the medical sector into nearly every other which demanded disciplined and trained thinking. Bearing in mind that most civilised countries were soon to be largely influenced either by the British or French in the wake of the Spanish decline, it can be seen how this trend produced world-wide effects.

The worst peril in which women physicians – particularly midwives – stood from the 14th century onwards was that of being accused of witchcraft. The pursuit of witches reached such intensity that it is estimated, in the 17th century, no less than 40000 were executed and many more tortured – most of them women who practised some form of medicine or healing. Small wonder, therefore, that women turned from medicine, and all the more laudable that many more took their lives in their hands in order to treat others. It is against a background of religious bigotry as well as masculine scepticism that women progressed in the sciences through the 17th, 18th and 19th centuries. Only the most brilliant, therefore, could rise to the top. For example:

Maria Cunitz (German, 1610–64), an astronomer, who rationalised Kepler's tables of planetary motion in 1650 in her *Urania propitia* and won a notable reputation. Yet she was no less renowned in her day than **Christina of Hesse** (German, 1578–1658), a celebrated mathematician and scientist.

Gabrielle du Châtelet

Gabrielle du Châtelet (French, 1706–49) was the first person to translate Sir Isaac Newton's *Principia Mathematica* into French and her long essay *Les Institutions de Physique*, written in 1740, also introduced into France the ideas of Leibniz. As well as being an accomplished linguist, she was also a mathematician and physicist. In 1744 the Académie des Sciences published, at their expense, her dissertations on the nature of fire. She wrote, too, on living forces and, after her death, several of her treatises on philosophy were published. For many years she lived with Voltaire – to their mutual intellectual stimulus and with emotional upheavals – for he liked to work surrounded by guests, pandemonium and crises whereas she needed peace and solitude.

At the same time in France was Mme **de Staël Delauney** (French, 1693–1750) who was considered by her colleagues to be the most expert anatomist in France of the day. There followed on, **Geneviève d'Arconville** (French, 1720–1805) who, in addition to translating other people's writings, for example Dr Alexander Monro's two-volume *Anatomy*, wrote 16 works of her own, such as *Description of the Movement of Systole and Diastole of the Heart*; *Description of the Lacteals*; *Ulcers, Fistulae, etc.*; *Colonic Hernia*; *Bones and Periosteitis* and *Muscle Fasciae*. She also studied putrefaction and the substances which caused or hindered it and the effects of acids on the human bile, besides being a chemist and anatomist of some importance.

Maria Agnesi (Italian, 1718–99) a mathematician, whose best-known work, written in 1748, was translated into several languages and contained a discussion on special geometric curves. She was a child prodigy who, mastering Greek, Hebrew and Latin, in addition to several modern languages, achieved the satisfaction of seeing her Latin discourse in defence of higher education for women printed when she was only nine years old.

Some women who played important parts in medicine were started on their career by their husbands and then became the more proficient. For example, **Salomea Rusiecka** (Polish, 1719–*c* 1786) was married, at the age of 14, to an elderly physician and it was from him she acquired her knowledge as an oculist. After the breakdown of her marriage she set up in business alone, travelling in the Balkans, Russia, Austria and Poland and performing a series of successful operations for eye cataracts, which gained her court recognition. Returning to Istanbul, she became Medical Adviser to the Sultan's harem among whom she applied psycho-analysis to treat numerous nervous disorders brought about by these women's unnatural existence in their luxurious prison. However, she continued to specialise in eye diseases and was medically and financially successful.

Another woman who was launched on her career by her husband was **Anne Manzolini** (Italian, 1716–74) who loathed the sight of the dead bodies he, a Professor of Anatomy, used for making anatomical wax models. Unfortunately he had to work on these at home – and they lived in a small house. Five years and six children later, with a husband who was slowly dying from TB, Anne Manzolini had also become an expert modeller in order to support the family. To make her work faultless, she studied anatomy in addition and, incidentally, discovered the correct termination of the oblique muscle of the eye. One thing led to another. From necessity she started to lecture in her husband's place, dissecting the body and explaining the anatomical relationships of the various parts, and did so with such clarity that she was allowed to take his place, appointed Lecturer in her own name after his death and elected Professor of Anatomy in 1766. She also lectured in Russia, where she was made a member of the Russian Royal Scientific Society, and in Britain, where she was elected to membership of the Royal Society.

Angélique du Coudray (French, 1712–89), an accoucheuse, was the first person to use a manikin of a female torso to teach the delivery of an actual foetus, putting her ahead of Smellie in this practice. It was typical of the state of the elevated medical atmosphere in France that, in 1759, she was paid an official fee of 3000 livres per annum and sent on a tour of hospitals to train 4000 students in her method.

Yet the rising bureaucracies were already making it difficult for women to train and become doctors. As a rule midwives were the highest order of women in medicine, and their chances of survival improved with the cessation of witch-hunting at the end of the 17th century. In Germany, for example, the only woman to obtain a medical degree in the 18th century was **Dorothea Erxleben** (German, 1715–62), for many Germans were convinced, like the majority of other nationalities, that woman's place was in the home even when her mental and practical abilities were undeniable. Dorothea Erxleben gained her knowledge with her brothers at home and only obtained entry to the Halle University by personally appealing to Frederick the Great in 1741. In 1742, however, she married and spent the next 11 years raising a family. When her husband died in 1753 she returned to her studies, qualified in 1754 and practised until her death. Yet she was merely a continuation in the long line of her country's scientific women and of those to come. **Dorothea von Rodde** (German, 1770–1824) became a Doctor of Philosophy at the age of 18 years and **Dorothea Hentschel-Guernth** (German, b 1749) carried out research into dietetics while writing numerous books and articles (many under the pen-name 'Amalia') on cookery and gardening besides medical matters.

Nevertheless, only highly qualified women actually struck out on their own because the social system made a total independence of the sex insecure. To be secure a woman did better to work in close association with a relative. To be independent and effective it was essential to have a substantial private income and, since commerce was not usually associated with higher education, that generally meant being an unmarried heiress.

Caroline Herschel (German, 1750–1848) was one important woman of science to make her name by collaboration with a man. She was the sister of Friedrich Herschel who became domiciled in England. He, a musician whose hobby was astronomy, had his hobby develop so promisingly that, in 1772, he asked his sister to leave Germany and help him in England. Together they built their own telescope, including the immensely precise grinding and polishing of the lenses, and then began deep study of the Universe. She took down the data and performed the innumerable calculations connected with them: her brother read his first papers to the Royal Society in 1780. In 1781 he discovered a new planet – Uranus – and in 1782 became Court Astronomer. All of this involved Caroline Herschel who, meanwhile, carried out her own investigations and, independently, made discoveries of nebulae and no less than eight comets between 1786 and 1797. That year she was in a position to inform the Royal Society of 560 stars missing from the *British Catalogue*, and after Friedrich's death in 1822 she compiled a new catalogue of the 2500 stars found by him.

Caroline Herschel

One of the medical students to enrol at the male-only Edinburgh College in 1809 was a James Barry who qualified in 1812 to become Dr James Barry – a name which was maintained, and shielded the actual and mysterious **Miranda Stuart** (British, 1795?–1865) until after her death.

After qualifying, and still in the male disguise necessary then to study and practise medicine, she joined the British Army as a medical officer, was sent to South Africa a year later and gained a reputation as a first-class surgeon (in 1826, without antiseptics, of course, she carried out the first successful caesarian operation there). As Colonial Medical Inspector

Miranda Stuart

at the Cape she imposed strict control upon apothecaries and the supply of drugs, and also improved the health standards in the gaols and leper colonies. At St Helena she was court martialled for a certain over-zealousness in attempting to improve the conditions of women patients in hospital. This strutting, bombastic, outspoken little doctor once found herself in a duel and was wounded but managed to conceal her sex.

Eventually 'Dr James Barry' was promoted to become Inspector-General Surgeon to the British Army and in the Crimea, where she remained four months at the nadir of that Army's medical history she was the only medical officer with the invective and temerity to reprimand an equally formidable woman, **Florence Nightingale** (British, 1820–1910).

Florence Nightingale, the attractive younger daughter of well-to-do parents, was endowed with dynamic energy and considerable intellect. On many occasions she dreamed of voices which helped her in making crucial decisions and at 17 claimed '. . . God called me to his Service', which helped to concentrate her mind upon putting service before self. She resisted marriage and in 1844 irrevocably declared that her mission in life was nursing the sick in hospitals. The profession of nursing had fallen upon bad times along with an ignorant acceptance that squalor and lack of sanitation went with hospitals where, to quote her, 'It was preferred that nurses should be women who had lost their characters . . .'.

Because of strong parental opposition her ambition was delayed until 1850 when she had a fortnight's experience of a well-run German hospital at Kaiserworth. She also visited many institutions and acquired a wide, critical knowledge of their systems and administrations. The

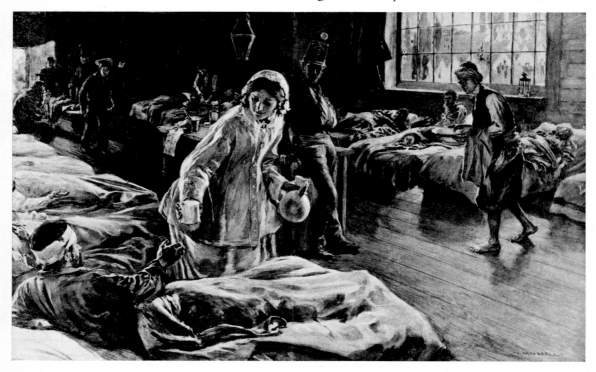

following year she returned to Kaiserworth to undergo a few weeks' intensive nursing training, and passed her examinations brilliantly – though not without some trenchant comments upon those of the hospital's methods which she considered wrong.

In 1853 she was appointed Supervisor to the Hospital of Poor Gentlewomen at 1 Harley Street, London, there to practice the latest nursing systems and to impose those strict routines upon nurses which, today, are the accepted minimum of hygienic and methodic treatment. In the process she became embattled with the first of those governing bodies who, out of ignorance, sought to limit her functions: against this obstruction she began to mobilise a deep understanding of committee procedures and reports which was to make her the greatest nursing administrator of all time. Against the wishes of her committee she insisted that the hospital should be non-sectarian, run with business-like acumen. Striking hard bargains with contractors, she also established herself as a steely authority on nursing.

The war in the Crimea had been going for a few months when, in 1854, reports arrived that the medical care of the troops was disorganised and appalling. She was requested by the Secretary of War to lead an official team of nurses to the base hospital at Scutari, near Istanbul, and within a week, with a team of 38 nurses – all that were sufficiently qualified and were available – she was on her way to start the team's task of caring for thousands of sick and wounded soldiers. As she was straightening Scutari's administrative muddles, Florence Nightingale was not only founding new rules and methods of Army nursing procedures but of general nursing throughout the world. She was also raising a nurse's status from disrepute, through that of a superior domestic servant, to a trained professional in a class of its own.

She returned to England as a heroine and an unchallengeable authority on nursing. Her *Notes on Matters affecting the Health, Efficiency and Hospital Administration of the British Army* became a bible of reform, while her *Notes on Nursing* published in 1859 sold 15000 copies in the first month at the then high price of 5s a copy, going on to sell hundreds of thousands at a lower price. This book presented revelations in sanitation, diet and general nursing. The money she received as public testimonials of her service was used to found the Nightingale Training School for Nurses at St Thomas's Hospital in London, which became a prototype for similar schools throughout the world.

She became an authority not only on the Army's hospitals but also on their barrack plans for India. Government Commissions sent reports of their findings for her approval. Her best student nurses were directed towards correcting the horrors of workhouse infirmaries and, perhaps her greatest achievement, she won the absolute confidence of men of good conscience who willingly carried out essential reform under her guidance and command. Most of this work she did from seclusion so that when, in 1907, she became the first woman to receive the Order of Merit, it came as a surprise to the public to learn she was still alive.

In 1910 she was carried to her grave in a country churchyard by six sergeants of the British Army.

Florence Nightingale at Scutari

It is important to appreciate that at least from the mid 19th century the story of women in science and medicine becomes more than ever intermingled with their struggle for universal equality with men in education and almost every other activity (see, in particular, sections on Education and on Equality) and to persuade their sex to take full advantage of the opportunities offered. Because of this a tendency has arisen to confer the accolade of 'first' on those doctors who qualified as part of that struggle. In point of fact they were merely first to breach the existing restrictive practices.

The first woman to gain a medical degree in the USA was the tiny blonde **Elizabeth Blackwell** (British, 1821–1910) (naturalised American 1849) who, when aged 11 years, went with her family to settle in America. In the USA women were not allowed to study medicine in the medical colleges – nor did many other colleges allow them in. But she was accepted, at last, by Geneva Medical College, in New York, in 1847, graduating in 1849. From there she continued her medical education in Europe, for a short spell in Paris (where they would only accept her as a student midwife), but mostly at St Bartholomew's Hospital, London.

However, on her return to New York she faced seven years of loneliness and difficulties, from being ignored by her medical colleagues and barred from the city's hospitals and dispensaries, to receiving abusive anonymous letters and finding it impossible to persuade anyone to rent her suitable consulting-rooms. The last situation was not really surprising because, at that time, the much-vilified New York abortionist **Ann Lohman** (British, 1812–78) was calling herself a 'female physician' in the running of her business (in fact Ann Lohman was also selling contraceptive materials and operating a clandestine maternity unit with an adoption agency combined – a very lucrative business in those days of hypocrisy with their double set of morals).

Despite the initial difficulties, Elizabeth Blackwell was responsible for the establishment in 1857 of the New York Infirmary for Women and Children and, in 1868, founded the Women's Medical College of the New York Infirmary. The following year she returned to England for good and there encouraged Elizabeth Garrett and Sophia Jex-Blake in their desire to become doctors, and Florence Nightingale in her life's work. She left behind her, in America, another woman she had encouraged to become a doctor, **Marie Zakrzewska** (German, 1829–1902), who had helped raise the funds for the New York Infirmary for Women and Children (America's first hospital to be staffed by women) and was its first Resident Physician and General Manager. Marie Zakrzewska went on to found the New England Hospital for Women and Children with a training school for nurses in 1863. It also attracted the ablest female doctors in America. Certainly **Susan Dimock** (American, 1847–75), who was the hospital's surgeon and probably America's first female surgeon, was considered brilliant, but tragically she was drowned at sea when only 28 years old.

Although by no means the first woman to practise dentistry in America, **Lucy Hobbs** (American, 1833–1910) was the first to obtain a dental degree. She had studied medicine and dentistry privately but began practising dentistry even though unqualified (as was common in the profession). She even had to make money from the struggling practice before she could buy a dental chair, but in Bellevue, Iowa, her skill became so well recognised that, in her first year, a profit of $3000 was made. On the way towards a belated graduation she was elected a member of the Iowa Dental State Society in 1865, then admitted into the Ohio College of Dental Surgery where she passed her Finals in 1866 and, as a member of the senior class, was rated 'second to none'. America also trained the first German woman dentist, **Henriette Pagelson** who, because she was not allowed to study the subject in her own country, learnt English and went to the USA where she gained admittance to the Pennsylvania Dental College, taking her diploma and, in 1869, returned to Berlin where she practised for the next 30 years.

On both sides, during the American Civil War, innumerable women were to be found nursing the wounded and copying the example of Florence Nightingale by insisting upon higher standards than had been the accepted minimum in many places. To take examples from either side:

With the Confederates there was **Sally Tompkins** (American, 1833–1916), a rich woman who ran a hospital from her own resources and staunchly resisted attempts by President Jefferson Davis to close it down in 1861 along with all the other private hospitals. Her hospital was a lot better run than others, and so Davis got out of a difficulty by commissioning her into the Army and thus militarising her hospital. It is to her credit that of the 1333 men who passed through her hospital during four years, only 73 died. She was buried with military honours in 1916.

With the Federal Army of the Mississippi there was **Mary Bickerdyke** (American, 1812–1901) who, when the Civil War broke out, was already supporting herself by 'botanic' medicine (it was not unusual in those days for American doctors to make up their own medicines from wild plants they had picked). When aged 43 she went to a field hospital to distribute funds from her local church and was horrified at the primitive conditions she found. A woman of action, she just rolled up her sleeves and started cleaning, cooking and nursing. Nine months later this human dynamo was still there. A brief spell at a base hospital confirmed her belief that the greatest need for help was at the front. She moved forward with General Grant's army and 'Mother' Bickerdyke, as the troops called her, was once more either up to her elbows in suds as she laundered mountains of linen, maybe assisting at an amputation or preparing vast quantities of food and distributing supplies. By midnight, after the Battle of Fort Donelson, she was out on the battlefield looking for wounded among the dead.

If something needed doing, she did it without further ado and heaven help anybody who tried to get in her way. When an army surgeon wanted to know on whose authority she was acting, she replied 'On the authority of the Lord God Almighty; have you anything that outranks that?' Lazy or corrupt medical officers and their orderlies hated her because, caring not for army 'channels', she went straight to the top. Grant, Sherman, Logan and Hurlbut all knew her and harboured an amused respect for this rough-tongued woman who did so much for their soldiers. She was the only woman at the battles of Lookout Mountain and Missionary Ridge, preparing hot drinks and food and doing all she could for the comfort of the 1700 Union wounded amid the mud and freezing rain. During the battle at Resaca she worked almost without break for five days and nights.

Mary Bickerdyke

The first registered women doctors in many countries in the 19th century often avoided restrictive regulations by taking foreign degrees and acquiring sufficient practical knowledge through nursing. The extraordinary thing, as far as Britain was concerned, was that the old statutes of 1511 were still extant: not until 1856 were these superseded by an Act excluding women from registration unless they had graduated from a recognised foreign university. As **Kate Hurd-Mead** (American, 1867–1941) points out in her admirable *History of Women in Medicine* (upon which we have drawn with great gratitude): 'The only reason for the oversight and non-enforcement of the Act of 1511 was the carelessness of the men and women concerned, and their lack of information on the whole subject.' Thus, **Elizabeth Garrett** (British, 1836–1917) celebrated as the first British woman doctor, was merely trying to re-establish women's ancient rights and the authorities and students who objected so forcibly to her and others, such as **Sophia Jex-Blake** (British, 1840–1912), though legally in the right were historically in the wrong. Elizabeth Garrett, who eased her way in as a nurse, beat all the male students in an examination at the Middlesex Hospital and they promptly had her banned. She eventually qualified as an apothecary in England in 1865 and as a doctor in Paris in 1869. Eventually she received approval from the British Medical Register by virtue of her apothecary's qualification. Sophia Jex-Blake was allowed to study at Edinburgh under constant harassment and impossibly restricting conditions. Sued when she spoke out fearlessly she lost for a farthing damages while legal costs of £1000 were paid by supporters. She would not give up and finally found her way on to the British Medical Register via successful examinations in Berne and Dublin in 1877.

The production of official medical qualifications from other countries helped to demolish the temporary bureaucratic bar to women. Switzerland was a haven for women students, Russia was in slow transition in their favour and France reopened her medical faculties to women in 1863. The achievements of the 'new' medical women were not so much in the field of medicine as in breaking through the bureaucratic barriers, illustrated by the efforts of the Russian doctor **Nadezhda Suslova** who qualified in Zürich in 1867; the Swiss **Marie Heim-Vögtlin** (1845–1916) who qualified in 1872; the French **Madeleine Brés** who qualified in 1875 and, although gainfully employed as a dresser and house surgeon during the Franco-Prussian War, was afterwards refused a degree until officialdom could be overcome; the Polish **Anna Tomaszewiczowna** who qualified in Switzerland in 1878 and in St Petersburg in 1879 but was not recognised by the Warsaw Medical Society until 1896; the first Australian woman to qualify, **Constance Stone**, in 1890, followed by the first Filipino woman **Honorie Sison** in 1909.

The 19th century saw an awakening of women to opportunities in fields other than medicine. The USA had its female astronomer **Maria Mitchell** (American, 1818–89) who at 12 years of age was already recording the time of a solar eclipse. On 1 October 1847, with a 2 in Dolland telescope, she discovered a new comet, 'Miss Mitchell's Comet', which was to gain her entry into high scientific circles in the USA and Europe. Appointed in 1865 to be in charge of the observatory at Vassar College, with its 12 in (304 mm) telescope – the third largest in the

Maria Mitchell

country – she proved to be not only the greatest of Vassar's teachers but also a maverick in her methods of instruction, class discipline and assessment of learning. This she did on half the salary which would normally have been paid to a man. Among her 25 pupils who became of national repute there was the psychologist and logician **Christine Franklin** (American, 1847–1930), the chemist **Ellen Richards** (see section on Homemakers) who became the first woman member of the American Institute of Mining and Metallurgical Engineers and the astronomer **Mary Whitney** (American, 1847–1921) who took over from Maria Mitchell and throughout her life pushed the cause for women's education and for women to be accepted in science.

Mention must also be made of the ethnologist **Alice Fletcher** (American, 1838–1923) who, when she was 43, started her great life work for the American Indians. It was entirely through her efforts that the Bill was passed in 1882 which apportioned the Omaha Indian tribal-held territory among its individual members, so helping them to become self-supporting. She personally inspected and allocated the strips of land, as she later did with the 1000 or more plots for the Winnebago Indians of Nebraska and the Nez Percés in Idaho, after the Dawes Act of 1887. All this time she closely studied the Indians' customs, rituals and music and recorded them in such works as *The Omaha Tribe* in 1911 and in the only complete record of a major Plains Indian ceremony *The Hako: A Pawnee Ceremony* in 1904. Her many scholarly writings established her as the leading authority on American Indians, with the honours that followed including, in 1896, becoming Vice-President of the American Association for the Advancement of Science and, in 1903, President of the Anthropological Society of Washington which, only four years previously, had an all-male membership.

A highly distinguished scientist of the time was **Sonya Kovalevski** (Russian, 1850–91) who studied mathematics in Germany and won a degree *in absentia* in 1874 from Göttingen University for a brilliant thesis on partial differential equations. Later, in 1888, when a Lecturer at the University of Stockholm, her paper on the rotation of a solid body round a fixed point won the award of the Prix Borodin of the French Academy so overwhelmingly that the value of the prize was doubled. The following year she was appointed a Professor and two years later, shortly before her death, was elected to the St Petersburg Academy of Science. She had also gained a reputation as a novelist, writing on the contemporary Russian way of life. Britain also had a scientist of note in **Hertha Ayrton** (British, 1854–1923), whose work on the electric arc started in 1883. It was her book *The Electric Arc*, published in 1902, which brought her an individual reputation and her reports for the Admiralty on electric searchlights which involved her in defence work. She invented an anti-gas fan to help repel poison gases during the First World War and to assist in the ventilation of gun emplacements. After the war she investigated the distribution of industrial gas over greater distances than hitherto.

The most famous of all women scientists, **Manya Sklodowska** (Polish, 1867–1934), the daughter of a mathematics and physics teacher, is better known by her married name, **Marie Curie**. She was born and educated in Warsaw and, by the time she was 16, this slight, bird-like creature with her remarkably retentive memory had already won a Gold Medal at the Russian Lycée upon the completion of her secondary education. There was no money to spare and so she worked as a governess to finance her sister Bronia's medical studies in Paris on the understanding that, later, this help would be reciprocated. So in 1891, almost penniless, she arrived in Paris to study at the Sorbonne. Hers really was the poor student's garret in which she worked ceaselessly, late into every night, virtually living off bread and butter. But it was here that she demonstrated her outstanding ability to the best scientific brains of the day. From then onwards her life was one of immensely hard work attended by successes of the first magnitude. The principal events were:

1893   First in the examination for a degree in physical sciences at the Sorbonne.

1894   Second in the examination for a degree in mathematical sciences.

1895   Married Pierre Curie, a physicist with whom, until his accidental death in 1906, she was to be closely associated in all her work.

Marie Curie losing her hair
due to her work

1896   Began her study of what she named 'radioactivity' which had just been discovered by Henri Becquerel.
1897   Birth of her first daughter, **Irène** (see below).
1898   Discovery of 'Polonium' by extraction with a new chemical method from pitchblende.
        Discovery of 'Radium' from pitchblende.
1900   Discovery of 'excited radioactivity'. Appointment as Lecturer at the École Normale Supérieure for Girls at Sèvres.
1903   Award of a Doctorate of Science for the research which culminated in her obtaining pure radium in the metallic state and, with Pierre, the Davy Medal of the British Royal Society. The award with Pierre and Becquerel of the Nobel Prize for Physics for the discovery of radioactivity – she was the first woman to be so honoured.
1904   Birth of her second daughter, **Eve**, who was to write her mother's biography.
1906   Accession to Pierre's professorship, thus to become the first woman teacher at the Sorbonne.
1910   First preparation of the element of Radium (with A. Debierne). Publication of her fundamental treatise on radioactivity.
1911   Award of the Nobel Prize for Chemistry for the isolation of pure radium. Thus she became the first person to receive two Nobel awards.

Awards came thick and fast, but they allowed no cessation of work; she was either lecturing or continuing research with hardly any abatement, and making sure of the accumulation of adequate radium stocks for their most beneficial use of tackling cancer and for research into nuclear physics. For it must be remembered that as well as the life-saving benefits from her discovery of radium she also laid the very foundations of contemporary nuclear science and technology. Her hands had already become scarred by radium when, in the end, her work proved lethal. In 1934 she died of leukemia caused by excessive accumulations of radium.

Lise Meitner

Following in Marie Curie's footsteps came the physicist **Lise Meitner** (Austrian, 1878–1968) (naturalised Swede 1949), a Jewess, who took her doctorate with relatively no opposition in 1906 in Vienna and began to work with Otto Hahn in Berlin. Together they were to run the Kaiser Wilhelm Institute for Chemistry after 1917 and to make the discovery of protactinium. Their work on radioactivity included the bombardment of uranium by neutrons and from this, with Otto Frisch, Lise Meitner propounded the correct interpretation of 'fission' in 1939 as a process for liberating great energy by dividing a heavy atomic nucleus into two approximately equal parts: the fragments, thus becoming unstable, would undergo a chain of disintegration. The Nazi occupation of Austria forced her into exile in Sweden where she was elected to the Swedish Academy of Science, but the results of her discoveries found their way elsewhere until, in due course (when linked to the discoveries of other scientists), they led to the first nuclear reactor, and also the atomic bomb.

The way for able women to penetrate the inner sanctums of scientific and medical establishments was open and their subsequent progress in these places marks a prime index of their advancing education and ambitions. The outstanding members had to make a worthwhile impact to continue breaking down the artificial barriers erected by prejudice, by associating scholarly attributes with organising ability and by originality in addition to perseverance. Among their number, as the 20th century emerged, were:

Emmy Noether (German, 1882–1935), a mathematician who became Lecturer at Göttingen University in 1919 (after the customary opposition), and thereafter made a significant contribution to modern algebra with her studies on abstract rings and ideal theory.

Annie Cannon (American, 1863–1941), an astronomer who not only discovered 5 new and 300 variable stars but also compiled the *Henry Draper Catalogue* of stellar spectra which, with her two-volume extension, gave a total classification of the spectra of some 350 000 stars. She built up Harvard College Observatory's card catalogue of the literature on variable stars from 14 000 to about 250 000 and their astronomical photographs from 200 000 to 500 000, making Harvard's records the largest in the world and invaluable for the observatory's future research.

Ruth Benedict (American, 1887–1948) whose anthropological studies of American Indian tribes led her to the deeper study of races and their different values. Her findings were embodied in her book *Patterns of Culture* published in 1934 and in *Race, Science and Politics* in 1940. After doing Government work during the Second World War by analysing the modern societies of Romania, Thailand and Japan for overseas intelligence, she made a closer study of the patterns of Japanese culture. This led to her presiding over America's most ambitious anthropological research to that date – 'Research in Contemporary Cultures' – which was financed by the Office of Naval Research. A year before her death she became President of the American Anthropological Association.

Libbie Hyman (American, 1888–1969), a zoologist, whose research into the physiology and morphology of lower invertebrates made her an authority on the subject. She produced six knowledgeable volumes *The Invertebrates*, and her revised *Comparative Vertebrate Anatomy* was still being used as a textbook when she died. She was awarded the British Royal Society's Gold Medal of the Linnean Society in 1960 for her zoological work.

Aileen Cust (British) became the first woman to be admitted to the British Royal College of Veterinary Surgeons in 1922.

Verena Holmes (British) was the first woman member of the British Institution of Mechanical Engineers in 1924 and a Fellow in 1944.

Jane Delano (American, 1862–1919) was, in a way, the Florence Nightingale of the US Army's nursing service in that she helped put it on a sound administrative footing and materially raised its standards by getting the pay scale raised to attract better graduates. Moving from post to post, she rose to become President of the American Nurses' Association and Superintendent of the Army Nurse Corps in 1909 and, from 1910 to 1919, Chairman of the National Committee of the Red Cross. She insisted upon the American Red Cross Nursing Service being confined to professional, graduate nurses and during the First World War administered the flow of 20000 such nurses to keep pace with the Army's needs. She accepted the view that trained, lay women did have their place in the Red Cross and developed the auxiliary 'Volunteer Nurses' Aides', at the same time helping to write a home nursing textbook for them.

Fanny Harwood (British, 1889–1973) became in 1912 the first woman in Britain to be a Licentiate of Dental Surgery of the Royal College of Surgeons. Later, in 1916, to satisfy the custom of the day, she took a degree in medicine but already, in 1912, she had been engaged to run what may have been the first school dental clinic in the country. She practised for most of her working life, encouraged at the beginning by her father, a doctor, and later by her dental surgeon husband with whom she was also in business partnership.

All cultures throughout history, irrespective of their religion, show evidence of a wish to regulate fertility. The ancient Egyptian *Petri Papyrus*, written about 1850 BC, describes several means to avert pregnancy and in keeping with medicine of its day it contained mostly magical rites and incantations: other means had value. Aristotle in the 4th century BC and Soranus in the 2nd century AD describe methods of contraception – physical and chemical methods were accepted in ancient Greece and Rome as a preventive medicine to maintain the health of women. But this knowledge became lost and unused until about the 19th century.

In England in 1797 and later, in 1822, birth control was advocated by two lone voices, but country-wide publicity was given to the subject when **Annie Besant** (see section on Religious and Social Reform) won a court case in 1877 on the right to publish in Britain the writings on methods of contraception by Charles Knowlton – a work which had received considerable opposition in America and caused his prosecution there in 1832. However, it was in Holland that the first systematic work on contraception began. It was started by Dr **Aletta Jacobs** (Dutch) and her colleagues in 1881, and they gave considerable professional assistance and support to birth control pioneers from other countries.

Margaret Sanger

The term 'birth control' was coined by **Margaret Sanger** (American, 1883–1966) who, as a nurse in the slums of New York, saw the results of uncontrolled fertility with its intensification of poverty and high rate of infant and maternal mortality. Close contact with these unfortunate mothers convinced her that every woman had the right to plan the size of her family. She determined to see the repeal of the laws which, by forbidding the dissemination of information on contraception, were causing such misery.

In 1912 a New York newspaper published her first article advocating birth control. In 1914, after a visit to Europe for further study on the subject, she was indicted for sending through the mail copies of a periodical called *Woman Rebel* which stated she intended breaking the law by disseminating birth control information in a pamphlet *Family Limitation*. This she did. Two years later the case was dismissed, but that year she further tested the law by opening America's first birth control clinic in Brooklyn. Charged with 'maintaining a public nuisance' she was convicted and jailed for 30 days.

In 1921 she founded the American Birth Control League, being its President until 1928. In 1929 she entered the political arena by starting the National Committee on Federal Legislation for Birth Control. The police raided her clinic, taking away the files and records. However, by then she had enough support from social reformers and doctors to bring pressure – the case was dismissed: public opinion was slowly changing. In 1936 the law classifying contraceptives and contraceptive instructions as obscene was modified to allow doctors to prescribe birth control for health reasons. Three years later the American Birth Control League amalgamated with the Education Department of the Birth Control Clinical Research Bureau. The new organisation took the name, in 1942, of the 'Planned Parenthood Federation of America'.

Margaret Sanger looked beyond America, and in 1953 the International Planned Parenthood Federation was started with her as its first President. She did much work for birth control in India, where the poverty and high birth-rate is well known, and in Japan which provided a concentrated example of the wider span of population control practised by humanity – first infanticide, followed by abortion, followed by contraception. In Japan's feudal days infanticide was common; in 1948 abortion was legalised and became the prime means of family control; in the 1960s more Japanese used contraception than abortion. By the late 1960s, 75 nations gave some assistance to birth control measures within their countries.

Marie Stopes (British, 1880–1958) helped spread the knowledge of birth control in the Far East. As a graduate in geology and with a doctorate of botany she had unlikely qualifications to become a pioneer of the birth control movement, yet her writings on the subject showed a deeper intellectual understanding than Margaret Sanger's. In 1918 she published *Married Love* and *Wise Parenthood* which went into many translations and, besides the economic issues of family control, emphasised the importance of husband/wife emotional relationship without constant fears of unwanted pregnancies. When her *Contraception: Its Theory, History and Practice* was published in 1923 it was the most comprehensive work on the subject to date.

Marie Stopes

In 1921 she started Britain's first birth control clinic and founded the Society for Constructive Birth Control. But many independent clinics started around Britain in the 1920s and in 1930 they all amalgamated into the Family Planning Association.

As well as lowering the birth-rate, women were also working to reduce the death-rate and an outstanding contribution to the control of sleeping sickness was made by **Muriel Robertson** (British, 1883–1973) by her investigation into the transmission of this disease in Uganda. Her study (at risk to herself) of the life cycle of the organism trypanosoma in the tsetse-fly, begun in 1911, led to a sharp reduction in deaths caused by this (then) incurable disease which used to kill thousands of people. She also did invaluable work upon the identification of gangrene which, prior to the First World War, was one of the principal causes of death among the wounded.

The new leaders in the sciences included many women. For example:

Virginia Apgar (American) who created the now internationally used 'Apgar Score' for evaluating a baby's over-all condition within one minute of birth. This drill immediately highlights the baby's chances for survival, thus enabling rapid, specific aid to be given if necessary.

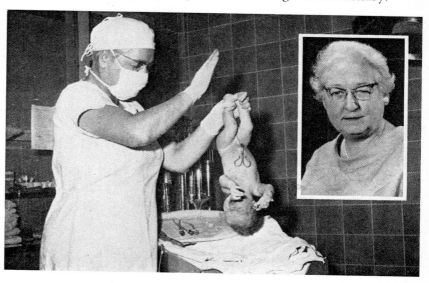

Virginia Apgar

Irène Joliot-Curie (French, 1897–1956) who, like her famous mother, Marie Curie, was also a physicist and, by working as her assistant from 1918, acquired a great knowledge of radioactivity. Also, like her mother, she married a physicist and formed a brilliant partnership in research. They discovered they could make certain elements artificially radio-active, which was an important step towards releasing the energy of the atom, and for this discovery they were jointly awarded the Nobel Prize for Chemistry in 1935. For her sympathies with Communism she was dismissed her post at the French Atomic Energy Commission. In 1951, like her mother, she too died from leukemia as the result of her previous work.

Marguerite Perey (French, 1909–75), a member of Marie Curie's staff from 1929 who in 1939 discovered the element she called 'francium' (actinium K). A brilliant, hard-working scholar and research worker, she was to become head of the Nuclear Research Centre at Strasbourg and, over the years, to be loaded with honours by her country that included one which had eluded women for the entire 200 years of its existence – membership of the Académie des Sciences. She died of radiation diseases.

Gloria Hollister (American) who at 15 became an expert in breeding chickens and turkeys, obtained degrees in zoology and took part in an expedition to British Guiana with the female explorer Mrs Mitchell. Shortly after returning to the USA she was made a Fellow of the Geographical Society and in 1929 invited to join the deep-sea expedition of William Bebe. Thus she became associated with the discoveries made when Bebe was lowered to record depths in the bathysphere. In August 1931, she was lowered to a depth of 1208 ft (367 m) – a record for a woman which so far seems unbroken.

Kathleen Lonsdale (British, 1903–71) who gained her DSc in Physics and became a distinguished crystallographer. Her publications included *Structure Factor Tables* in 1936 and *Crystals and X-rays* in 1949. She was also Editor of the three-volume *International Tables for X-ray Crystallography*. In 1945 she became one of the first two women Fellows of the British Royal Society, and in 1960, its Vice-President and was awarded the Royal Society's Davy Medal for her work on crystallography.

Nina Matikashvili (Russian), a veterinary surgeon who rose to become head of the Arachnology and Protozoology Laboratory at the Georgia Zooveterinary Research Institute, is an expert on ixoliid ticks and has written more than 50 works on the subject.

Maria Mayer (German) a PhD in theoretical physics also married a physicist and went to live in America. Researching in nuclear physics she worked on the unusual stability of various nuclear structures and for this work won the Nobel Prize for Physics jointly with J. Jensen and E. Wigner in 1963. During the whole of the period of the Second World War she worked on isotope separation for the atomic bomb project. Afterwards, in 1955, she and Jensen wrote together the *Elementary Theory of Nuclear Shell Structure*.

Nuzhet Gökdoğen (Turkish), an astronomer who took her PhD at Istanbul University in 1937, became a Member of its Senate in 1952, its Dean of Studies in 1954 and Director of its observatory in 1958. Later she also became President of the Turkish Astronomical Society.

Ida Macalpine (German, 1899–1974), a specialist in psychosomatic medicine, who wrote the standard reference work *Three hundred Years of Psychiatry 1535–1860* in 1963.

Lyudmila Keldysh (Russian) whose work on physico-mathematical science at the Mathematical Institute of the USSR produced a number of deep studies with very long titles – such as this one in 1957: *Conversion of a Monotomic Irreducible Mapping in a Monotomic Open Mapping and Enlarging Monotomic Open Map of a Cube.*

Zdenka Samish, a Jewess, who went to Israel in 1924 and played a prominent part in developing food technology at the Volcani Institute for Agricultural Research.

Letitia Obeng (Ghanian) who, as founder and Director of the Institute of Aquatic Biology at Accra, Ghana, was in charge of all the work on waterborne diseases in connection with the vast Volta River project.

Joan Whitmore (South African), the Director of the Hydrological Research Institute in north-east Pretoria, who was the prime mover behind the launching of this establishment in an effort to solve South Africa's water shortage.

Dorothy Hodkin (British) who was awarded the Nobel Prize for Chemistry in 1964 for determining the structure of biochemical compounds essential in combating pernicious anaemia.

Katherina Zaleska

Women have made great breakthroughs in scientific research, with subsequent world-wide acclaim. But for each one of these women there are today thousands unknown who play their smaller part in science or medicine for the benefit of humanity. There is not room to list even a fraction of them, the difficulties they overcome, and their achievements. And so, in conclusion, we have taken just one of these, **Katherina Zaleska** (Polish) whose achievements are little known but which, nevertheless, are a fine example of what one woman can do for medical science even in primitive and under appalling difficulties.

She was born at Lvov in 1919 and separated from her parents in September 1939 when her father was among those captured and later killed at Katyn Wood and her mother was deported to the Gobi Desert. During the early days of the occupation she and her sister were couriers for the clandestine Polish forces, taking messages to Hungary via the German-occupied zone and Czechoslovakia. They were caught 13 miles from the Hungarian frontier and spent a long time in five different prisons answering questions put by the Gestapo. Fortunately for them they had managed to destroy the messages and were able to convince the Gestapo that they were just 'silly girls'.

Katherina Zaleska made her way, penniless and practically naked, to Cracow where she enrolled, through the Red Cross, as a nurse to perform sanitary duties. When the Germans closed that hospital in 1941 she began studying by day at the Rockefeller Nursing School in Warsaw and looked after wealthy people in nursing-homes during the night in order to pay her tuition fees. At the same time she joined the secret Home Army and operated under the nickname of 'Juka' as a courier. She describes this as 'the most fascinating and wonderful period of my life . . . in spite of the hunger, the bitter cold, the lack of clothing and the separation from our families. Our sense of humour and our high spirits were our only means of defence.' Weariness she never recalls. By chance she was outside Warsaw when the siege began in 1944 and suffered agonies of torment that her comrades in arms and relatives were fighting without her. All she could do was help the survivors escape and watch the Russians occupy her country in place of the Germans. She was twice decorated for valour. In this period she lost 18 close relatives, including 5 boys who were only sons, one of whom was her brother.

In 1945 some of the Polish universities began to revive and Katherina

Zaleska was able to obtain admittance at Poznan to study medicine while working as a nursing sister to pay her way. In her second year she was asked if she would actually perform laryngolical work since there was a dire shortage of doctors and specialists. Thus she began to specialise in ENT work even before she had qualified as a doctor. In her third year she was performing minor operations under supervision and in her fifth was offered the post of Assistant ENT at Stettin University where she gave lectures to the medical students and at the same time completed her training as a doctor.

After the Hungarian uprising in 1956 it became possible for Poles to get exit visas. This practically coincided with her discovering that her mother was alive and in London. To earn enough money to buy proper clothing for a six weeks' visit she took three jobs, which ran concurrently, for one year, in the ENT Department of the Medical Academy in the morning, in the ENT Clinic of the Stettin Harbour in the afternoon, and in the Casualty Department every second night. Eventually she arrived in London in 1957 to spend a breathless time looking at luxuries and breathing a freedom to which she was totally unaccustomed. Quite by chance she met somebody who told her that Mr A. B. Alexander, the ENT Consultant at St James's Hospital, Balham, was looking for an assistant. At this time Katherina Zaleska could speak hardly any English – only Polish, French and German. She was invited, along with six other applicants for the job, to write a diagnosis on 15 patients. When Mr Alexander asked for her passport, however, and began dictating quickly to his secretary, her nerve gave way. She was sure he thought she was an impostor and that she was to be arrested for falsification of documents. 'All the souvenirs of the Stalinist terror went through my head. I became hysterical, begging Mr Alexander not to drag me to the police but to let me return to my mother and my home country.' He was flabbergasted and explained that she was the only candidate not to make a mistake, that the job was hers and he was merely arranging an extension of her visa. Within 18 months she was Registrar of St James's Hospital – but this proved '. . . too easy and uninteresting when compared with the tremendous amount of serious and complicated cases I was used to handle in my practice in Poland. . . . Also I felt somehow ashamed to earn in one week what would be two and a half months' pay in Poland. . . . However, I was sending my money to help the relatives I had left there.'

In 1959 she married a Pole who was working in Nigeria. She went with him to Lagos where she began work as ENT Specialist in the General Hospital. Her marriage failed, but her love for Africa blossomed and she stayed on. Now she deals with 60 patients a day (20 000 per annum). She bought a house in London for her mother and continues to help her family in Poland. She loves her work and Africa, but remains 100 per cent Polish in mind and heart.

IN TRADE

Women have always lived close to the soil, extremely close in those peasant communities where their labour has been vital to survival. The latest research indicates that in primitive communities it is the women who provide food from the land and make clothing while the men hunt and prosecute war. It is not unreasonable to suppose, therefore, that in early days women took part in barter and marketing as improved communication led to trade between groups. Thus they learned how to strike a fair (perhaps hard) bargain in the exchange of goods and services. When the men left for war the women often controlled a home or estate. In the upper hierarchies when a woman ruled she would be responsible for higher trade policy, as the section on Politics and Statecraft mentions in respect of those who placed commerce uppermost in their order of priorities. The Egyptian ruler Hatshepsut and the English Elizabeth I, for example, strongly encouraged trade despite a background of war. But there is only scanty evidence showing women involved with the development of trade and industry in the days when Guilds were formed leading to the Mercantile System becoming merged with the Industrial Revolution: they mostly supplied the work force – often receiving a mere pittance for their sweated labour in the new factories (see section on Religious and Social Reformers). Nevertheless the 17th century produced many female craftsmen in the trades of printing, plumbing, carpentry and as silversmiths and wig-makers.

An outstandingly successful and hard businesswoman of the 16th century was **Kenau Hasselaer** (Dutch, 1526–c 1588) from a brewer's family who married a shipwright. Widowed and left with four children in 1561 she registered the following year in Haarlem as an independent shipwright

Kenau Hasselaer

and continued to run the business with enormous drive and perception. To acquire materials and win orders she travelled extensively in rough conditions throughout the Low Countries and Scandinavia, dealing directly with some of the shrewdest men of the day. Naturally she operated at an initial disadvantage and attempts were made to cheat her: she retaliated with lawsuits – and won. Her fame in Holland rests upon her part in the defence of Haarlem during the siege of 1573, but her main achievement was a persistent demonstration of commercial acumen and toughness in expanding her commercial enterprise. Dutch women were well known to be good at business and the following century saw the avaricious **Margaret Philipse** (Dutch, d 1690) holding her own in international mercantile affairs. It is known that by 1660 she was a business agent for various Dutch merchant traders plying between Holland and America. She carried on this business in her maiden name and upon losing her first husband became in addition a trader and shipowner. Her second husband was a New York (then called New Amsterdam) merchant but she still carried on her own trading business, frequently travelling between America and Holland. On one occasion a passenger noted with strong disapproval how she insisted that her ship circled for an hour and a half while everybody, passengers included, had to make a fruitless search for a mop which had fallen overboard.

The first English daily newspaper was published by **Elizabeth Mallet** (English) on 11 March 1702, and called *The Daily Courant*. Very probably hers was the first of all daily newspapers published by a woman, but she had to give it up after only nine days for it to be resumed a month later – by a man. The first woman to publish a newspaper in America was **Elizabeth Timothy** (Dutch, d 1757) who, as part of her education in Holland, had been taught accountancy. A mother of six, in 1738 she took over the weekly *South Carolina Gazette* when her husband, the publisher, was killed. She did not miss an issue and proved a better business executive than him, eventually buying a printing-works, three houses, land and eight slaves.

A sound and profitable agriculturist, being also a good businesswoman, was **Elizabeth Pinckney** (British, *c* 1722–93) who, when in her teens, was left by her British Army father in charge of a plantation he had inherited in South Carolina. At her father's suggestion she diversified crops and, in particular, experimented with indigo raised from seed he sent her from the West Indies. After achieving the most favourable growing conditions and then the best methods to obtain the dye from the plants, she was able to produce indigo blue dye which was superior to that supplied by the French and in 1744 sent 6 lb (2·7 kg) on trial to Britain. In 1746 40 000 lb (18 144 kg) was exported by the State and in 1747 100 000 lb (45 359 kg) – continuing exports which sustained Carolina for the next 30 years. At his own request George Washington was one of her pall-bearers.

The first woman to operate an iron-mill in the USA was **Rebecca Lukens** (American, 1794–1854). In 1810 her father converted a saw-mill

A London sweat shop in the 19th century

at Brandywine Creek, Pennsylvania to iron-making. She and her husband later took it over and began expansion at her instigation. She, in the meantime, had studied the manufacturing processes involved. At a critical moment when, in 1825, they received a large order for plate for the first American ironclad warship and were financially overstretched, she became pregnant and her husband died. She took over as ironmaster, arranged finance for the deal, obtained the essential raw materials and organised production. The mill prospered and expanded under her direction, survived the financial panic of 1837 and went on supplying the Pennsylvania Railroad as it grew, in addition to the new iron ships. Its boiler plate was famous. Moreover the work people were quite well cared for according to the standards of the day. The first Englishwoman to run an ironworks was **Charlotte Guest** (British, 1812–95) whose husband owned, in the mid 19th century, the enormous Dowlais Iron Company of Merthyr Tydfil in Wales. For many years she acted as Company Secretary, showing close interest in all the technical processes in addition to finance and control (and producing ten children). When her husband died in 1852 she became sole trustee of the works and almost at once was faced with a strike affecting all the other British ironworks. The other ironmasters proposed a lock out. Charlotte Guest remonstrated, since she felt the workers should be consulted but, 'I suspected my objections arose from a woman's weakness, and succumbed for the moment with extreme reluctance.' Nevertheless she did not sign a joint document with other ironmasters and gave her work people a wage increase. At once the other ironworks were faced with the same demand. She lost patience: 'If the men threaten or make any demonstration of a strike, I will resist them to the end. . . . I will be their master.' She did just that, not as a distant figurehead, but as an on-the-spot expert, where she could be seen scrambling round furnaces or through mineshafts. Eventually she was to reliquish her command after a second marriage.

The most inspired industrial system of the early 1830s was a weaving factory near Boston, USA, staffed by female labour and begun in 1823. The girls' welfare was put first and they lived in carefully managed boarding-houses. Francis Lowell, the founder, believed in educating the girls and improving social conditions as a means to higher productivity. The elevated state of the 'reading' ladies of Lowell (compared with their oppressed fellows in Europe) attracted world-wide attention: one 'graduate' was a well-known poetess, **Lucy Larcom** (American, 1824–93) and there were others among her colleagues who moved towards higher education – and dissatisfaction. By 1845 the owner's philanthropy was giving way to his personal greed at a moment when the better-educated girls had learnt to query their exploitation. Strikes occurred. **Sarah Bagley** (American) formed the Lowell Female Labor Reform Association and fought along with the embryo men's unions for a ten-hour day. Her organisation spread throughout the USA but did not achieve its aim in Massachusetts law until 1874. The other States copied in the years to follow, but she faded from notice in 1847 having become, in the meantime, America's first woman telegraph operator.

Lydia Pinkham (American, 1819–83) made a fortune from patent medicine and by the time of her death was earning $300 000 a year from

Lydia Pinkham's portrait on her patent medicine label

a 'remedy' first concocted in her kitchen and sold in 1875. Her Vegetable Compound, a mixture of roots (mainly *Aletris farinosa* and *Asclepius tuberosa*) plus 18 per cent alcohol to preserve it, produced a medicine, the curative claims of which were extensive and bold – and in which she seems to have believed. She and her Vegetable Compound have been immortalised in songs and jest. The most successful feminine financier of the later 19th century was probably **Henrietta Green** (American, 1835–1916). She inherited $1 000 000 and the income from her family's $10 000 000 shipping business in 1865 and speculated, mostly in Government bonds, railroad stock and real estate, with such success that, by 1916, it was valued at about $100 000 000, making her, reputedly, the richest woman in the USA. She was also, by repute, the greatest miser – distinguished by wearing the oldest of clothes, using free clinics and living in run-down boarding-houses. She is said to have eaten her porridge cold because she begrudged the fuel to heat it.

To meet their everyday needs in the home, women have always displayed a measure of invention often through improvisation, but few are found on the rolls of recognised inventors with patents to their names. Perhaps the most prolific of all feminine inventors was **Margaret Knight** (American, 1838–1914) who, when only 12, thought up a safety device for shuttles in a cotton-mill, though her first patent, for a machine to fold square-bottomed paper bags, was not applied for until 1870. She seems to have taken out about a dozen patents, mostly connected with industrial machinery, though little money was made from any of them.

American females were certainly using their initiative at about this period and their first woman stockbroker, **Victoria Woodhull** (*née* Claflin) (1838–1927) could well have been the first in the world. With her equally

The *Claflin* sisters

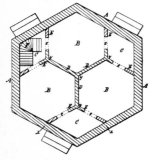

Harriet Irwin's hexagonal house

attractive sister, **Tennessee Cook** (1845–1923) she posed as a clairvoyant and caught the fancy of the 'King' of Wall Street, Cornelius Vanderbilt. Backed by him they operated unofficially from a carriage during the Panic of 1869 and made $700000, using the proceeds to open officially in an opulent office bought cheaply from a failed rival. In 1870 Victoria announced she would stand as President of the USA (the first woman to try) and began a campaign which proposed almost any subject from free-love to spiritualism, abortion, legalised prostitution, divorce, women's suffrage, and exposure of fraud in Wall Street. Unfortunately for her, however, she defamed a distinguished preacher, Henry Beecher, for having an affair with a parishioner, and not only was indicted but also lost her business and candidacy in the ensuing scandal. In 1877 the sisters arrived in England where Tennessee Claflin married a merchant baronet and Victoria married a banker. Victoria also began publishing a monthly paper dealing with palmistry, astrology, and the explanation of high finance, founded the International Agriculture Club, joined the Ladies' Automobile Club and organised the Women's Aerial League.

Bricks and mortar as well as financial construction claimed women's increased participation. The first woman to design and patent an architectural innovation in the USA was **Harriet Irwin** (American) who created (and had built) a hexagonal house in 1869 which still remains standing. She was the pioneer among modern female architects even though she had no formal training, and plump little **Louise Bethune** (American, 1856–1913) became, in 1888, the first woman to be admitted to the US Institute of Architects. As a real professional she had set up jointly with her future husband in a practice in 1881 and designed some 18 schools, also factories, flats and banks. Women's part in architecture has been continuous but slow ever since: even now this is a profession in which they are heavily outnumbered by men. The first woman to become an Associate of the Royal Institute of British Architects, **Ethel Charles** (British, 1871–1962), did not qualify until 1898, though today among comparatively few British women in the profession or allied professions is the eminent British landscape architect **Sylvia Crowe**, President of the Institute of Landscape Architects. Since 1945 she has practised on her own as a consultant to New Town developments (Harlow and Basildon) besides planning restoration work after floods, arranging the layout of a nuclear power station and US Air Force bases in Britain. Also, as an expert on re-afforestation, she is Consultant to the Forestry Commission, and was a founder in 1948 of the International Federation of Landscape Artists. Now a spattering of women architects can be found in most countries; for example, an inhabitant of Liberia, **Betty Carter** (American) builds low-cost housing duplexes and cottages. In addition she has founded a fishing company and that country's first garbage-disposal company – City Better Cleaners Co.

AGRICULTURISTS

Crucial improvements to agriculture are made as much by scientists as by tillers of the soil and many women who have contributed in the laboratory.

Cora Hind (Canadian, b 1861), who began wheat inspections in 1898 and, who from 1901 as a writer in the *Winnipeg Free Press*, exploited her knowledge and judgment of crops to such effect that for the next

25 years her estimates helped to determine in advance the price paid for Canadian wheat.

Agnes Arber (British, 1879–1960), with a DSc from London University in 1905 for research on fertilisation, also did research on monocotyledons, wrote papers and published *Herbals, their Origins and Evolution* in 1912. She was called '. . . the most distinguished as well as the most erudite British plant morphologist'.

Vera Higgins (British, 1892–1968), a scientific officer at the National Physical Laboratory who worked on temperature measurement and later on radiology. She translated and edited many books on plants and at one time (until 1945) was Editor of the Royal Horticultural Society's publications besides being a pioneer woman writer for gardening books. **Frances Perry** (British) has for 26 years written articles, broadcast on television and radio and is the author of 15 books on gardening. She is the first woman member of the Council of the Royal Horticultural Society and in 1973 was awarded America's premier gardening award from the Garden Club of America for her book *Flowers of the World*. A leading ranch-owner and manager in Argentina, **Carmen de Perkins**, was also a Delegate of the UN Status of Women Conference and President of the Argentina Federation of Business and Professional Women from 1962 to 1966. She is one of the comparatively rare cases of a woman farming on a large scale and holding her own. In the horticultural branch of agriculture perhaps the most successful businesswoman has been **Tillie Lewis** (American) who, in the 1920s, did research into the growth of tomatoes and concluded that the variety most favoured for purées, canning and sauces, the pear-shaped pomodoro type, could be grown in the San Joaquin Valley. Knowing that practically all America's tomato sauces and pastes were imported from Italy, she obtained financial backing and pomodoro seedlings from an Italian canning firm but later bought them out, continuing the firm herself under the name 'Tillie Lewis Foods'. She converted the initial capital of $10 000 into such a successful business that when the firm was bought out in 1966 she realised almost $9 000 000.

Some of the most important research into horticulture in underdeveloped lands has been performed by women. For example – **Mariya Gocholashvili** (Russian) became head of her country's Laboratory of Plant Physiology in the All-Union Research Institute of Sub-Tropical Crops in 1929 and between 1935 and 1946 worked in Batumi on the winter-hardiness of sub-tropical crops. She has since carried out biological studies of tea plants. **Yelizveta Ushakova** (Russian), a rural economist as well as a specialist in vegetable cultivation, became Director of the Gribovo Vegetable Selection Station in 1948 and has written many papers on advanced vegetable production. **Elizabeth Bokyo** (Austrian), a Viennese Jewess who arrived in Israel in 1935, grew vegetables during the Arab siege of Jerusalem in 1948 and since then has explored the Negev and founded an experimental desert garden at Eilat. After becoming a senior research officer she was appointed a member of the Research Council of the Prime Minister's Office. And **Wendy Campbell-Purdie** (New Zealander) has experimented with tree-planting in desert regions and, over a period of 13 years, successfully established eucalyptus, acacia, cypress and pine trees along with grain and root crops in what was once Algerian Saharan desert. Her 260 acres with 170000 trees is the pilot scheme for something much bigger and the Algerians are now developing a green belt on their own. Even if the reclamation of just 260 acres of Sahara desert appears a negligible amount to the whole, it at least showed the people of Bou Saada what could be done in under a decade with land they had considered uncultivatable.

A woman who put the fruits of the earth to good use was **Nicole-Barbe Clicquot** (French, 1777–1866) who first took an interest in vineyards and champagne when she married the heir to a vineyard in 1799. The following year her husband took over the business and her interest grew, but by 1805 the war with Britain, with its naval blockade, had brought about a sharp decline in business. Her husband died, leaving her with a young daughter and an ailing business. Veuve (widow) Clicquot carried on under her own new title and experimented with easier methods to remove sediment from bottles of champagne. Her method of storing them up-ended (or *sur pointe* – her expression and method which are now widely used) brought a clearer champagne than any of her competitors could produce; once Napoleon was deposed in 1814 and foreign trade resumed, her business soared ahead of other champagne-producers.

Nicole-Barbe Clicquot

Esher Ocloo (Ghanian), started her own fruit drink and bottling industry in 1943, came to England to study methods of preserving fruit and jam-making and has continued expanding her industry to canning of soup. She was the founder of many women's associations, and is involved in introducing cottage industry work – tie-dying, hand-weaving, hand-made pottery, and garment-making – to encourage village women to raise their standard of living.

FINANCIERS

It is difficult to say when women first started to take a direct interest in banking. It is certain that throughout history there have been women with capital who have acted as money-lenders, laying down legally sound terms for interest and capital repayment. However, in modern banking the Woodhull sisters, mentioned above, seem to have been well to the fore since they included a banking firm in their many early activities on Wall Street. Perhaps the bank run by women for women in Britain, Farrow's Bank Ltd, founded in 1911, was the first of its kind in the world. Unhappily it failed with disastrous results for depositors. Since then women have gradually infiltrated banking, starting as clerks and easing their way towards the highest posts. In the USA **Catherine Cleary** (American) became President of the First Wisconsin Trust Company which has assets in excess of $1·25 billion. She trained as a lawyer and rose through the administrative side of the business to become Chief Executive in 1970. But she has also reached the Boards of General Motors, Kraftco, Northwestern Mutual Life Insurance Co. and American Telephone and Telegraph. The first woman to be appointed a Director of the Belgian National Bank was **Elizabeth Malaise** (Belgian) in 1968. She did so as pressure was rising for more posts to be given to women throughout the financial world. And the first woman Director of the world's largest bank, the Bank of America, was **Claire Hoffman** (American) – who may have had something of a start since her father was its founder. Indonesia opened its first women's bank in 1933 as a way of encouraging saving, better home management and small business enterprises by women. They have expanded well and usually are run from homes on a voluntary basis.

In France a successful investment trust was started in 1970 by **Micheline Courty** (French) and **Monique Kaplan** (French). In 1972 and 1973 their 'Intercroissance' achieved the top performance of all French investment funds and had risen 50 per cent in value. They managed over £10 000 000 which represented, in 1973, a fivefold increase in growth since 1970. Both have degrees in economics, were the first women to be admitted to the French Association of Financial Analysts and met while working for the Banque de Rothschild. They ascribe their success to hard work and sound investing determined by their own joint conclusions – and are aided, just a little, by the exploitation of feminine charm to obtain better information than their rivals. Israel, too, has its top female financial executive. **Margot Hamberger** (German) and her husband jointly own and manage the largest insurance company in the country – the Hamishmar Insurance Services – which has world-wide contacts and deals in marine insurance.

Gradually, with a stiff rearguard action, stock exchanges are opening their doors to women. Antwerp's first woman broker, **Hélène**

Oboussier (Belgian), was admitted in 1922, but it took exactly half a century before Lloyd's in London admitted their first female member and broker **Liliana Archibald** (British) who is, in addition, not only a university lecturer specialising in 18th-century Russian history but also head of the Export Credit Insurance Division at the European Commission – so being in a strata of its executive grades where women are almost as rare as orchids on Everest. Following Lloyd's lead, the London Stock Exchange admitted in 1973 their first female stockbrokers, **Anthea Gaukroger**, **Audrey Geddes**, **Susan Shaw** and **Muriel Wood** (all British) all of whom had, in fact, been working for firms for some years and handling large transactions. The same year, 1973, heralded Switzerland's first woman stockbroker, **Ingrid Elgenmann**.

SHIPPING

Possibly the only woman in the world to run a big shipping company is **Sumati Morarjee** (Indian). As the daughter-in-law of Narottam Morarjee, who owned the Indian Scindia Steam Navigation Co., she and her husband became partners in running the firm when Narottam died in 1929. She learnt all there was to know about the business and not only expanded the firm until it now owns more than 50 ships, but personally negotiated exemption for Indian shipping from the wealth tax on companies in 1957. She works a full day in the office and has been indefatigable in informing the Indian public of their maritime interests.

In the same line of business, but on a smaller scale, the London Thameside has been enlivened by the personality of **Dorothea Fisher** (British, 1894–1974) with her cropped hair, monocle and Savile Row suits. An ex-pupil of Cheltenham Ladies' College, she must have caused a considerable gasp of horror among society when she married Billy Fisher, a lighterman. Together they bought a barge for £20 and gradually built up a fleet of 200, all named after fishes. As the administrative head of their business she directed operations, kept the records and paid the lightermen's weekly wages. After her retirement this woman, who was awarded the OBE for her charity work, continued to preside at the annual contest between sailing-boats from London Bridge to Chelsea Pier – a race which is claimed to be the oldest continuously held sporting event in the world.

MANUFACTURING

As shown earlier in this section, women have not limited their manufacturing skill to producing purely feminine commodities. For example **Melainie Schwarz** (German), was the first, and maybe only, woman to construct a rigid airship. When her husband David Schwarz, who designed the first rigid airship, died in 1897 she determined to carry on and in collaboration with Carl Berg and others had the craft ready that year. Unfortunately, a combination of inclement weather, bad design and panic on the part of the male pilot brought about the destruction of the airship on its first flight.

However, a woman's knowledge of women's needs can give a female a head start in specialised business ventures and some of the wealthiest and most successful businesswomen in the world made their fortunes out of cosmetics and other beauty aids (see section on Fashion). An immense business and a personal estate of over $1 000 000 was amassed by the negro women **Sarah Walker** (American, 1867–1919) – (known

English factory girls
during the First World War

as 'Madame C J Walker') – for her invention and marketing of a system for straightening and adding shine to frizzy hair and, therefore, specially suited to the needs of negro women. This treatment consisted of a shampoo, 'hair-grower' pomade plus vigorous brushing and a heated comb to be drawn through the hair with reverse effects to the then popular heated curling-tongs. Sarah Walker started this venture in 1905, when a young widow with a daughter and whose only means of support was taking in washing. Mixing her soaps and ointments in her wash-tubs she sold 'The Walker System' door to door, advancing to employ agents and own a factory so that her employees eventually numbered some 3000 – mostly women. The products were increased in variety, distinctively packaged and well advertised. 'Walker Agents' wearing white shirt blouses tucked into long, black skirts and carrying black satchels containing the preparations and apparatus, became familiar throughout the US. By 1920 the idea spread to Europe.

By the contractual binding of her agents to a hygienic régime she anticipated later state cosmetology laws. Her money was not only used for extensive philanthropic work during and after her lifetime but also, in the 1920s, supported a salon where coloured and white intellectuals and masters of the arts met, so helping to stimulate the 'Harlem Renaissance'.

Helena Rubinstein (Polish, 1872–1965) made her fortune from cosmetics, and was a pioneer of the present mass-production and wide marketing of such products. As an emigrant in Australia she started her business by preparing and selling beauty preparations. Her Crème Valaze, made from a herbal recipe obtained from a Hungarian friend of her family's, had a soothing, whitening effect on sun-dried Australian

Helena Rubinstein

skins and was mostly the reason for her initial success. By the turn of the century she had opened her first salon in Melbourne and a few years later a salon in Mayfair, London, 'to attract the carriage trade' and from then on her empire spread throughout the world. The business was run on family lines with each new salon put in the charge of a relative. She pioneered coloured face powder and foundation, also the use of silk in cosmetics. When this self-confessed matriarch died she left $100 000 000.

Control of the business is still being kept within the family, for the present President is a nephew, and the Executive Vice President Polish-born **Mala Kolin** – now taking the name Mala Rubinstein – a niece, is in charge of sales promotion activities spread over more than 100 countries at a salary, in 1973, of $104 000 per annum, including expenses.

Another woman to make a fortune from cosmetics was **Florence Graham** (Canadian, 1884–1966), a very poor girl who trained as a nurse and then turned to the manufacture and selling of beauty preparations through her first **Elizabeth Arden** salon in New York in 1912. Apart from the urge to make money, which was pre-eminent in her order of priorities, she was dedicated to promoting feminine health by eliminating unhygienic and dangerous practices in beauty preparation and teaching women how to improve and tone their bodies. A martinet with both her staff and herself (the managers of her pink-hued salons had to obtain permission to marry) she was finally responsible for devising 450 different beauty preparations in 1500 different shades and for establishing a world-wide selling organisation.

Other types of industries have women at the top and although the motor-car industry can claim only one such woman, **Dorothée Pullinger** (British), who ran Galloway Motors Ltd, of Tongland, Kirkudbright-shire in 1921–2, the aircraft industry can boast **Olive Beech** (American) who was reputed to be the highest-paid woman industrial chief in the USA in 1973. She began work as a secretary to the aircraft-designer Walter Beech in 1924, founded the Beech Aircraft Corporation with him in 1932 and for most of its existence has run the company finances. It was her negotiations in 1940 which raised the enormous funds needed for expansion to meet wartime orders, and her leadership as Chairman which has kept the company flying high since her husband's death in 1950. At 69 she was receiving a salary of $123 694 – and ruling the company with as much determination as ever.

Ruth Handler (American) with her husband founded in 1945 the Mattel Toy Company. In 1955 it was mainly her decision to advertise on television direct to children and in 1959 she conceived the idea of the Barbie teenage doll – erupting the firm into the world's largest toy company by 1970. In addition to being Mattel's President she became the first woman on the Business and Industry Council, White House conference.

Top women in British industry are:

June Warrington, the owner and Chairman of the Hanmade Conveyor Company, making mining equipment, which she took over in 1962 after her husband died. It is part of her achievement that her firm has an unusually low turnover of employees and a matter for congratulation that, in 1973, she became the first woman to win the 'Women in Industry' Award given by the Institute of Works Managers.

Marion McQuillan who is rated one of the leading experts in special metals became, in 1973, managing director of Enots, a subsidiary of Imperial Metal Industries which produces the largest slice of Europe's titanium, hafnium, tantalum and niobium. Previously she had been involved with aeronautical research and atomic energy research. At IMI she was made Technical Director in 1967 at the same time as she was awarded the Rosenhain Medal of the Institute of Metals.

Stella Brumell, Managing Director of Benfords Ltd, Britain's largest manufacturer of concrete-mixing machinery has done particularly well with the number of export contracts she has secured.

The profit motive drives and so does the spur of ambition even when, as in the Soviet Union, profit is said not to be the motive. There, women provide 33 per cent of managers and experts in industry and have risen to top posts. For example:

Alla Yevdokimova (Russian), in 1970 became head of a municipal services department after being chief engineer in a chemical works. She had under her 7000 workers who included hairdressers, cloth-cutters, shoemakers, nurses and polishers.

Tatiana Nikiforova (Russian) has managed a clothing factory from the age of 35 and said that, except on Women's Day, she forgets she is a woman and remembers only she is a manager. Tough and yet compassionate, she knows her job from beginning to end. Of her methods her Chief Engineer, a man, said: 'There is something maternal in her attitude . . . and for this reason it's easier for her to deal with all sorts of personal problems in addition to questions of management.'

A successful businesswoman in Pakistan is **Razia Ghulamali** who, despite the inhibitions imposed by the Muslim faith, owns and runs a Karachi cement factory, while the Middle East's leading construction company, CAT, is run by **Myrna Boustany** (Lebanese) who inherited it from her father. She has been in active business for 11 years. However, the Middle East's biggest domestic textile centre, Domtex, is solely the brain-child of **Charlotte Esseily** (Lebanese) who still directs, having started the firm ten years ago. In the less well-developed countries women have had to struggle even harder than in the West to make their presence felt in industry: those who have done well are quite rare. In Indonesia, however, several women have become directors of small firms and in Ghana women have a strong financial influence upon all sorts of operations as well as upon politics.

PUBLISHING

The most famous newspaper proprietor of today is **Katharine Graham** (American) of the Washington Post Company which controls not only *The Washington Post* and *Newsweek* but also extensive magazine, radio and television outlets. Educated at Vassar College and the University of Chicago she was sensibly encouraged by her parents to work at a career, despite the fact that her father was a millionaire.

After about a year as a reporter on the *San Francisco News* she joined

Katharine Graham

The Washington Post in 1939 – a paper her father had bought in 1933. In the 1940s her lawyer husband also joined the paper, and in 1948 Katharine Graham's father sold the couple all his voting stock. This arrangement lasted until 1963 when her husband committed suicide and she was left with the responsibility of raising their four children. She also became President of the company, quoting from her father '. . . In the pursuit of the truth, the newspaper shall be prepared to make sacrifices of its material fortunes.'

She runs the company in conjunction with the Chairman, Frederick Beebe, and all divisions report to her. She does not dictate editorial policy but chooses the best professional journalists and backs them up. Before the Watergate affair flared up it was her paper which fearlessly nagged away about suspect deals and the facts behind them until official investigation became a necessity. For obvious reasons continual checking and rechecking for accuracy was necessary before this anonymous information was reported in her papers and she claims that there was only one minor error in all the 200 articles written in *The Washington Post* about Watergate. Heavy legal fees involved in the papers fight with the Government over its rights to publish the Pentagon Papers illustrated the upholding of her ideal. Early pressures, with accusations of over-playing the story, which the papers had to bear, gradually decreased as later events showed the event to be of a magnitude to topple the President. If any one woman has helped to change the history of the USA it is Katharine Graham.

SERVICES

The most important invention so far as women's entrée to commercial life was concerned was that of the typewriter in 1868. The highest net recorded speed attained in one minute on a manual machine (with a ten-word penalty per error) was 170 in 1918 by **Margaret Owen** (American) and the highest net speed on an electric machine over a period of one hour was achieved by **Margaret Hamma** (American) in 1941 at 149 words per minute. Several women have exceeded 250 words per minute at shorthand but the world's record is held by a man.

Passing from the outer office to the executive suite, the highest paid woman in the USA is thought to be **Mary Wells** (American). As a dynamic member of a highly creative group in the advertising agency of Doyle, Dave, Bernbach, she achieved quite startling results and in due course set up her own agency, Wells, Rich, Greene. In five years it boomed, one of her most startling innovations was that of painting Braniff's aircraft many different colours and she then went on to captivate the airline's owner, Mr Lawrence, and take him to the altar. Her annual salary in 1973 was said to be $385 000.

And in South West Africa a successful business service has been run by **Johanna Schoeman** who is Director of Schoeman's Office Equipment Service and Fastkopi Ltd, besides being the founder and President of South West Africa's Federation of Business and Professional Women as well as Vice-President of the Council of Women.

Britain's most successful businesswoman is probably **Margery Hurst** (British). Born the second of four daughters to loving, kindly parents she was a domineering, strong-willed and not a particularly likeable

Margery Hurst

child who decided at an early age that, since chances of real success come rarely, they have to be grasped without hesitation and used to the full. After two mediocre years at the Royal Academy of Dramatic Art she worked first as a typist and then ran the clerical side of her father's building business, which employed about 50 people, rising to Office Manager. The war came and Margery Hurst married an Army major after a whirlwind romance. When he was posted overseas, she, at 27, joined the Women's Auxiliary Territorial Services as a Welfare Officer. It was in the army's officer training unit and later, as an officer, that she learned invaluable lessons in personnel management. After about two years in the services she had a nervous breakdown, probably from becoming too emotionally involved with her welfare cases, and left for civilian life and her newly returned husband. At the age of 31, with a three-week-old baby daughter, Margery Hurst was deserted by her husband who left her penniless and crushed. Starting by taking in typing at home she realised she had to think on a bigger scale to support herself and her child – but all she could do was type. With a £50 overdraft, guaranteed by her father, she opened, in Brook Street, London, an office to do typing, duplicating, etc. – with herself as the only member of the staff. The obvious result of strain on her made her reassess the possibilities of the success of the business, and she decided to offer firms top-grade temporary secretaries. She sold the idea to the first firm by working there for half a day free – as a sample; they were impressed and embarrassingly requested six temporary secretaries immediately. But friends rallied round, the request was met and Brook Street Bureau born. There followed a licence to supply permanent staff and by the end of the first year, with an average of six to seven placements a week, low overheads and taking a minimal salary from the profits, the business was established.

With Brook Street Bureau leading the way in original advertising, and rigidly testing and interviewing prospective temporary employees for efficiency and suitability, it soared ahead. In 1965, with valuation at over £1 000 000 and liquid assets of well over a quarter of that, Brook Street Bureau, the largest multiple secretarial bureau in the world, went public. By 1973 it had 210 branches throughout the world of which 35 were in Australia, 7 in the USA and 1 in Asia with the first Common Market branch about to be opened. Now Margery Hurst, with her colossal energy and self-confessed streak of intolerance, is a millionairess and the founder of a college for administrative and secretarial studies. She is also a wonderful example of courage to widows or deserted wives.

From business activities to leisure and relaxation, women are slowly rising in the ranks. The first woman tourist guide in Europe was **Enid Lockhart** (British) who, already having a fair knowledge of French history, drifted into conducting tourists in 1923 when her husband, the Paris Manager of Frame's Tours, was short of a guide. When he left her and their four-year-old son she made guiding her career and in due course married one of her clients. She is now an expert on French history and probably the only British person to hold the exclusive badge of French guides – which, because she was a woman, was awarded to her somewhat begrudgingly after a fierce struggle and success in an exhaustive examination designed to ensure her failure.

Lebanon's luxurious St George's Hotel is owned and managed by **Nadia El Khourey** who is also Vice-President of a bank, Director of a contracting firm, a member of the Middle East Airlines Board, Chairman of the Hotel Society in the Middle East – and the mother of five children. The number of children a businessman has sired has no bearing on his business achievement, but a universal and main difficulty a business or professional mother has to overcome is the emotional fulfilment of being a good mother and organising the day-to-day running of a home after a long, exhausting business day.

The first woman chef at the Waldorf Astoria Hotel, New York, was **Leslie Arp** (American) who took over in 1973. She remains something of a rarity still since women rarely rise to the zenith in the catering profession. Skill in the preparation of food is one thing – over-indulgence in consuming it another, and the most successful attack by a woman on excess weight has been made by **Jean Nidetch** (American) the founder of Weight Watchers in the USA. In the ten years which have elapsed since her thirty-eighth birthday, she has reduced from 214 lb (97 kg) to 142 lb (64 kg) and established an organisation which has put over 4 000 000 people through its routine – known as 'the programme'. Scientific dieting is the key to the programme but, in selling it, Weight Watchers has produced a magazine, distributes frozen diet dinners and soft drinks to supermarkets, runs special summer camps for overweight teenagers and is on the threshold of starting restaurants. All this adds up to a world-wide company worth £17 000 000 of which Jean Nidetch's share is £2648 333. The Weight Watchers record for reduction is held by **Florence Jaffee** (American) who removed 335 lb (152 kg) in two and a half years, although the world's record for this sort of feat by a woman belongs to a circus lady, **Celesta Geyer**, who lost 401 lb (182 kg) in 14 months during 1950/1.

SALES

For generations women have served in shops and as saleswomen, slowly working their way from the counter into more important work as buyers, floor managers and directors. As in every other business activity they remain in a minority at the higher levels.

A woman with diverse interests, and the proprietor of Lindy's Stores in Nairobi, is **Grace Ogot** (Kenyan) who was educated as a nurse and midwife, became a scriptwriter, author and broadcaster for the BBC and then a public relations officer for Air India in East Africa. Lindy's followed and with it involvement in local government and women's interests. One of her books is *Family Planning and the African Woman*. One of the biggest British supermarket chain stores, Tesco, has a woman as its Managing Director of Wholesale with executive control of buying. She is **Daisy Hart** who joined the firm when aged 18 as an assistant book-keeper clerk at a wage of £2 per week.

CONSUMER AFFAIRS

The profit motive and the problems frequently related, of quality control, have led in recent years to the growth of consumer protection groups. The first effective non-profit-making consumer protection group in Britain was formed in 1957 and called the 'Consumers' Association', its Research Director, **Eirlys Roberts** (British), also becoming the Editor of its magazine *Which?*. The expansion of CA functions, as measured by *Which*'s soaring circulation (over 650 000 in 1974) in response to private subscription (not one bit of revenue coming from advertisements), was a testimony to CA's methods. Sixty local consumer groups have been formed: above all effective pressure was brought to bear to strengthen legislation in many commercial fields, with Eirlys Roberts regularly giving evidence and goading the authorities besides disciplining wayward manufacturers.

One of the USA's leading women in consumer matters has been **Bess Myerson–Grant** (American), Commissioner of the New York City Consumer Affairs. Maybe she has too many other interests to devote enough time needed to attract sufficient nation–wide attention to the subject, for she is also connected with several foundations dealing with disabled children and is active in Zionist promotion. She has been awarded the title 'Woman of Achievement' by the Anti-Defamation League.

The highest peaks of achievement in commerce have been scaled by only a very few women. Out of 6500 officers and directors earning more than $30 000 each in the USA in 1973 only 11 were women. Tillie Lewis in the USA thinks women are not generally inspired. Margery Hurst makes it clear that higher executives, like herself, have to work long hours to succeed and in doing so put their home life at risk. It is a fact that many materially successful men and women find they have sacrificed their marriages for their careers.

14

IN LITERATURE, JOURNALISM AND PUBLISHING

Women's involvement to the world of letters has been immense and represents, perhaps, the most persuasive contribution to their attempt to achieve parity with men. Sheer output of creative, emotional works of deep perception are only part of this contribution, however, since writing itself is an act of psychological independence that takes on hard, practical reality if it can be made to pay – and one of women's most hampering problems through the ages has been lack of financial freedom. Among the most emancipated women are to be found the writers, and few among the emancipators were not highly literate.

Of course literature was non-existent until writing materials became generally available and even then only an élite among the educated participated and evolved distinctive styles. Women, whose participation in educational processes was so severely circumscribed, were indeed to be admitted to the facilities enjoyed by the élite. Early among these was **Psappho of Lesbos** (Greek, 610?–580? BC) who was well to do, with plenty of spare time. Her poetry, which is greatly admired, was frank and mainly dealt with personalities, particularly women, for whom she entertained deep, probably homosexual, feelings. Not only did she communicate in a simple, concise style and originate a special four-line stanza, known as 'Sapphics', but her works were preserved because they were written on papyrus – a rare departure at a time when story-telling was generally handed down by word of mouth.

Despite a Greek antithesis to the mention of women (Pericles thought that the best should never be mentioned) **Anyte of Tegea** (Greek, 3rd century BC) achieved great fame as a poetess. Unlike Psappho she ignored personalities and described nature, writing dedications for fountains or

Greek female reading
from a box of rolls

epitaphs for animals. The latter were probably literary expressions of her appreciation of nature and the landscape around her. Even three centuries later the statesman Antipater referred to her as 'a woman Homer'. But literary women's struggle for survival was hard, and though the best known of Arab poetesses, **Al-Khansa** (*c* AD 645), was famed for her elegies, these were the last free utterances of Arab women's art before their tribe embraced Islam and demanded that they should be relegated to more mundane pursuits. Yet women everywhere continued in their attempts at expression – Al-Khansa's daughter, **Amra**, was one – and in the Orient the oldest full-length novel in the world, and still considered of literary merit, was written by a woman who is identified by the name of her heroine, **Murasaki Shikibu** (Japanese 978?–1026?). It is called *The Tale of Genji* and concerns the several loves of Prince Genji, a study of the psychology of a narrow society seen through the eyes of the dominant Fujiwara family. She was privileged at a time of peace, elegance and slow tempo and made her book a conversation-piece about people living in thin-walled houses where nearly everything could be overheard and much else seen. Its crucial importance, and that of her diary, lies in the knowledge that she was merely one of a great many Japanese women writers in that period. In fact men rarely ventured into literature and at least one male diarist preferred to disguise his sex. Murasaki Shikibu and her contemporaries on the other hand made constructive use of their opportunity, for it was largely they who weaned their nation away from an obsession with things Chinese, and developed the Japanese phonetic script. Thus they helped impose independence both on their nation and their sex. If Buddhism later reduced women's status, while polygamy undermined their security, it seems that being an author remained a way to freedom at a time when Japanese women were allowed by law to inherit.

Although there was a spell of femininity in Chinese literature after the 10th century (for example a verse form known as 'Tz'u' was principally employed by women folk-singers and reached its peak of development in the hands of **Li Ch'ing-Chao** at the beginning of the 12th century)

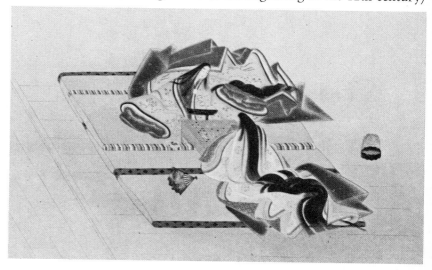

Japanese court ladies of the time of *Murasaki Shikibu*

this was only transition. Nevertheless, the literary women of the Far East were better off than their European sisters, the latter finding expression mainly through restrictive religious orders. **Hrosvitha** (German, *c* 935–1000) besides writing religious works for the edification of the other nuns at Gandersheim, composed poetry and six prose comedies from which, it is said, miracle plays derived.

One of the earliest known examples of a woman who made her living by writing was **Christine de Pisan** (Italian, *c* 1364–1430), domiciled in France and thrown on to her own resources with three children when she was widowed at the age of 25. She began composing ballades mourning her husband, and diversified her output (which rose to the equivalent dimension, in manuscript copies, of 'best-sellers') as success brought the nobility and then royalty as patrons. Besides her verses on themes of courtly love she wrote, in 1401, the more positive *Dit de la Rose* which was probably the first feminist book. In 1405 she turned to biography with *Cité des Dames*, a collection of stories about celebrated women of the past, and a year later an autobiography, *Avision Christine*, in defence of herself. She advocated the emancipation of women through better education and clubs. But she was too far ahead of her time and France was preoccupied with the Hundred Years War (to be defeated in 1415 at Agincourt). It must have meant much to Christine de Pisan that her last work would eulogise a modern heroine – Joan of Arc, the saviour of France (see section on War).

Christine de Pisan

Soon, in 1445, the advent of the first printing-press would begin slowly to make mass-production of books possible. There is no evidence that women helped with Gutenberg's invention or that they played any part in early publishing, though there were convents where the nuns worked as compositors sometime after 1476.

Yet, although Germany provided the technology and Italy so much of the inspiration behind the Renaissance, it was in France that literary women abounded in the years to come. Within the salon of **Catherine de Vivonne** (see section on Salonnières) was to be found **Madeleine de Scudéry** (French, 1607–1701) who prospered as the author of prodigiously long and, sometimes, historically unreliable novels such as *Ibrahim* (in four volumes 1641), *Artamène* and *Clélie* each of ten volumes between 1649 and 1660. Published with the aid and in the name of her brother Georges (and translated, too, into English) her books followed the custom of the day in their verbosity besides providing a record of the Golden Age of the Sun King by basing the characters upon close contemporaries. On the other hand **Marie La Fayette** (French, 1634–93) while having her heroines re-enact her own experience, broke from tradition by writing far shorter novels – in effect producing a 'modernised' psychological novel, of which the masterpiece is probably *La Princesse de Clèves*.

Rising from poverty and imprisonment for debt, **Aphra Behn** (English, 1640?–89) is said to have been the first woman in Britain to earn her living by writing. Of her 15 plays, mostly comedies, *The Rover* was the most popular. But she was versatile and, besides beautiful poetry, wrote novels which included the philosophical *Oroonoko, or the History of the Royal Slave*, it being the first time that sympathy for slaves was expressed in English literature. Her knowledge of the subject had not been all hearsay for she had spent her early life in Surinam. The first American poetess, an immigrant to Massachusetts, came to public notice rather to her own surprise, however. **Anne Bradstreet**'s (English, 1612–72) poems, written for her own amusement, were published in London in 1650 (without her knowledge) by her brother-in-law under the title *The Tenth Muse, Lately sprung up in America*, though later she published a revised edition of her own in America. Of course it would be several years before an original American style established itself, but the many women who kept diaries recorded experiences which were both memorable and important in a fast-developing country.

The dawn of the 18th century coincided with great advances in the art of propaganda. Newsheets began to appear and with them the first British woman journalist, **Mary Manley** (English, 1663–1724), who published political tracts aimed at the Whigs and, in particular, the Duchess of Marlborough. She was arrested for libel because of her *Secret Memoirs . . . of Several Persons of Quality* published in 1709 but gained a discharge. In 1711 she became Editor of the *Examiner* after Jonathan Swift had completed that phase of his campaign against the Whig Government.

Travel promoted some of the best feminine literature in the early 18th century, notably from **Celia Fiennes** (British, 1662–1741), a spinster who journeyed the length and breadth of the land from one health resort to another writing in her journal of what she saw and ate in her forays down by-ways, noting the everyday way of life with an observant, inquiring eye. From mines to local workshops, ancient archaeological sites to enclosures and manors, she assembled a comprehensive picture of England on the move towards industrialisation in a journal that presaged Cobbett in the 19th century and Ronay in the 20th. Her journeys, moreover, were made extremely dangerous by the prevalence of high-waymen and the dankest of rural squalor. Less thorough in her observations, though more intellectual, **Mary Montagu** (British, 1689–1762) went with her Ambassador husband to Turkey, recording the things which interested her. Above all, as a disfigured survivor of smallpox, she recommended and popularised smallpox inoculation in England having seen it work in Turkey. She practised her belief that education was the key to feminine emancipation and dabbled in politics. As the author of novels, poetry and a play (first performed in 1967!), flexibility of approach and a remarkable contemporary open-mindedness were her keynotes in the composition of 1000 and more celebrated letters. Yet it was through her position in society she got a hearing – which is more than can be said of the brilliant **Juana de la Cruz** (Mexican, 1651?–95) who exhibited literary skill at the age of eight and by nine had obtained a complete grasp of Latin after only 20 lessons. Not for her, however, a privileged place in the University of Mexico. Instead, after a brief, vivacious spell at court, she was sent to a convent in 1669 where she created a library of over 4000 volumes, studied science and wrote poetry and plays. When, in 1689, some of her written works were published in Spain there was a reaction from the Church with the result that the woman who was to be called Mexico's 'Tenth Muse' was instructed to study only religious subjects. Against two years' pressure she resisted strongly, but at last was forced to give way. Shut off from the world she eventually died while combating disease in her own convent.

It was in the 18th century that women accelerated their break away from restrictions in the literary world. Some, like **Elizabeth Carter** (British, 1717–1806), did it by sheer hard work that damaged their health. She studied ten languages besides astronomy, history and music and at 17 published her first poems. This diligence earned the praise of Dr Johnson for whom she wrote two numbers in his *Rambler* periodical series of 208 (only five numbers were not written by Johnson himself and of these four were by women). Similarly, brilliant women were coming to the fore in Germany as well, leading them **Sophie von la Roche** (German, 1731–1807) whose *Geschichte des Fräuleins von Sternheim* in 1771 was the first original novel written by a German woman. Significantly it is the story of a girl's struggle through life, for its author, to whose salon Goethe came in his formative days, was keenly interested in radical politics, social improvement and women's education. In 1782 she founded and edited a women's journal called *Pomona* which struggled to survive in mediocrity for two years. Fortunately Sophie could afford to experiment, unlike **Anna Karsch** (1722–91) who, as the first professional German poetess, scraped a living from her work. For Anna Karsch, as a peasant, had to overcome many discouragements to survive until at last, during the Seven Years War, she won recognition and even was presented to the King. **Theresa Heyne** (German, 1764–1829) was to take a step further when, in 1794, she became co-Editor of the *Allgemeine Zeitung* and from 1817 to 1824 sole Editor of the Stuttgart *Morgenblatt* and at the same time raising a family of ten children. But generally speaking German women's literary works were overshadowed by the men and much credit due to them was purloined. It was in Britain where the greatest strides were made. There **Fanny Burney** (British, 1752–1840) wrote *Evelina* and had it published in 1778. In line with tradition she at first maintained anonymity, but when the book was an immediate success and her identity became known she was lionised by Johnson and the other critics of the day. Writing thereafter under her own name, she encouraged other women writers, though never again would she excite as she had with *Evelina* which was the original simple novel of home life. Of those she inspired was **Maria Edgeworth** (British, 1767–1849), an Anglo-Irish girl, who took up a popular theme of 1795 and wrote a plea for women's education. Far more sincere and effective was her first novel in 1800, *Castle Rackrent*, which sold well and encouraged her in the next 15 years to write many novels about Ireland. In the postscript to Sir Walter Scott's original edition of *Waverley* he said he aimed 'in some distant degree to emulate the admirable Irish portraits drawn by Miss Edgeworth'.

It is an irony that the most celebrated of British women novelists was hardly aware in her lifetime of the high regard in which she was already held. For this **Jane Austen** (British, 1775–1817) was herself partly to blame since as the youngest daughter of a country rector she rarely ventured far from the family circle, never married and left the business side of publishing her books to her father or brothers. And yet this curly brunette whom children adored seems to have made little effort to make a home of her own but, while gracing the family household, concentrated upon becoming a thoroughly professional writer. She once remarked that if she married at all she would fancy being the wife of the author George Crabbe, whose books she admired. The urge to write fiction originated from childhood and with it a determination to perfect what she had written – within the compass of her acknowledged limited experience. As models she took Samuel Richardson's books but her reading was catholic. Of the works that appeared before she was 16 many were later revised, a habit she fastidiously cultivated. Not until 1795, however, did she begin her first major novel, a piece called *Eleanor and Marianne* which later grew into *Sense and Sensibility*, and in 1796 she began *First Impressions* that later appeared as *Pride and Prejudice* – both of which she prepared for publication in 1797. Thus her system was evolutionary in all respects, but not at first her sales. In 1798 she began *Susan* that became *Northanger Abbey* and it was this book which was first accepted for publication in 1803 for a mere £10, the publisher taking no steps to put it into print. Indeed it was nearly ten years before at last she got one of her books upon the market. In this period she seems to have begun nothing else to be completed that was of importance which, from the lack of encouragement except within the family, is hardly surprising. In any case a major war was in progress and two of her brothers were naval officers. But at last in 1811 *Sense and Sensibility* was published – at her own financial risk, it is true – but the event stimulated her and once more she began to compose, this time with the book that was to become *Mansfield Park*.

Jane Austen

At least she did not make a loss. *Sense and Sensibility*, published anonymously (as were all her books during her lifetime even though it was quite well known who the author was) earned £150, but her total earnings from the five books published before her death (that is from *Pride and Prejudice* in 1813, *Mansfield Park* in 1814, *Emma* in 1815 and *Northanger Abbey* in 1816) was only £700. Yet by 1815 she had won a form of renown, and recognition by the Prince Regent, along with permission to dedicate *Emma* to him.

Like her style of composition, Jane Austen's fame developed steadily by degrees. If *Persuasion*, published posthumously in 1818, achieved better sales in the aftermath of its author's recent death, and her first biographer that year condescended to mention her as just on a par with Fanny Burney and Maria Edgeworth, that was as nothing to the deluge of praise that was to carry her posthumous fame to the heights.

Opinions about so famous an authoress are bound to vary. Certainly Jane Austen suffered from the limitations imposed by her background. And yet this is one reason why her books provide an accurate as well as a witty historical account of her class in the period to which she belonged. In the final analysis, her books and the various plays and films that have been made from them, give good entertainment – not a bad sort of aim for any author. The influence she had on the future was purely literary.

It was for others to give the lead which would have an impact upon serious affairs of the world, women such as **Bettina von Arnim** (German, 1785–1859). The dominant theme of her letters was a sense of democracy and a desire to see an advancement in social conditions without destroying the fabric of society. In an epoch of revolution in 1848, she sent an essay to the Prussian King, called *This Book Belongs to the King*, in which she attacked his Ministers, the existing system of government and, for good measure, the Churches, her aim being to avoid revolution by reducing poverty and disease. But the King was displeased and the Revolution, to Bettina von Arnim's dismay, came that year, with methods that were too radical for her.

An increasingly articulate feminine minority began to communicate forcibly with the massed underprivileged. In Sweden there was **Fredrika Bremer** (Swedish, 1801–65), the well-educated daughter of a wealthy man, who adopted the English novel as the basis for hers and argued the case for women's emancipation in the 1850s. In America **Lydia Child** (American, 1802–80) a pioneer for the emancipation of slaves and women, was well known by her popular writing and was nationally celebrated in 1826 as the editor of *Juvenile Miscellany*, the first US children's periodical. But her attack on slavery in 1833, in *An Appeal in Favor of That Class of Americans called Africans*, and the publication of the *National Anti-Slavery Standard* in 1841, which she edited, carried her into the lead among the growing numbers in favour of ending slavery. While she drifted into general journalism, and then to writing anti-slavery pamphlets, **Harriet Stowe** (American, 1811–96), a minister's daughter, endured poverty and tried to eke a living by writing, her first collection of stories, *The Mayflower*, appearing in 1843. In 1850 Congress passed the Compromise Act which temporarily secured slavery but saved the Union. The Stowes, who lived in the North, were appalled and Harriet, a dedicated Calvinist, was prompted to write about the subject (see section on Reformers). The result was *Uncle Tom's Cabin*, first published by instalments in an anti-slavery newspaper in 1851. Eventually it grew into the book which, in its first year, sold 305000 copies – equivalent to over 1500000 at today's population figure – and earned the author $10000 in three months. Aimed purely at slavery, not the political factions, it defined the problem and led to such a counter-blast from the South that the issue could no longer be ignored. Moreover it fascinated the world and was translated into 23 languages (in Germany by 1910 there were 41 translations and 75 different editions) and frequently was dramatised for the stage. Harriet Stowe played no significant part in the Civil War she did so much to start, but went on writing, on average, a book a year about a wealth of subjects, many of them related to improving human dignity among the white as well as the black people.

Far more deeply plunged in revolution and the politics of the day was **Margaret Fuller** (American, 1810–50), a precocious child reared on the classics, which she read analytically and critically. Among the books she wrote was *Woman in the Nineteenth Century* (1845) which influenced contemporary American feminists, but her greatest contribution to literature was her *Short Essay on Critics*. Heavily involved in intellectual circles, she drifted into journalism as Literary Critic of the *New York Tribune* in 1844 and in 1846 was the first US woman to become a Foreign Correspondent. In Italy she secretly married an Italian and became involved in the Revolution of 1848. During the Siege of Rome in 1849, in which her husband fought, she nursed the wounded and wrote a history of the Revolution. Unhappily, with her family and manuscript, she was lost at sea when returning to the USA in 1850.

It was not only political revolution which stirred women writers. For example, **Charlotte Yonge** (British, 1823–1901), a novelist, realised that outbreaks of cholera and typhoid were caused by poor drainage and this led her to tackle the peril. In *The Three Brides* (1876) she made this subject the central issue in a well-informed attack upon medical conservatism and the indifference and ignorance of local councils to waterborne sewage, an assault that had a profound effect upon changing the situation by means of the Public Health Acts in Britain in the 1870s and 1880s.

George Sand

Not all writers were so public spirited, of course. The notorious **George Sand** (Armandine Dudevant) (French, 1804–76), whose books are now scarcely read outside France, was devoted to free and erratic expression. She caused a stir in her own time by her predilection to wear male dress and her succession of love-affairs after her marriage. And even the fascination engendered by the **Brontë** (British) sisters – **Charlotte** (1816–55), **Emily** (1818–48) and **Anne** (1820–49) – may be enhanced by the brevity of their lives. Of the lasting popularity of their writing, Emily Brontë's *Wuthering Heights* is probably the family's supreme contribution, yet it is hard to claim that they advanced literature since their style was mainly the copy of an earlier period. As imaginative intellectuals, the Brontës' stimulated each other. Handicapped by ill-health and shortage of money, they turned to writing under pseudonyms and, although their life was sheltered, some of their material was drawn from personal experience, such as the school 'Lowood' in Charlotte Brontë's *Jane Eyre*.

Foremost among the biographers of Charlotte Brontë was **Elizabeth**

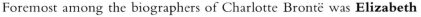

Gaskell (British, 1810–65) whose fame as a novelist was established with her first novel *Mary Barton* in 1848, a controversial book dealing with industrialists' exploitation of people. In between producing six children she was to write short stories and many more searching novels of the highest quality. *Ruth*, in 1853, by its attack on ethics, caused a storm. *Sylvia's Lovers* (1863) is rated her masterpiece, while *Cranford* (1851) was the most popular publication. But the *Life of Charlotte Brontë* which, through first-class organisation and use of material, defined and criticised the Brontë family, has been described as 'one of the few literary biographies that is at once a work of art and a well-documented interpretation of its subject'. Elizabeth Gaskell's wish that no biography be written about her has so far been respected.

In contrast, at the lower end of the literary market, was to be found **Ann Stephens** (American, 1810–86) a novelist, professional journalist and editor who wrote a deluge of adventure tales about Frontiersmen versus Red Indians. In 1860 her *Malaeska* was first of the series of Beadle's Dime Books which were among the first paperbacks. It sold 500000 copies, introduced the author to literary circles (which included the President), and encouraged her to keep up production of serialised, popular novels – a pastime which supported her family over the years.

Of far deeper understanding by her insight into a child's mind was **Johanna Spyri** (Swiss, 1827–1901) who wrote many books, but whose *Heidi* (1880) became famous and sold most in a variety of different languages. Women authors of the 19th century were every bit as respected as their male counterparts and quite as prosperous. For each one of renown there were a hundred or more who struggled on the periphery of success or failed to achieve publication. Financial reward more than ever became dependent on good fortune in producing what a fickle public desired. But, in the final analysis, sheer merit was rarely denied. **George Eliot** (Mary Cross) (British, 1819–80), the daughter of an estate agent, was assured of success from childhood. Her passion for reading, particularly books by Scott, developed when she was eight in parallel with marked musical talents that were held in check by shyness when asked to perform. Throughout her life, in fact, she was to be of a somewhat retiring disposition though by no means an unattractive person. With a strong religious bent and an enthusiasm for languages her first literary efforts were the poetry published in the *Christian Observer* in 1840. Encouraged by a few close, radical friends, who steadily widened her knowledge and broke down an initial bigotry, she took an editorial post with *The Westminster Review* in 1850. Simultaneously she carried out translations from the German of a religious work. Work for the *Review* brought her into contact with prominent people of the literary world and in particular with George Lewes, a critic and editor who was estranged from his wife. In 1854 they began to live together, creating a situation that was entirely in line with her professed objection to marriage's indelibility. When her friends stood back in distaste, Lewes's boundless enthusiasm for her obvious talent, launched her in September 1856 upon her first novel – *Amos Barton*. Its appearance in January 1857, its immediate success and subsequent binding into a volume, at once convinced discerning critics that a new novelist of immense power and stature had arrived. A few were fooled by her adoption of a man's name –

George Eliot

George Eliot – but not Charles Dickens, who lavished high praise upon the book, regardless of its author's sex.

George Eliot now became a dedicated professional. Though she produced books at regular and quite short intervals, there was no decline in quality. Quite the reverse, for the entire range of the original series, *Scenes of Clerical Life*, are distinguished for a steady improvement in style and thoughtful content. Moreover she began to receive considerable sums for copyright – fees that were entirely justified by mounting sales. For example *Adam Bede* (1858) fetched £800 (later doubled), sold 16000 copies in the first year and attracted the flattery of a claim to authorship by a Mr Liggins which merely led to the disclosure of her true sex. Her life was one of great contentment. The partnership with Lewes brought four children and a steady flow of books of improving merit that won her recognition as an author of the front rank whose originality carried the novel a stage beyond the point at which it had been left by Jane Austen. The semi-autobiographical *Mill on the Floss* appeared in 1860, *Silas Marner* in 1861, and an illustrated historical novel, *Romola* (1863), is considered by some as her masterpiece though the same claim is sometimes made for *Middlemarch* (1871) which fetched £7000 for the part-work copyright. (In fact she turned down £10000 for it in book form since she preferred her readers to digest her lengthy books slowly.) After Lewes's death in 1878 she concentrated upon publishing his unfinished works and in 1880 got married to a Mr Cross but died the same year. By general consent she remains enshrined alongside authors of the calibre of Hardy, Tolstoy and Zola.

By comparison with her **Louisa Alcott** (American, 1832–88), with one major work *Little Women* (1868), was a tyro, since she was unable to raise her intellectual standard above that required for children, though she was not without merit in style. And the same can be said of **Frances Burnett** (British, 1849–1924) whose *Little Lord Fauntleroy* (1886), *A Little Princess* (1887) and *The Secret Garden* (1918) delighted children and adults in their day and are still welcomed by television and radio producers in search of a popular Sunday series.

Patriotic motivations often influence writers and women are no exception in this. The poetry and novels of **Rosalia de Castro** (Spanish, 1837–85) were profound writings of her nation, while **Emilia Pardo Bazán** (Spanish, 1851–1921) not only tackled the theoretical aspects of literary reform (with considerable influence upon Spanish literature) but pointed out the weaknesses of certain social aspects of Spanish life, particularly in Galicia: her reward in 1916 was rare – the Chair of Literature in Madrid University. In South Africa **Olive Schreiner** (South African, 1855–1920) became a world-renowned name (as 'Ralph Iron') with *The Story of an African Farm* in 1883. But she also joined strongly into politics, with pro-Boer propaganda against the English colonists and publishing in 1911 her *Woman and Labour* which some took as the bible of the responsible Woman's movement when it neared fulfilment. And the doyen of German female writers, **Ricarda Huch** (German, 1864–1947), one of her country's first women to take a Master's degree at Zürich University, was also a patriot as well as a reformer, though her first novel, *Memoirs of Ludolf Ursleu Junior* (1893), was a record of the conflict in her own love-life. Deeply involved with the Socialist Revolutionaries in Switzerland, she came to write about poverty in Italy, at the same time attacking prostitution and anything else which downgraded her sex. In 1912 she began publication of what amounted, in description of suffering, to a prophetic attack upon war entitled *The Great War in Germany*. The coming of the Nazis she regarded with horror but also with unflinching courage: in 1933 she rejected the title of 'Member of the Prussian Academy of Arts' and spoke openly against the new régime, and in 1941 appealed to the Bishop of Münster to 'arrest the reign of evil'.

Among the mass of literary outpourings of the late 19th and of the 20th century it became increasingly difficult to detect the truly important works and writers. Writers of quite low merit, from both sexes, began to amass fortunes while the better deserving, from a purely meritorious point of view, were dismally living on the breadline. For example, although the Irish-born **Isabella Crawford** (1850–87) has been rated as Canada's first poetess of note, even though her standard was by no means exemplary, she could barely scrape a living from her offerings to newspapers and magazines and the single volume she published in 1884 was produced at her own expense. Meanwhile, in England, **Marie Corelli** (British, 1855–1924) turned out a steady flow of popular, moralising Victoriana and became a rich woman.

Selma Lagerlöf

The introduction of international literary prizes sometimes managed to promote serious writers who might not otherwise had received widespread mention – though many would probably have won recognition without a prize. The first woman to win a Nobel Prize for Literature (1909), **Selma Lagerlöf** (Swedish, 1858–1940), began writing when a teacher and published her first historical heroic novel, *Gösta Berlings Saga* in 1891. Vastly encouraged by its success she developed her art, won a travelling scholarship in 1895 and turned professional. Several new novels financed journeys, the backgrounds of which she used in her forthcoming novels of legend and saga.

Among the most distinguished winners of literary prizes was **Laura Richards** (American, 1850–1943), a prolific writer from a home permeated by vibrant, intellectual people, who in 1917 became the first woman (in collaboration with her sister **Maud Elliott** (American, 1854–1948)) to win the Pulitzer Prize for Biography with the biography of their mother – **Julia Howe** (American, 1819–1910), author of the *Battle Hymn of the Republic*. In Europe **Hélène Văcărescu** (Romanian, 1866–1947), whose love-affair with Crown Prince Ferdinand of her country led to banishment to France, wrote verse and novels in French and to such good purpose that she was awarded the Prize of the French Academy (1886). Much later, in 1925, she was allowed back into the Romanian fold and elected an Honorary Member of the Romanian Academy. Then, in 1946, as a final tribute, she was appointed a Romanian Delegate at the Paris Peace Conference. And **Grazia Deledda** (Sardinian, 1875–1936) who won the Nobel Prize for Literature in 1926 and was elected to the Italian Academy, in due course wrote nearly 50 novels based upon the Sardinian peasant community in all its primitive violence and passion.

As the struggle for woman's equality got into its stride during the 19th century, feminine writers not only added their weight to the scales of debate and action but gained materially from the opportunities offered to them. Taking advantage of the success of their predecessors, they almost entirely dropped the convention of using a man's name and stormed to the top of the literary ladder in swarms. A glance at any universal bibliography of women almost invariably shows authors in a vast majority to other activities. So it is only possible here to select a few of the most celebrated. These include:

Mary Bateson (British, 1865–1906), a specialist in medieval sociology, who wrote both popular and academic history, made important discoveries in monastic and municipal history and became a member of the Council at Newnham College, Cambridge.

Willa Cather (American, 1873–1947) who entered journalism as a critic but became the successful Managing Editor of *McClure's* magazine in 1908. Her first book about the West appeared in 1912 and thereafter the frontier spirit played a prominent part in her works, which were aimed at a public who liked to believe in pioneering (but were no longer pioneers). Sales were good and in due course (in 1922) she became the first woman to win the Pulitzer Prize for Fiction with *One of Ours*.

Sigrid Undset (Norwegian, 1882–1949), whose bent for close research and intense personal experience of an office environment, enabled her to penetrate and explain lower-middle-class women's problems. But in addition to current affairs she explored the Norwegian medieval scene, her *Kristin Lavransdatter* (1920) being rated among the great European novels of the 20th century and which won her the Nobel Prize for Literature in 1928.

Sarah Millin (South African, 1889–1968) who wrote objectively about her native land. A Lithuanian Jewess, brought up in Kimberley, her first novel, *The Dark River* (1920), tackled the problems of the half-castes, but later she was to analyse South Africa closely through authoritative biographies of both Rhodes and Smuts. Deeply involved in the fate of her race in Europe, she endeavoured to impart common sense to the racial political issues in Africa.

Rebecca West (British) who began work as a political journalist in 1912, grew in stature until her many books won her an unassailable reputation for integrity and style on both sides of the Atlantic. *The Meaning of Treason* (1949), which was a report on the trials of traitors who had worked for Germany during the Second World War, achieved high sales.

Among the journalists are to be found:

Elizabeth Seaman (American, 1865–1922) who wrote under the name **'Nellie Bly'** and was, perhaps, the most sensational of them all through her work for the *Pittsburg Dispatch* and later the New York *World* and *New York Journal*. A demon at treading forbidden ground and exposing poor social conditions, she once feigned insanity in order to examine a lunatic asylum from the inside and lambaste the conditions she found – to the ultimate benefit of the inmates. But her most notable exploit was a well-publicised journey round the world in 72 days 6 hours 11 minutes and 14 seconds to beat the 80 day record of Jules Verne's Phileas Fogg. Over 1 000 000 people entered a competition to guess the time her voyage would take.

Dorothy Thompson (American, 1894–1961) the personification of the hard-driving newspaper woman – a plump human dynamo who kept three secretaries busy. As Foreign Correspondent for the *New York Herald Tribune* in Germany in the 1930s, she earned a colossal reputation and in 1936 began to write a column for her paper called *On the Record* which was syndicated to no less than 166 papers and had an estimated readership of 7 500 000. She also broadcast extensively.

Nora Beloff (British) began her career in the British Foreign Office and joined Reuters in 1946. As a writer for the British *Observer* with experience as a political correspondent in all the major capital cities, she has acquired the authoritative manner of Dorothy Thompson without giving way to quite the same impression of frantic haste. As one of the few British female political journalists she claims an advantage: 'Men behave much better to us than to each other.'

Rachel Katznelson (Russian), a journalist who married the future President Shazar of Israel. Coming from St Petersburg in 1912, she was among the pioneers of the evolving Jewish homeland. As co-founder of the Women's Workers Council and also founder and Editor of the weekly paper *Davar Hapoelet*, besides being heavily involved with the Histradut (General Federation of Labour), she virtually created the directives on feminine policy in the evolving State.

Begum **Zeb-Un-Nirsa Hamidullah** (Pakistani) the publisher and Editor of the Pakistan magazine *Mirror* which began in 1951 and, through its popularity, has helped the women's cause in that country. She has also written several books and poems.

As an index of writers' performance, however, it is the story-tellers – above all those who win status with 'best-sellers' – who catch the public's attention and, sometimes, adulation. For example:

Sidonie Colette (French, 1873–1954), a libertine who wrote beautifully about love and life and had an enormous success with *Chéri* (1920). As wife of the Editor of *Le Matin* she presented almost anything from theatrical critiques to fashion or law reports – and at an earlier moment in her career mimed, partly in the nude, on the stage: versatility was her watchword and rewarded at the end by the honour of Grand Officer of the Legion of Honour, among other distinctions.

Pearl Buck (American, 1893–1973) who knew China from childhood as the daughter of US missionaries became a missionary herself before turning against some of the reforming practices. Her second novel, *The Good Earth* (1931), luckily coincided with the Japanese invasion of Manchuria; and the sales went skywards. More books about the 'inside' of Chinese family life followed and, in their train, criticism from fellow missionaries and the Chinese. However, she was awarded the Nobel Prize for Literature in 1938.

Edna Millay (American, 1892–1950), first acclaimed at the age of 19 with her poem *Renascence*, also wrote verse plays and the libretto for Deems Taylor's opera *The King's Henchman* which enjoyed more success than any other American opera to date. In her early thirties she had travelled Europe as Foreign Correspondent to the magazine *Vanity Fair*, but it was for her poetry *Ballad of the Harp Weaver* that she was awarded the Pulitzer Prize in 1923.

Agatha Christie (British) has written an immense number of thrillers and plays and holds the record for the longest consecutive run by any play with *The Mousetrap* which, on 21 August 1975, achieved an unrivalled 9478th performance. By 1975 there had been translations into 103 foreign languages and global sales of more than 300 000 000 copies.

Dorothy L. Sayers (British, 1893–1957) who rates as among the astutest of detective novelists but who later turned to writing religious dramas of which *The Man Born to be King* (1942) received particular acclaim.

Margaret Mitchell (American, 1900–49) wrote one of the biggest bestsellers of all time – *Gone with the Wind*. Set in the Southern States during the American Civil War and published in 1936, it sold 50 000 copies in a single day and by 1965 over 12 000 000 authorised copies had been sold in 40 countries. The book won the Pulitzer Prize in 1937.

Daphne du Maurier (British) the daugher of Sir Gerald du Maurier the celebrated actor-manager, inherited his sense of drama and, in

Agatha Christie

Vera Panova

addition to plays, has written best-selling novels which were readily adaptable for stage, screen and radio. Among the most praised were *Rebecca* and *Jamaica Inn*.

Vera Panova (Russian, 1905–73), one of the more successful Soviet Russian novelists and playwrights who retained a measure of integrity, was widely read, became a member of the USSR Union of Writers, won three Stalin Prizes and stayed out of gaol. Her novel *Travelling Companions*, about a hospital train and its occupants during the Second World War, is well known. Twice she survived an occupational hazard, endured by so many Soviet writers, of being accused of objectivism and deviation from Socialist Realism.

Enid Blyton (British, 1897–1968) who wrote over 400 adventure stories for young children and had her works translated into the record number of 165 foreign languages, suffers now from a form of censorship in that many libraries withhold her books on the grounds that there is a danger of saturation by books, the literary content of which is low and repetitive of theme. She once sued a librarian for suggesting she did not write the books herself, books which, nevertheless, continue to give millions of children enormous, innocent pleasure.

Ursula Bloom (British) who, since 1922, has written 564 books totalling 40 000 000 words under her own name and that of 13 aliases, and includes several best-sellers and even the odd non-fictional work.

Jacqueline Susann (American, 1921–74) whose *Valley of the Dolls* sold 350 000 hardback copies plus 4 000 000 paperbacks in its first week, another 4 000 000 by the end of 1967 (its first year of publication) and the film rights, produced a strictly commercial endeavour of small literary merit. Stuffed with the seeds of popularity, its formula of violence, sex and intrigue, set in Hollywood, overrode the universal slatings of critics. By June 1975 world-wide sales had reached 18 100 000.

There are a great many 'experimenters' in literary style, notably **Virginia Woolf** (British, 1882–1941), who made a studied attempt to change the form of the novel by placing greater emphasis upon what she called 'the stream of consciousness' than the hard external facts of life, and **Edith Sitwell** (British, 1887–1964) whose poetry rarely achieved popularity except in the desperate days of the Second World War. They are revered by a small circle of intellectual devotees but it is unlikely that they or their kindred spirits will achieve a lasting readership. On the other hand **Anna Akhmatova** (Russian, 1888–1966), a poetess who studied law at Kiev and who could translate from French, Chinese, Korean, Romanian, Bengali, Polish and Hebrew may do better. She rejected symbolism and wrote briefly and intelligibly, with the result that she was widely read. Her poetry was genuine, original and essentially feminine although later, under Communist Party pressure, she followed the required party line of patriotism. It availed her little. Under the Stalin régime she was ostracised as 'a frantic "fine lady" pandering to the bourgeois culture of the West', and although some of her poetry was published during the Second World War it was again rejected as 'alien' in 1946. Not until 1959 was she granted official absolu-

Ursula Bloom

tion and raised to the heights of praise as the greatest poetess in Russian literature. Similarly the works of **Nelly Sachs** (German, 1891–1970) the doyen of Jewish poetesses who has become known as 'the poet of the holocaust' may survive. Neither her poetry, plays nor prose made an impact until she arrived in Sweden in 1940, having been rescued from a concentration camp at the instigation of Selma Lagerlöf and in response to the pleading of the King of Sweden with Hitler. Having learnt Swedish she translated modern Swedish poetry into German, but it was her poetry mourning the genocide of the Jews that catches at the heart with evocative titles such as: *In the Abodes of Death, Eclipse of the Stars, And no one knows where to turn* to speak for themselves. In the aftermath of German contrition, as it overspilt in the 1960s, she received the adulation of German authorities whose predecessors would have destroyed her.

One of the more successful modern appeals by publishers is the persuasion of women to buy women's books and, therefore, to have women authors write deliberately for selected feminine groups. For example, Bantam Books of the USA, with **Grace Bechtold** (American) as Executive Editor and **Esther Margolis** (American) as Publicity Director, made the women's market a speciality, printing, by 1970, 20 000 000 paperbacks of **Emilie Loring's** (American) 44 romances, and vast numbers of **Georgette Heyer's** (British, 1902–74) and **Grace Hill's** (American, 1865–1947) works, along with *Diary of a Mad Housewife* by **Sue Kaufman** (American) which was specifically aimed at the bridge–club set.

Fortunately writers who are prepared to concentrate on promotion before art are in a strict minority. The vast majority, in rising numbers, are dedicated to literature and journalism in their traditional roles. Three contrasting writers are mentioned in conclusion.

Lucila Alcayaga (Gabriela Mistral) (Chilean, 1889–1957), the poetess whose *Sonnets of Death* in 1914 established her reputation as the possessor of deep, emotional feelings. Translations into five languages were to come and in 1945 the award of the Nobel Prize for Literature. Her poetry seemed to reflect the idealistic aspirations of the Latin American world.

Gudrun Tempel (German) who suffered in youth from the results of bombing and the deprivation of Russian occupation of her country and has distinguished herself by writing frankly and fearlessly about current problems. She upset her own class in Germany by relating their complicity in permitting the Nazis to take power; she offended the firm of Unilever by writing penetratively of their operations (to the extent that they tried to withhold publication); industrial tycoons everywhere she has put on guard by her book *The Chairman as God*.

Iona Opie (British) who, with her husband Peter, has compiled *The Oxford Dictionary of Nursery Rhymes* and *The Oxford Book of Children's Verse* which have received much praise from the critics not only as notable operations in deep research, but as welcome contributions to literature for saving much of value from extinction. In this joint effort the wife does the research and much of the typing but is an equal partner with her husband in the venture.

15

AS ARTISTS

Recorded women classical artists date from the 7th century BC in ancient Greece, although very little is known about them. There was **Kora** (Greek *c* 600 BC), daughter and assistant to the potter Butades, who sketched her departing lover in charcoal on a wall of her home and so inspired her father that he outlined it in clay, thus forming the first medallion. At the time of Alexander the Great several women artists are said to have existed – **Helena** (Greek, *c* 330 BC) whose original painting of Alexander beating Darius in battle was supposed to have influenced the famous mosaic in Pompeii; **Cirene** whose painting of Proserpina was preserved: **Aristante** who painted Esculapius and **Calypso** among whose work is reputed to be the now named *A Mother superintending her Daughter's toilet* which was removed from the ruins of Pompeii to Naples.

Miniature-painting was pioneered by a woman named **Laya** (Greek, *c* 100 BC) who excelled in this skill, working on ivory. Also at this time there is mention of a Greek girl called **Lala** who was celebrated for making busts in ivory and to whose honour the Romans erected a statue.

The coming of Christianity with its trend towards simplicity as opposed to pagan decorations, brought a dearth of artists. Creative art did not start again until about AD 1200 with the illuminating of religious manuscripts in convents and monasteries. For example, **Agnes, Abbess of Quedlinberg** (German, *c* 1200) was a celebrated painter of miniatures and some of her works still survive.

The first known sculptress was **Sabina von Steinbach** (German, *c* 1300) who was responsible for most of the figures in the Cathedral at

Strasbourg, built between 1230 and 1365. The sculptured groups, particularly those on the portal of the south aisle, have remarkable beauty. The Apostle John is shown holding a scroll on which is written in Latin:

> The grace of God be with thee, O Sabina,
> Whose hands from this hard stone have formed my image.

In the Carthusian convent in Germany between 1459 and 1470 a nun named **Margareta** (German) copied in Gothic letters and illuminated with pictures in miniature eight folio volumes of religious works, blending the scribe's and the painter's arts so typical of the Middle Ages. The founder of the Corpo di Cristo Convent, Saint **Caterina Vigri** (Italian, 1413–63), painted many large works with immense sympathy – particularly of women – and also executed miniatures.

There were some things women would not sacrifice for art, according to the story of **Onorata Rodiana** (Italian, d 1472) born at Castelleone in Cremona. So great was her reputation as a painter that the Marquis Gabrino Fondolo engaged her to decorate his palace, but while painting a mural a courtier tried to rape her. She stabbed him, and escaped disguised as a man. The furious Marquis unsuccessfully sent soldiers after her but later, when he realised no one else could finish the murals, he offered her a pardon for her return. It was too late; she had joined a band of Condottieri, gaining a command. After thirty years of soldiering along with painting, she was killed when relieving her besieged native town of Castelleone from the Venetians.

The first sculptress of repute in Italy was **Properzia di Rossi** (Italian, 1490–1530), born in Bologna, who carved in miniature. In the silver filigree Grassi family coat of arms were placed eleven peach stones she had carved, each stone having on one side one of the Apostles with an article of the Creed underneath and on the other side a holy virgin. On each stone the name of a saint and her special virtue were inscribed. But she also sculpted larger works in white marble, and two angels in bas-relief in the Church of San Petronio are hers.

A skilled portrait-painter, famous enough to be sent invitations from Emperor Maximilian, Philip II of Spain and Archduke Ferdinand to be the artist at their respective courts, was **Marietta Robusti** (Italian 1560–90) the daughter (and also the pupil) of the celebrated Tintoretto. Her father, however, did not want her to leave him and betrothed her to a wealthy German jeweller on condition that she remained under the paternal roof. Here she continued painting until her early death. Her self-portrait is in Florence.

Of the great number of 16th-century Italian women artists of renown the most famous, in her lifetime, was **Sofonisba Anguisciola** (Italian, *c* 1533–1626) who was born in Cremona, one of six gifted and artistic daughters. By 1559 her name was already famous throughout Italy and Philip II of Spain invited her to the court of Madrid. She was conducted there with regal pomp and entertained lavishly by Philip and his Queen. Philip was so delighted with the portrait she painted of him as part of a history in portraits, that he gave her a diamond worth 1500 crowns and a pension of 200 crowns. This project included pictures of the Queen and

Sofonisba Anguisciola's picture of her sisters by herself

the nobility but unfortunately is no longer in existence. Those of her many pictures which do survive, however, exhibit a quite remarkable freshness and vitality compared with so many others of her age. The one showing three of her young sisters is full of fun – as she was herself full of laughter – and prompted the critic Giorgio Vasari to exclaim that 'The figures wanted only voice to be alive.' She was her own woman too – sincere yet quick to publicise herself by sending a self-portrait to Pope Julius III in 1555 and determined to marry the man of her choice even when the King of Spain tried to arrange a match for her.

For her first marriage the Spanish King and Queen gave her rich presents, a dowry of 12 000 crowns, and a pension of 1000 crowns. Soon her husband died but, despite an invitation to return to the Spanish court, she remarried and lived in Genoa where she painted and received many distinguished visitors. Even up to her death many artists of repute came to this, now blind, old lady. Van Dyck was a frequent visitor who greatly admired her works and is said to have stated on several occasions that he had learnt much about the principles of art merely from talking to her, and much more than from his other teachers. A medallion was struck at Bologna in her honour and a poet wrote of:

'La belle e saggia dipintrice,   (The beautiful and wise painter
La nobil Sofonisba da Cremona.'   The noble Sofonisba of Cremona.)

Many women of the Middle Ages and the Renaissance became engaged upon creating works of art because it was expected of them that they should remain at home while the men went about their business. Apart from ordering the home, which took as little time as there were servants to do the work, the prescribed pastime for well-to-do ladies was chiefly gossip, writing, embroidery, painting, sculpting and engraving. Much of their production was mediocre and amateurish – as was a large proportion of that produced by men – but it is perhaps symbolic that so little is known about their higher-grade works of art. Symbolic, that is, because the vast majority of art critics have been men who have made a practice of denigrating or ignoring the works of women.

Enormous prices were often commanded by women who painted professionally. **Lavinia Fontana** (Italian, 1552–1614?), was one who did and who was regarded highly by successive Popes (whose portraits she painted) and by society. And yet although she is recognised as a better portrait-painter than her father and a good painter of religious subjects, it is to her father that most credit is commonly given. Nevertheless, she was elected a member of the Rome Academy.

Even so there seems to have been some sort of equality for women artists in the 16th/17th centuries because **Artemisia Gentileschi** (Italian, c 1597–1651) was also able to ask and receive large sums of money for her pictures which have been described as 'masterful and ruthless'. A 'realist', she was invited to the court of King Charles I of England where she painted many pictures (her own self-portrait is now based on Hampton Court) and earned enough to live in splendour when she returned to Naples.

The first public commission received when only 15 years of age was achieved by **Elisabetta Sirani** (Italian, 1638–65), born in Bologna. She excelled at drawing, painting, sculpture, etching, engraving and music and was so good an artist and so quick to execute her work that rumour was spread by other artists that her father, also a painter, must work on the pictures. But visitors had free access to her studio and marvelled at the speed and sureness with which she worked, so these jealous rumours were silenced. However, the jealousy must have remained for it was claimed that this popular and clever young artist, who had already painted at least 150 pictures, was poisoned. It is said, too, that all Bologna wept at her funeral.

Ambition and remuneration encouraged women to seek independence using artistic endeavour. A well-known wood-carver, **Luisa Roldan** (Spanish, b 1656) who was born in Seville, made her name carving religious statues and was invited to Madrid where Charles II commissioned a life-sized statue of St Michael for the Church of the Escurial. As a result she became Sculptress-in-Ordinary to the King with a salary of 100 ducats. And a sizeable pension of 500 livres was given by Louis XIV to **Elizabeth Sophie Chéron** (French, 1648–1711), born in Paris, who is said to have been the best French miniature- and enamel-painter of her day and at 26 was elected a Member of the Academy in Paris. She was also a poet and, at 51, became a Member of the Academy dei Ricovatri in Padua.

A high peak in diamond-point engraving on glass was reached in the Netherlands in the early 17th century with the sisters **Maria** (Dutch, 1595–1649) and **Anna Visscher** (Dutch, 1583–1651). Anna (who was also a writer) was particularly skilled, though less so than the brilliant

Anna Maria van Schürman (see section on Education). Both escaped from the previous century's stiff and linear designs to create flowers and insects most exquisitely engraved, and often enhanced their work with epigrams in Greek or Latin capitals.

The first eminent Dutch flower-painter was **Maria van Oosterwyck** (Dutch, 1630–93). Born near Delft, she sold paintings to Louis XIV, and Emperor Leopold and the Empress (from whom she received their portraits set in diamonds as a token of esteem). William III of England paid 900 florins for a picture, and the King of Poland 2400 florins for three pictures. Yet she lived a quiet and comparatively simple life devoted to painting, taking a great deal of care and time over each of her works which are consequently scarce. She was followed by an even more illustrious flower-painter, **Rachel Ruysch** (Dutch, 1664–1750), from Amsterdam, who prospered despite a marriage in 1695 which produced ten children and also running an orderly home – initially on a low income. In 1701 she was elected a Member of the Academical Society of The Hague and in 1708 the Elector John of the Pfalz invited her to be Painter-in-Ordinary at his court in Düsseldorf, and sent her a 28-piece silver toilet set and 6 silver flambeaux. She entered his service and some of her paintings found their way to Munich as well as Düsseldorf, paintings for which the payments were always accompanied by rich gifts. On the death of the Elector she returned to Holland (where her work was very much in demand) and continued painting.

An important painter of insects, small animals and plants, who expanded the knowledge of botany and zoology, was **Maria Merian** (German, 1647–1717) who was born at Frankfurt-am-Main. She had a lifelong interest in her subjects which led in 1679 to the publication of a book called *The Wonderful Transformations of Caterpillars* illustrated with her own engravings. Then in 1699, accompanied by one of her daughters, after the termination of an unhappy marriage, she travelled to Surinam in South America (no easy undertaking), to study and draw the insects and their food. She returned two years later with enough material to publish her pictures in a work entitled *Metamorphosis Insectorum Surinamensium, etc. The text drawn up by Gaspar Commelin, from the Manuscripts of the author.* But her greatest work, *History of the Insects of Europe, drawn from Nature, and explained, by Maria Sibylla Merian*, showing each stage of the insect's growth, with its diet and in its natural habitat, was published in 1705.

Two well-known English painters were **Mary Beale** (English, 1632–97), who was a portrait-painter at Charles II's court and also was patronised by Archbishop Tillotson, and **Anne Killigrew** (English, 1660–85), who painted the aristocracy, historical works and still-life, before she died of smallpox. In addition Anne Killigrew wrote poetry – her works being published after her death.

An interesting artist in silk was **Mademoiselle Rosée** (French, 1632–82) who was born in Leyden. Instead of using oil-colours she applied coloured silk fibres, blending them to produce the effects required for her portraits or landscapes. Another original method was developed by **Joanna Block** (Dutch, 1650–1715) of Amsterdam. She painted in oils and watercolour and was a delicate glass-engraver, but she also cut out

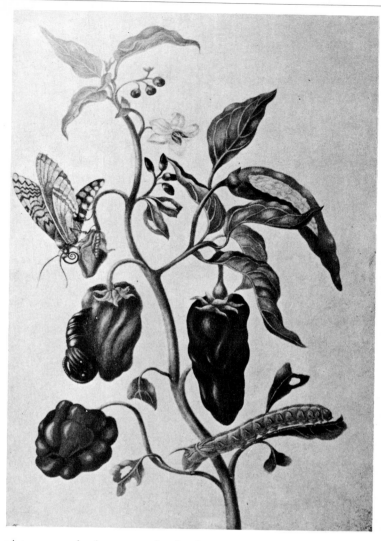

Plant study by
Maria Merian

her pictures – whether portraits, landscapes, seascapes, floral or animal studies – so that when the white cut paper was laid over black the effect was of a fine pen-drawing or engraving. The Elector Palatine offered 1000 florins for three small works by her but she refused, saying they were worth more. Once she was paid 4000 florins by the Empress of Germany for a coat of arms of Emperor Leopold I.

One of Switzerland's most eminent painters was **Anna Wasser** (Swiss, 1676–1710) who was born in Zürich. From an early age her skill brought commissions (including some from Germany, Holland and England), her most successful subjects being rural scenes. An avaricious father constantly pressed her to produce quantity rather than quality to keep himself and his large family, but for a spell she worked at the court of Solmo Braunfels where she gave the pictures the time and finish she desired. However, when her father demanded that she return home to once more augment the family income she was killed in an accident on the journey.

Considered as possibly being the first American woman painter was **Henrietta Johnston** (American, 1670?–1728/9) who worked proficiently in pastels even though she had little training.

Still considered the best artist in pastels was **Rosalba Carriera** (Italian, 1675–1757), although her initial reputation was made through painting miniatures on snuff-boxes and by being the first to paint on ivory using transparent colours – a method which had great advantage over opaque colours. Born in Venice, fame came when Pierre Crozat persuaded her to go to Paris in 1720 where she was appointed a Member of the Academy. French patronage enabled her to return to Venice within a year where she was visited by important people from all over Europe either to have their portraits painted or to purchase her works. These were delicately executed and of the Rococo style, then beginning to achieve popularity. She did work (and was well paid) for the Kings of Denmark and Poland and, while in Vienna in 1730, executed a portrait of Emperor Charles X. The latter was, according to her, 'the ugliest of men', who annoyed her greatly by remarking to his Court Artist, Bertoli, in her presence 'She may be clever, Bertoli mio, this painter of thine, but she is remarkably ugly!' Nevertheless her work impressed Watteau sufficiently for him to sit for a portrait and she converted Latour to the pastel medium and she became a member of the academies of both Bologna and Rome. In 1750 she went blind.

There were more known artists in the 18th century than the total of all known women artists of preceding history, for it was in art, more than any other vocation or profession, that the greatest increase of female participation took place. Even so, there was less originality than in the previous century – as was typical of the arts as a whole. But, whereas in the 17th century female artistic activity was centred on Italy (in the cities of Bologna, Florence and Rome) in the 18th century it increased most in Germany – in Berlin, Dresden, Nuremburg and Munich, as the Romantic movement grew in strength. Yet, as in previous times, there were still women who worked with their husbands, fathers, brothers or teachers (often combining efforts on the same picture) and selling under the man's name.

A great reputation as a gem-cutter was attained by **Susanna Maria Dorsch** (German, b 1701) who was born in Nuremberg. Following her father and grandfather in this art, she cut a vast number of precious stones. Another gem-cutter was **Rosa Elizabeth Schwindel** of Leipzig, though she made her name stamp-cutting for medals and was also a proficient wax-modeller – one of many women who practised this method of presentation.

And two painters of miniatures in Berlin who received special recognition were **Marianna Hayd** (German, 1688–1753) who gained an appointment at the Electoral Court of Saxony in Dresden and **Anna Liscewska** (German) who, in 1769, was admitted as a Member of the Academy in Dresden. In addition one of Anna's sisters, **Dorothea Liscewska** (German, 1722–82) was elected a Member of the Parisian

Academy on the merits of her portraits and historical pictures. None of these, however, matched **Angelica Kauffmann** (Swiss, 1740–1807), who already was famous when only 11 years old. A portrait and historical painter, as well as a talented musician, she studied painting in Como, Milan, Schwarzenberg, Naples, Florence, Rome, Bologna and Venice – during which time she was as much a social success as she was in demand as a portrait-painter. She arrived in London in 1766 where competition was less intense than on the Continent and, therefore, remuneration potentially higher. There she was accepted in court circles, painted portraits of several members of the Royal Family, including the Queen, and was one of the signatories of the petition to the King asking for the establishment of the Royal Academy. With Mary Moser (see below) she became one of its first women members and was part of the team appointed by the Academy to decorate St Paul's Cathedral. Her love-life was complicated and her name is romantically linked with Sir Joshua Reynolds, Fuseli and Marat. She received many proposals of marriage but at 26 married in good faith a man who claimed to be the Swedish Count Frederic de Horn. However, he turned out to be his already married manservant so that marriage was quickly annulled, and in 1781 she married Antonio Zucchi and settled in Rome.

Mary Moser (German, 1744–1819) was a very skilful flower-painter who had a German father but was educated in England. She decorated

Vase of flowers
by *Mary Moser*

one of Queen Charlotte's rooms at Frogmore for which she was paid over £900, and the Queen afterwards commanded that it would be known as 'Miss Moser's Room'. It was said of Mary Moser that she was 'skilful in painting flowers, sarcastic when she held the pen'. It was also said that she was in love with Fuseli who, as noted above, was looking elsewhere.

The majority of British women artists of the day were enthusiastic amateurs. For example, **Anne Seymour Damer** (1748–1828) who, determined to be a sculptress despite an aristocratic background, took modelling lessons from Cerrachi, anatomy from Cruikshank and also learnt the technique of working with marble. She covered her rich clothes with an apron, her hair with a mob-cap and worked hard at her hobby, which was to last a lifetime, using marble, bronze and terracotta. Two large heads representing Thames and Isis were made by her for the keystones of the bridge at Henley-on-Thames. She ordered that her apron and tools were to be buried with her.

Self-portrait in wax by *Marie Tussaud*

But the now world-famous exhibition of waxworks, made and staged by **Marie Tussaud** (French, 1761–1850) which opened in London in 1802 and later for 33 years toured the British Isles, was a collection of high professionalism. She was born in Strasbourg and learnt wax-modelling from her uncle, whose collection she inherited. From 1780 she was art tutor to Louis XVI's sister but at the outbreak of the French Revolution was imprisoned as a Royalist and given the job of making death-masks from heads freshly severed by the guillotine – some of the victims being her friends.

In fact the only centre in France for female art in the 18th century was Paris where the majority were engravers, mostly professionals. No artist, however, was superior to **Elizabeth Vigée Le Brun** (French, 1755–1842) who painted a grand total of 700 pictures, among them 662 portraits, and 15 large compositions also 200 landscape sketches. As a child she displayed a natural talent and by 1789 had earned more than 1 000 000 francs – but had less than 20 to her name due to her husband's extravagances. She had become friend and Painter-in-Ordinary to the Queen, Marie-Antoinette (of whom she painted over 25 portraits) and a Member of the Academy, achieved by a self-portrait in 1783.

   When the Revolution broke out in 1789 she fled to Italy and there was elected a Member of the Bologna and Parma Academies. In Naples she painted several portraits, including one of Lady Hamilton, and in Florence painted a self-portrait for the famous Pitti Gallery – to join those by Marietta Robusti and Angelica Kauffmann. She was fêted in Venice, Verona and Milan, and in Vienna and Berlin when her travels took her farther. From there she went to St Petersburg, where she lived under royal protection from 1795 to 1800, being elected a Member of that Academy of Arts in 1800. Through ill-health, she was compelled to leave Russia for Berlin, where she did more painting and was elected to the Berlin Academy. Eventually she returned to Paris in 1805 after spending three years in England where she fulfilled several commissions, including a portrait of the Prince of Wales. When Sir Joshua Reynolds was asked his opinion of two of her portraits he said they were 'as fine as those of any painter'. A woman of charm and wit she maintained in Paris a famous salon at a time when salons were important. Indeed 1808/9 found her in Switzerland, where she painted a portrait of Madame de Staël – one of the most distinguished of salonnières (see section on Salonnières). It was during her stays in England and Switzerland that she made her 200 landscape sketches. Returning from Switzerland she bought a country-house at Marly in France, and painted with undiminished vigour and skill until her death (the lively portrait of her niece, Madame de Revière, was painted at the age of 80).

The only woman to mix wax-modelling with spying was **Patience Wright** (American, 1725–86), who from an early age, became well known in some US cities for her true to life wax models. When widowed she travelled to London where prospects were brighter and where she helped support her three children by making likenesses of the people in power, including George III and his Queen. At one time she was a regular visitor to the royal household, but lost favour by the too-frequent and frank airings of her political opinions during the American War of Independence. She is said to have fed information of British troop movements, gleaned from families she visited, to the American, Benjamin Franklin, who was then in Paris, and throughout the war remained an ardent American – while continuing to live in England.

The 19th century, like the 18th, continued the downward trend in numbers of those with outstanding artistic merit. Perhaps the advent of photography had something to do with it!

The first effective photography dates from the mid 1820s and by 1850 was a well-developed art. Rated the most brilliant portrait-photographer of the 19th century was **Julia Cameron** (British, 1815–79) who was born in Calcutta, worked in 1846 to relieve sufferers in the Irish Famine, and who had a reputation as a superb conversationalist as well as being a poetess. She began photography in 1863 with a camera using a 30 in (76 cm) focal length lens and the necessity of making and developing her own plates – a complicated chemical process. Within a year she was producing artistic portraits which, to this day, astound at the way she made the camera reveal people's character. But she also produced fine illustrations for books, notably Tennyson's *Idylls of the King* in 1875, and wrote an autobiography. In 1974 an album containing 119 photographs, mostly hers, was sold for £52000 at Sotheby's, London.

A surge of newly awakened interest, both in France and England, in things medieval stemmed chiefly from the sculptress **Félicie de Fauveau** (French *c* 1802–86) who was inspired by medieval art and design. Modern events overtook her. She had ample commissions (paintings and sculptures) in hand when the Revolution of 1830 broke out, but because of her strong Royalist leanings and her dabbling in political intrigues, she was arrested and imprisoned for seven months (designing and modelling the while) and finally exiled. She moved to Florence, having lost the contents of her studio and all her money, and there worked on bronze sculpture, terracotta-modelling and wood-carving. For bronzes she returned to the forgotten art of casting a bronze statue in one piece with no finishing work required. Her statue of St Michael was cast seven times until she was satisfied that, with no further work, it was as perfect in bronze as it had been in wax. She also worked in silver and, for the Empress of Russia, made a silver bell, representing about 17 medieval household servants being assembled by the 3 stewards who formed the handle.

Still the most famous woman animal-painter of all is **Rosa Bonheur** (French, 1822–99) who was born in Bordeaux. She could not settle to a systematic education so her artist father taught and encouraged her in her leaning towards art. The family was extremely poor and the only way she could obtain the animal subjects she wished to copy was, firstly, by trudging into the country each day and drawing animals on farms and, later, by spending all day and every day at the abattoirs of Paris sketching the animals in the pens and being slaughtered. After exhaustive studies she shifted her attention to the Veterinary School of Afort. Although she was always treated with the greatest respect by the men at the abattoirs, she found that when sketching at cattle and horse fairs she attracted less attention if disguised as a man. Following a first entry in the Paris Fine Arts Exhibition in 1841, she entered something every subsequent year, gaining several Bronze and Silver Medals. In 1844 she added to her picture exhibits a clay model, *A Bull*, thus demonstrating her skill as a sculptor. In 1849 her *Cantal Oxen* took the Gold Medal. She was now among the top in her profession and need never go hungry nor want for money – a state which did nothing to alter her plain, drab working dress or change her ways of pleasure. She helped poor artists financially and was kind to all.

In 1853 Rosa Bonheur's picture *The Horse Fair* gained her the jury decision that she might enter anything she wanted, without prior committee approval, to the Academy of Fine Arts exhibitions. (When

Bull by *Rosa Bonheur*

'The Jetty'
by *Berthe Morisot*

Landseer saw the picture he is quoted as saying, 'It surpasses me, though it's a little hard to be beaten by a woman'). Previously this top award had always been accompanied by the Legion of Honour, but Napoleon III refused on this occasion – solely because she was a woman and a feminist. Even when she was invited to State dinners at the Tuileries and numerous efforts were made to get the Emperor to reverse his decision, he would not give way. However, in 1865, when the Emperor was on an excursion and the Empress was acting as Regent, the Empress walked, unannounced, into the studio where Rosa Bonheur was working, threw her arms round her neck, kissed her and then, after a brief interview, was gone again. It was not until the rumble of the carriage had died away that the artist looked down and discovered that she had pinned to her blouse the Grand Cross of the Legion of Honour. This was rapidly followed by her becoming the first woman to receive the Leopold Cross of Honour bestowed by the King of Belgium.

The distinctive lead taken by French art in the 19th century, particularly its second half, was shared by innumerable women artists apart from Marie-Louise Vigée Le Brun and Rosa Bonheur. Most important of the women Impressionists was **Berthe Morisot** (French, 1841–95) who was trained by Corot and married Edouard Manet's brother, Eugène. It was she who interested Manet in outdoor painting and persuaded him to change his technique by using the 'rainbow' palette. Her reputation was international and strengthened further when she fell under Renoir's influence after the death of Manet. There were also women from other countries who made their reputations in France. For example:

Marie Bashkirtseff (Russian, 1860–84) a precocious, ambitious girl who lived in Paris from the age of ten and intended to be a singer until tuberculosis prevented it. Turning to painting, it was not long before her work was accepted for exhibition and became greatly admired. Highly cultivated, she kept a diary which was published in many languages after her early death.

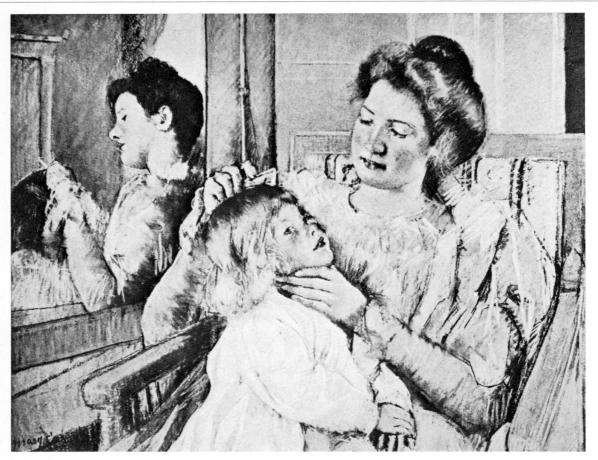

'Babies Toilette'
by *Mary Cassatt*

Mary Cassatt (American, 1844–1926) whose talents developed into Impressionism under the influence of Degas. Mostly she exhibited in Paris where she regularly had entry to the Salon after 1872, though she also showed works in the USA and had much to do with building up the New York Havemeyer Collection. Her favourite theme eventually became that of mother and child.

Of the American women artists of the 19th century mention can be made of **Anne Hall** (American, 1792–1863), elected a Member of the National Academy of Design in New York and who painted in water-colours on ivory, and of **Harriet Hosmer** (American, 1830–1908), the sculptress, whose bronze of Thomas Hart Benton, commissioned by St Louis for the Lafayette Park, brought her $10000 and whose *Sleeping Faun*, exhibited at the Dublin Exhibition in 1865, was sold on the first day to Sir Benjamin Guinness whose offer of $10000 she refused in favour of a price of $5000 which she considered sufficient.

The buying of works of art is as much affected by vogue as anything else. A widespread fashion of this sort was started by **Kate Greenaway** (British, 1846–1901) who began exhibiting in 1868 but who also created a revolution in book illustration for children. She produced the annual

An example of
Kate Greenaway's work

Kate Greenaway's Almanacs from 1883 to 1897 with only a break in 1896. The early-19th-century style in which she dressed the children in her illustrations added a humorous quaintness which so captured the imagination of her reading public that it was said 'Kate Greenaway dressed the children of two continents.' She was elected a Member of the Royal Institute of Painters in Water Colours in 1890.

The 19th century cannot pass without a mention that for the first time (1872) the Slade School of Art in London accepted women students – on condition that they did not study from the nude. An early woman student at the Slade (1898) was **Eileen Gray** (Irish) who afterwards apprenticed herself to a lacquer workshop and started to design and make furniture. In 1926 she opened her own gallery in Paris but by 1925 had already exhibited furniture in chrome, steel-tube and glass. She also designed and built two houses (the one at Castellar, owned by the painter Graham Sutherland, is considered by many experts one of the best examples of domestic architectural design of the period) and her models and plans for social and cultural centres are still being copied for holiday complexes.

A popular portrait-painter specialising in women and children was **Cecilia Beaux** (American, 1855–1942). She won the Dodge Prize at the New York National Academy, the Saltus Gold Medal of the National Academy of Design in 1913, the Gold Medal of the National Institute of Arts and Letters in 1942: and she painted Mrs Theodore Roosevelt and her daughter. But she was among the gentler creative artists of the violent 20th century, for, on the other hand, there was that stalwart advocate on behalf of victims of inhumanity, war and social injustice – the engraver **Kathe Kollwitz** (German, 1867–1945) who was born in Königsberg and studied art in Berlin. With her husband, a doctor, she lived in a workers' district of Berlin where he treated the poor and she made engravings that were severely influenced by her surroundings. A collection of engravings, *Revolt of Weavers*, was exhibited in 1898 and her finest work, a series entitled *The Peasant Revolt*, was completed between 1902 and 1908. Even her pictures of mother and child had a fierce symbolism.

Beatrix Potter

Later she linked with the Spartacist (in due course the Communist) Party in Germany and was the first woman to be elected a Member of the Prussian Academy of the Arts, though she resigned in 1933 as a protest against the Nazi régime. In 1927 and 1932 exhibitions of her work were staged in Paris, though in 1936 she was forbidden to exhibit in Germany. Her home in Berlin was destroyed by bombing during the Second World War but she ended her days at the Castle of Moritzburg, near Dresden, as a guest of a former royal Saxon family.

Many artists aim to stimulate just as others, like many people who look at their works, do so for relaxation. One of the most charming illustrators of children's books was **Beatrix Potter** (British, 1866–1943), a shy person who shunned society and who, paradoxically, personally frightened many children. But 30 years after her death her watercolours, painted in the best English tradition, are still being widely sold in print and poster form while she remains famous as author of 23 celebrated little books. These were started when, aged 27, she began sending illustrated letters to a sick child. They gave so much pleasure that she decided to publish *The Tale of Peter Rabbit* in 1902. The characters and models were taken from hedgerow animals she kept. The books went into many editions and translations: the original illustrations for *The Tailor of Gloucester* are in the Tate Gallery, London.

Stimulating art sometimes needs a sense of direction, and an important sculptress, **Malvina Hoffman** (American, 1887–1966) who studied under Rodin for four years in Paris, found it when she was commissioned in 1930 by the Field Museum of Natural History, Chicago, to create a series of 101 bronzes portraying ethnic types of man. In search of subjects she travelled the world and eventually created works with titles such as *Family Group of South African Kalahari Bushman* and *Hawaiian Surfboard Rider*. In 1911 she had won first prize at the Paris Salon with her *Russian Bacchanale* but her finest composition is often rated *The Sacrifice*, the war memorial in the Memorial Chapel at Harvard University.

Inevitably artists and sculptors have become involved in war subjects. **Kseniya Suprun** and **Lidiya Tverdyanskaya** (both Russian) specialised in painting women at war during the Second World War and in its aftermath **Laura Knight** (British, 1877–1970) sketched the prisoners in the dock during the trials at Nuremburg of the German war criminals. But for Laura Knight, the first woman Academician since Angelica Kauffmann and Mary Moser were appointed, her *métier* was the circus and Russian ballet, although she tackled other subjects including poster design for the London Underground.

Women with an international reputation as artists or sculptresses are quite rare, perhaps because critics search for manly qualities in their work and, finding only those of women, reject them as slightly inferior. **Barbara Hepworth** (British, 1903–75) overcame this difficulty by the uncompromising brilliance of her sculpting. She exhibited from Tokyo to New York, Buenos Aires to Germany and in 1953 won Second Prize in the International Sculpture Competition on the theme 'The Unknown Political Prisoner', besides many more prizes. Her development was steadily progressive and influenced by the bleaker landscapes. There is

Barbara Hepworth

an unusually sensitive feeling for surface and material about her works with a sensation of mysticism surrounding her sculptures.

An increasingly functional part is being played in modern art by women. For example **Iris Barry** (American) became a Director of the Museum of Modern Art in New York in 1949 and **Kathleen Fenwick** (Canadian, 1902–74) was Curator of the National Gallery of Canada, Ottawa for 40 years, the founding Editor of the country's first art periodical, *Canadian Art* in 1943, Chairman of the Canadian Film Awards from 1958 to 1973 and Director of the International Fine Arts Exhibition at Expo 67 in Montreal.

Departments of design are heavily populated by women: postage stamps are designed by **Mary Adshead** (British); mosaics and ceramics by **Audrey Blackman** and **Mary Keepax** (both British); carpets by **Helena Hernmarck** (Swedish). There are master glass-engravers, medical artists, such as **Patricia Archer** (British) illustrating scientific journals and illustrators of manuscripts on vellum such as **Irene Base** (British). In photography there was **Lotte Meitner-Graf** (Austrian, d 1974) who not only took pictures of the most distinguished people of the day while managing the Fayer Studio in London, but contributed to many book-jackets and record-sleeves with her photographic portraits.

A leader in present-day art is **Bridget Riley** (British) whose sharp-edged, monochromatic works cause interesting optical reactions. She is currently achieving effects by the balancing or repetition of different coloured lines. Her first one-woman exhibition was held in 1962, in London, and since then she has exhibited in the USA, France, Japan, Germany, Canada, New Zealand, Australia, Italy, Belgium, Ireland and South America.

The initial exhibition in America (New York) in 1965 sold out on the day of opening. She has won several prizes, including that of joint winner of the Internation Prize for Painting at the 1968 Venice Biennale. The results she has achieved are demonstrably commercial with little or no sense of emotional or political involvement. The trend may or may not be significant – a great many of the women artists in history worked mainly for remuneration, as has been shown – but whether or not this is the beginning of another renaissance remains to be seen. The trend whereby interest in women's art advances in proportion to their assault upon male chauvinism continues. In 1960, in that stronghold of masculinity, **Judy Cassab** (Australian) won her country's biggest art award, the Archbold Prize.

16

AS MUSICIANS

It is one of the incontrovertible facts of musical history that, although women have been music-makers in that they have sung as they worked or been members of choral and instrumental groups, they have so far played a relatively minute part in its creation – above all in composition. This seems all the more surprising when it is remembered that music sprang from the home and the Church, and that its public performance on an increasingly large scale has coincided with the improvements in women's status, particularly in literature. Many reasons for this can be advanced but, as usual no doubt, educational deprivation has been the principal cause. Composition is an art which demands a comprehensive grasp of musical technology besides sheer creative ability: performance at concert level requires an almost total dedication, besides long and meticulous training. For women, immersed in their homes in the 18th and 19th centuries (when musical technology was rapidly and essentially changing as instruments of far greater range replaced those of old), there was a relatively low chance of their keeping pace as a common traditional pastime advanced into a modern, specialised profession.

The first of the plucked string instruments in the harpsichord family were called virginals (dating from the 16th century), possibly because they were considered delicately fit for pure young girls to play (unlike the cello which, in Victorian times, was regarded as so indecorous an instrument that a ladies side-saddle model was produced). Early music printed for the virginal in England was, in fact, called 'Maidens' Songs', just as the first contribution by women to music was singing. Possibly some of the oldest known tunes were women's compositions, but there is no way of saying since many were religious and handed down from generation to generation.

It is from the Renaissance that the first important feminine musicians emerge by name as performers. From the Italian salons, notably that of the d' Este's (see section on Salonnières) come 'ladies' concerts' as they were called, by the Italian trio **Tarquinia Molza**, **Laura Paperara** and **Lucrezia Benedidio** in the late 16th century. There were Italian singers too who composed their own songs, among them **Barbara Strozzi**, **Laura Bovia** and **Francesca Cascini** whose fame spread beyond Italy.

The creation of traditions is as important to the evolution of music as in any other art. It has grown either from patronage in the courts and their associated schools, from family groups and the churches or from combinations of them all. When the French court was at the height of its glory between the 16th and 18th centuries it attracted many celebrated musicians. For example:

Antonia Bembo (Italian), a Venetian soprano and composer, who took Paris by storm in 1700 and became a musical leader at court, but whose compositions are now hardly known.

The **Couperin Family** which is among the most famous connected with music and extended its influence from the late 17th into the mid 19th century in France. As court musicians they once held the highest appointments and dominated French music. Of the most distinguished among their ladies were:

> **Marguerite-Louise** (French 1676?–1728), a clavecinist who was also a principal soprano in the Musique du Roi and regarded as the best interpreter of the family's compositions.
> **Marguerite-Antoinette** (1705–78), clavecinist to the King and also the first woman to become Ordinaire de la Musique in 1733.
> **Céleste** (1793–1860), a competent organist who had the unhappy task of winding up the family's bankruptcy affairs by selling their portraits to France.

Improvements to travelling facilities in the 18th century led to a more extensive exchange of players among the musical centres of Europe and, in due course, the rest of the world. Rivalries between touring artists of different nationality became prominent and newsworthy. **Gertrud Mara** (German, 1749–1833), who as a child suffered from rickets (due to her father's neglect) taught herself to play the violin scale. Her father then arranged lessons and, when she was five, presented her in a public performance which so impressed the listeners that subscriptions were raised to have her properly trained. During a visit to England, however, she was persuaded to give up the violin and concentrate upon her voice which developed into a powerful soprano that could range between three octaves. In due course she was the unwilling recipient of the appointment of musician at the court of Frederick II of Prussia, a contract from which she managed to escape later. Her great rivals on the concert platforms of Europe were **Luiza Todi** (Portuguese, 1753–1833) and **Josephina Grassini** (Italian, 1773–1850), and it was a matter of good timing for the success of their tours if they could avoid each other and thus prevent invidious comparison by audiences. Sometimes, however, they appeared in the same concert and this could lead to all sorts of embarrassing confrontations and squabbles.

One of the first women to compose songs of lasting popularity was **Carolina Nairne** (British, 1766–1845), a fervent Jacobite who, though born long after the 1745 Rebellion, helped perpetuate a lost cause since many of the songs she wrote made deft use of old Scottish tunes and were closely associated with the Stuart cause – songs such as *Charlie is my Darling*, *A Hundred Pipers*, *Will ye no come back again* and *Caller Herrin* touched the emotions.

Not until the 1820s was the art of listening to music fully developed for the public at large. An important technical contribution to the teaching of music was made by **Sarah Glover** (British, 1785–1867) who, in 1845, invented a 'movable doh' system which, when adapted by others, came into general use as 'Tonic Sol-Fa'. Despite imperfections, this system undoubtedly simplified teaching and brought music to a great many more people, popularising it by increasing public performances on a large scale. More important still were the technical improvements in musical instruments which began to appear during the 18th century, more so with the pianoforte than any other instrument. The lighter type of piano produced by the Viennese family of Stein was to have a direct influence upon Mozart and Beethoven. For a start, **Nanette Stein** (Austrian, 1769–1833) was almost as brilliant a child prodigy at the piano as was Mozart. In criticisms of her he wrote 'She sits right up in the treble, instead of in the middle of the instrument, so as to be better able to move about and make grimaces.' However, she was one day to assist Beethoven and become associated with the commercial side of the family business in a dynamic and capable manner by enlarging its operations in addition to improving its technology. Music benefited enormously from this.

Clara Wieck

It benefited too from inspired performances and criticism. **Clara Wieck** (German, 1819–96), an infant prodigy pianist was brought up strictly in a musical family by a father whose ambition for her – and his own enrichment – was strong. At the age of nine she gave her first concert performance and soon developed an unusual talent for those days of playing Mozart concertos from memory (a skill which she did not always practice later on). Her father, recognising her earning power as she developed into one of the finest pianists of her day, furiously resisted any suggestion of marriage to Robert Schumann, himself an excellent pianist and a rising composer of genius. Schumann claimed that the vivacious Clara Wieck was the only pianist in Germany who played his works as he wished, but it took more than flattery to turn the head of his intended wife. For although she returned his affection and dismissed her father's demands, she insisted that Schumann must find the means to support her. By persuasion that amounted almost to coercion she helped lift the standard and scope of his compositions, a pressure that led to his most inspired writing and which she maintained after their marriage (an event which took place in 1840 after a prolonged family wrangle and a court action setting aside her father's objections that Schumann was a drunkard). Yet Schumann was unstable and the marriage proved tumultuous – a whirl of concert tours between the bearing of seven children and the creation of ever-more ambitious musical works torn from her husband. He, jealously infuriated by the tag as 'the great pianist's husband', fell into depression, turned to drink and frequently threatened to commit suicide, particularly when they were kept apart during her concert tours.

Jenny Lind

And yet this jealousy, staunched by her constructive criticism, spurred him to greater endeavours and led him also to start conducting. Without her it is unlikely that he would have reached such heights and after his death in 1856, she redoubled in loyalty by giving up composing (she had 23 opuses to her credit including a piano concerto) in order to promote his music and that of Beethoven through a succession of highly successful concert tours. Brahms now became the principal recipient of her insistent encouragement, although perhaps he resisted it a little more strongly than her late husband, though glad enough of her support in the confrontations with Wagner's band of critics. To the last she was a teacher, both formally and by the nature of her influence upon the main European musical circle which radiated round her.

Extended tours by a great many concert artists became common in the 19th century. For example:

Jenny Lind (Swedish, 1820–87) who was said to be one of the most celebrated soprano's of all time, made her début in her native Stockholm in 1838 and then toured widely throughout Europe and the USA, where her promoter was P. Barnum of circus fame. Frail and unprepossessing to look at, it was when she sang that she seemed to 'light up' – her voice had an outstanding range between 'G' and 'E', that was pure and controlled. People jammed the streets outside her residence in London, calling upon her to sing. Three times they were without a quorum at the House of Commons because Members flocked to hear her at the opera. She lived finally in England and taught at the Royal College of Music, London. Of her voice Clara Schumann wrote that it was not large '. . . for it is all soul'.

Clara Novello (British, 1818–1908), rated by Grove as one of the greatest and most professional of British sopranos, was quite as well known as Jenny Lind and also drew large audiences in tours of Europe. Using her mother **Mary Novello** (British, d 1854), as business manager (the first organiser of celebrity concerts) she frequently sang at the opening of public buildings including that of the Crystal Palace in 1854.

As composers women have usually been more prolific in sheer output than memorable in quality. **Fanny Crosby** (American, 1820–1915) who was blinded in childhood, taught for 11 years in the New York Institute for the Blind and married one of her pupils, a blind musician. Though she did not begin writing hymns until 1864, she then wrote continuously, turning out about 8000 of which *Safe in the Arms of Jesus* is the best known. But women did figure among the musical best-sellers. **Thekla Badarzewska** (Polish, 1834–61) wrote *The Maiden's Prayer* which was still selling at more than 10 000 sheet copies per annum in the 1920s. Of her the *Oxford Companion to Music* remarks that she 'provided the piano of absolutely every tasteless sentimental person in the so-called civilised world with a piece of music which that person, however unaccomplished in a dull technical sense, could play'. The fact remains that even composers have to live and no sooner was it apparent that 'popular' music (like popular literature) could give a woman financial independence, then more turned to make money that way. For example **Elizabeth Stirling** (British, 1819–95) a fine organist, particularly strong in pedal work, did much to bring the music of Bach to the attention of London audiences and she wrote many fugues and songs including one 'best-seller' – *All among the barley*.

But the demand for best-sellers depended on people to play them and an important contribution to their popularity in the USA was made by the pianist **Amy Fay** (American, 1844–1928) not so much because of her talent at the keyboard, which was competent, but through the publication in 1881 of letters she had written between 1869 and 1875 while studying music in Germany. The book ran into 21 editions and inspired some thousands of Americans (mostly women) to make the pilgrimage to Germany to learn music and thus stimulated the whole process of music making in homes.

The first women to compose large-scale classical music fairly prolifically were:

Alice Smith (British, 1839–84) whose numerous works included 5 cantatas, 2 symphonies, 2 concertos, 4 overtures, 7 quartets, a trio and many songs. The cantatas were written with immense feeling and her compositions in general were frequently played throughout her career even if they are practically forgotten now.

Augusta Holmès (French, 1847–1903), born in France but of Irish parentage, a musical prodigy who overcame her parents' objections in order to play the piano and sing in public. Eventually her studies were channelled into serious composition by Caesar Franck under whom her output both increased and improved, to the point at which she won important prizes and heard her work performed in preference to men's. She wrote symphonic works, operas (with her own libretto), songs and choruses in the grand manner – and was accorded typically sententious praise by Grove which refers to her better pieces as having 'masculine spirit'.

Amy Beach (American, 1867–1944), a good concert pianist whose theoretical musical education was limited to a single year's study of harmony. Nevertheless she was the first person in America to write a symphony of importance (the *Gaelic*) and composed 150 opuses (of which only 3 were never published) including a symphony and a piano concerto, plus a great many songs, many of them popular. Even more popular for songs was **Carrie Bond** (American, 1862–1946) who wrote sentimental pieces such as *I love you truly* and *A Perfect Day* – the latter selling 5 000 000 copies in 60 different arrangements, plus recordings, by 1925 – swiftly converting its composer into a rich woman.

At last, towards the end of the 19th century, the means to evaluate generations of performers were provided. We cannot be sure how **Katharina Klafsky** (Hungarian, 1855–96), who was renowned for her powerful rendering of Wagnerian roles (she was in the cast of the first *Tristan* in 1882) would have sounded by comparison with Jenny Lind or today's singers. Had she lived a little longer she might have recorded for the gramophone. For the first sound recording was made in 1877 when Thomas Edison recited *Mary had a Little Lamb* on to a cylinder and commercial recording arrived in the 1890s to bring music to the masses from the best singers and instrumentalists. With the early recordings voices reproduced themselves much better than instruments and so female singers with their higher pitch were, quite literally, first to make a good impression on discs and cylinders. In due course, the full range of musical composition entered people's homes, a process redoubled when commercial radio began in the 1920s.

Women were soon involved in record production. The first to be found in an educational department of a gramophone company was **Frances Clark** (American, 1860–1958) of the Victor Phonograph Company of the USA in 1911. As a keen protagonist of musical appreciation she used this opportunity to expand her activities to encompass a wider influence. But it was the singers whose talents were vital; pioneers in the recording studios such as **Adelina Patti** (Spanish, 1843–1919), whose coloratura soprano voice (one of the purest in the world) was past its best when she recorded; **Luisa Tetrazzini** (Italian, 1871–1940), a short rotund, prima donna in the grand style; **Nellie Melba** (Australian, 1861–1931), whose stage-name was based upon that of the city of her birth and who was first recorded in 1905; and **Clara Butt** (British, 1873–1936), the massive contralto, a fine singer of ballads and renowned for her rendering of *Abide with me*, and as the first British woman musician to receive the title 'Dame'. By making recordings these women became household names throughout the civilised world in a way totally unknown before. And their finances greatly increased, the richest of them being **Amelita Galli-Curci** (Italian, 1889–1963) who received $3 000 000. A superb coloratura soprano, self-taught, she made her first important appearance when aged only 19, her last in 1936. With 28 operas in her repertoire she sang in all the important opera-houses and concert-halls, toured extensively and made many gramophone records.

Amelita Galli-Curci

It now became possible for women to make a far greater impact on music by widening their activities. **Wanda Landowska** (Polish, 1877–1959) the harpsichordist, made deep research into ancient music and, by her virtuosity on the harpsichord family of instruments, rescued them from obscurity. Besides being a very good teacher who founded a school of music in Paris, she also became a leading exponent of music by Bach and the Couperins and, in addition, inspired the writing of the first modern works for the harpsichord, herself composing numerous pieces of music besides writing influentially on ancient music.

Marjory Kennedy-Fraser (British, 1857–1930), an indefatigable collector of Scottish folk-songs, made an extensive study of Hebridean music and published her work for posterity in *Songs of the Hebrides*.

Mabel Daniels (American, 1878–1971), not only wrote romantic orchestral music (of which *Deep Forest* is perhaps best known), but explored the less used instruments, particularly the harp. Her *Songs for Elfland* was scored for soprano, women's chorus, flute, harp, strings and percussion – a combination which definitely suggests a distinct bias towards feminine players.

Of all the feminist musicians the most formidable and renowned was **Ethel Smyth** (British, 1858–1944), a general's daughter who fought

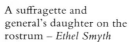

A suffragette and general's daughter on the rostrum – *Ethel Smyth*

mainly for two causes – music and women's emancipation. She studied in Leipzig and it was there, in 1884, where the first public performance of her music – a quartet – took place. Her Mass was performed in 1893 followed in 1901 by an opera *The Forest*. *The Wreckers*, her best-known opera, was performed at Leipzig in 1906 and repeated in Prague and in London in 1909 under Thomas Beecham. By now she was famous both as a composer and a suffragette – she composed the latters' marching song, *The March of the Women*, and in 1911 she spent two months in gaol as punishment for her militancy. But the Establishment forgave her, creating her 'Dame' in 1922. Grove praises her compositions by saying 'they were very masculine'. In 1916 she had written *The Boatswain's Mate* as a demonstration that women were as efficient as men – and she certainly endeavoured to prove it by the heartiness of her campaign for a British National Opera. In later life Ethel Smyth was to go deaf and turn to writing books – eight in all, plus a resounding autobiography in which her trenchant tweed-skirted personality stands out. By then she had composed 6 operas, 5 pieces for chorus with orchestra, 5 unaccompanied chorus, 7 orchestral works (including a concerto for horn), 3 songs with orchestra, 16 chamber works, 2 organ pieces and many solo songs, and throughout employed a wide range of instruments, including the harp and, in her opera *The Prison* appropriately, the bugle.

In a different key, almost literally, was **Nadia Boulanger** (French), a child prodigy who could read music fluently at 5 and who, by the age of 16, had won many musical prizes including a second in the Prix de Rome. As composer, conductor, pianist, organist and, particularly, teacher at the Ecole Normale and the Conservatoire, and then, in 1921, the Conservatoire Américain in Paris, she was outstanding. Mostly, however, her pupils were American – Lennox Berkeley, Piston, Virgil Thompson and Aaron Copland, but only one French student composer of note, Jean Francaix, passed through her hands and so she is not regarded with nearly the same adulation in France as in Britain and the USA. In 1937 she was the first woman to conduct the London Royal Philharmonic orchestra and in 1938 the US Boston, the New York Philharmonic and the Philadelphia orchestras. However, it is as yet too early to assess Nadia Boulanger's role in music for it remains to be seen if her pupils' compositions stand the test of time.

The rising popularity of music in a period of rapidly improving fidelity of sound on the gramophone and in broadcasting led to a far better educated appreciation of artistic qualities. More performers achieved fame, reaching peaks of excellence higher and more difficult to scale in face of immense competition. It may not be an exaggeration to say that a Golden Age was reached in the 1930s when faithful techniques of sound reproduction appeared. The period became starred by performers such as:

Elizabeth Schumann

Elizabeth Schumann (German, 1885–1952), who was rated one of the greatest *Lieder* singers as well as a supreme interpreter of Richard Strauss, who wrote specially for her. From the oldest records emerges a mystic quality in her voice unmatched by any of her successors. On stage she had a captivating charm. When the Nazis occupied Austria she left her native land.

Lotte Lehmann

Kirsten Flagstad (Norwegian, 1895–1962) who is rated by many the greatest Wagnerian soprano of the 20th century. Hers was a voice which grew more powerful with the passing years as she improved to Wagnerian stature and acquired an aura which belongs only to the great. From 1958 to 1960 she was a founding Director of the Royal Norwegian Opera.

Myra Hess (British, 1890–1965), who was perhaps the most distinguished of British female pianists and made her début at the age of 17. She developed a wide-ranging repertoire in which, as a player of Schumann, she became celebrated. The deep affection felt for her by the British public was largely won by her lunchtime recitals at the National Gallery during the Second World War and in that connection she was a leader in the people's bourgeoning interest in live performances.

In a world packed with good specialists, versatility is much prized. **Lotte Lehmann** (German) a great Wagnerian who made her début in Hamburg, sang throughout the world, and as the Marschalin in Strauss's *Der Rosenkavalier*, was almost unmatched. An outstanding soprano with variety of talent, she went on singing professionally until she was 65, taught and produced opera, sculpted, painted, wrote ten books (including a novel) and dabbled in musical journalism. At 85 she was still vibrantly involved with life.

The earliest women's choirs and bands were probably those which performed at religious ceremonies and sang in convents and churches, though social prejudice often curtailed their activities. A change began to take place in the 1870s when women's music clubs began to be formed throughout the Western world. From these came musical groups, choirs and the brass bands which were to be found leading processions

Bessie Smith

by suffragettes. A landmark in the evolution of women's choruses goes to the credit of **Margarethe Dessoff** (German, 1874–1944) who took her choir to the USA in 1912 to make public appearances and where they were very impressive. From 1925 to 1935 she conducted in New York the Adesdi Choir whose 50 women only sang music which had been specially composed for female voices, her infectious example leading to women's choirs springing up everywhere and attracting large audiences. In the world of jazz and blues music, women have played no more important a part than in the realms of the classics. No great woman jazz composer stands alongside Gershwin, simply many singers whose performance, too frequently, depended upon the projection of personality and physique, and the help of a microphone and electronics rather than vocal excellence. Yet certain names are memorable for the impact they had in their day and the immense sales of gramophone records they made.

The first distinctive 'blues' singer was **Gertrude 'Ma' Rainey** (American, 1886–1939), but her successors – all negresses – are generally rated greater, above all:

Bessie Smith (American, 1894–1937) who made the first of approximately 160 released recordings in 1923 and became known as 'The Empress of the Blues'. With a voice that carried the power of emotional conviction, she provided the essence of 'blues' music even without the aid of electronics.

Billie Holiday (American, 1915–59), a prostitute who began singing in Harlem night-clubs in 1931, first recorded in 1933 and came into prominence in 1935 with what are now regarded as masterpiece recordings of jazz. Celebrated though she was, her technique depended much more upon phrasing than pure singing. There have been many imitators, among them the myriad pop-singers whose achievements are vast sales with scanty musical merit.

All-women bands are unusual, but, the longest-lasting professional women's dance band, led and managed by **Ivy Benson** (British), seems

Ivy Benson and her Band

Two Dagenham Girl Pipers

to have been going for about 40 years though its conductor is evasive on this point. It has a very strong brass section and plays in the tradition of the 'big' dance bands, but unlike its successful male competitors has never made a gramophone record – it did once get as far as a contract but the Musicians' Union called a strike and the recording company dropped the idea. Of course women have formed musicians' groups for centuries and today one of the best quartets in the world is the Russian all-women Prokofiev Quartet. Perhaps the most unusual, among the successful ones, has been the **Dagenham Girl Pipers** from England. Formed in 1932 by the Reverend Joseph Graves, a Canadian Congregationalist, they quickly mastered the Scottish pipes and at once attracted the attention of newspapers and newsreels. Overnight they became famous with their public performances, recordings and films and in 1933 turned professional, though the Congregational aspect of their foundation remained: each rehearsal began with a prayer and Bible reading. They were to tour widely and eventually become not only entirely female in composition but also in leadership and instruction when **Edith Turnbull** (British) became their Pipe-Major and thus the first woman Pipe-Major in the world. Perhaps their greatest achievement was that of convincing kilted Scottish audiences of their prowess with that difficult instrument, the bagpipes, and to dumbfound those who believed that only men could play them.

The second half of the 20th century has produced a flood of talented female musicians in nearly every department of the profession. For example:

As impresario there is **Lina Lalandi** (Greek), a harpsichordist and singer who organised the successful English Bach Festival.

As conductor **Kathleen Riddick** (British, d 1973) who formed and conducted the Riddick Orchestra and had also conducted the London Symphony Orchestra and the Surrey Philharmonic Society; **Emma Steiner** (American) who led the New York Anton Seidl Orchestra; **Veronica Dudarova** (Russian) who in 1961 took over the Moscow Symphony Orchestra as Artistic Director and Chief Conductor.

As instrumentalists the violinist **Ida Haendal** (Polish) who at nine was a gold medallist in the Warsaw Conservatoire, and of international repute were the French cellists **Ginette Neveu** (1919–49) and **Jacqueline du Pré** and the flautist **Elaine Shaffer** (American, 1926–73). The last, who toured extensively as a soloist three times to the USSR and, in all, to 26 different countries, sometimes had **Hephzibah Menuhin** (American), a distinguished pianist, as her partner in sonatas.

As singers the sopranos **Victoria de los Angeles** (Spanish), **Maria Callas** (Italian), **Rita Streich** (German), **Joan Sutherland** (Australian) and **Elizabeth Schwarzkopf** (German) and the contraltos **Marian Anderson** (American) and **Kathleen Ferrier** (British, 1912–1953) were supreme. Few singers have so entranced the public as Kathleen Ferrier for she avoided the antics sometimes associated with prima donnas and sang with simple sincerity and enlightened purity. Not until she was 28 did she begin singing seriously but in the ensuing 13 years was to develop quite astonishingly into a great contralto and a specialist in the work of Mahler. Her courage in continuing to perform even when cancer was well advanced set a wonderful example.

Thea Musgrave

As composers there are **Priaulx Rainier** (French) who came to the vocation at the age of 33; **Verdina Shlonsky** (Israeli) who has won the Béla Bartók Prize for a string quartet and has many orchestral and choral works to her credit in addition to children's songs; **Galina Ustovolskaya** (Russian) who has written for Russian films besides composing many orchestral works and concertos; and **Thea Musgrave** (British). The last is enjoying a vogue, but it is founded upon a fine musical education at the Paris Conservatoire, followed as Lecturer at the London University and the University of California. The first public performance of her opera *The Decision* was at Sadlers Wells in 1967. She has choral works and a concerto, *From one to another* which is for viola and electronic tape.

As women feel their way forward in the world of creative music, time alone will show if they are to achieve a dominant place throughout the world of music, to becoming top composers and impresarios in addition to holding pre-eminence as performers.

LIST OF WOMEN MUSICIANS NOT INCLUDED ELSEWHERE IN THIS SECTION

There are thousands of women singers and instrumentalists of whom only a few, such as those mentioned in this list, have achieved fame in their lifetime. Of composers there are very few and, again, only those of particular note are included in this list.

Licia Albanese (Italian). Soprano.

Anna Amalia, Prinzessin von Preussen (German 1723–87). Composer of military marches.

Gina Bachauer (Greek). Pianist.

Isobel Baillie (British). Soprano.

Janet Baker (British). Mezzo-soprano.

Theresa Berganza (Italian). Mezzo-soprano.

Monserrat Cabaille (Spanish). Soprano.

Harriet Cohen (British). Pianist.

Régine Crespin (French). Soprano.

Suzanne Danco (Belgian). Soprano.

Mabel Daniels (American, 1878–1971). Composer.

Jeanne-Marie-Madeleine Demessieux (French, 1921–71). Composer and organist.

Mattiwilda Dobbs (American). Soprano.

Shula Doniach (Russian). Pianist and composer.

E.T.P.A. – Ermelinda Talia Pastorella Arcadia – the Arcadian name of Antonia Amalia Walpurga, Princess of Saxony (fl.1760–70). Composer.

Joan Hammond (New Zealander). Soprano.

Imogen Holst (British). Composer, conductor and promoter of Gustav Holst's (her father) music.

Eileen Joyce (Australian). Pianist.

Sena Jurinac (Yugoslavian). Soprano.

Marguerite Long (French, 1874–1966). Pianist.

Maura Lympany (British). Pianist.

Elizabeth Maconchy (British). Composer.

Zinka Malinov (Yugoslavian). Soprano.

Birgit Nilsson (Swedish). Soprano.

Alexandra Pakhmutova (Russian). Composer.

Lily Pons (French). Soprano.

Erna Sack (German, d. 1972). Soprano.

Renata Scotto (Italian). Soprano.

Irmgard Seefried (German). Soprano.

Oda Slobodskaya (Russian, 1895–1970). Soprano.

Ebe Stignani (Italian). Mezzo-soprano.

Rita Streich (German). Soprano.

Germaine Tailleferre (French). Composer and pianist.

Phyllis Tate (British). Composer.

Renata Tebaldi (Italian). Soprano.

Jennie Tourel (Russian, 1910–73). Mezzo-soprano.

Helen Traubel (American, 1899–1972). Soprano.

Joan Trimble (Irish). Composer and piano duettist with sister **Valerie**.

Gioconda de Vito (Italian). Violinist.

Ljuba Welitsch (Bulgarian). Soprano.

Maude White (British, 1855–1937). Composer.

Stages are open spaces where dance, mime, songs and plays may be performed either in private or public for entertainment and relaxation. This type of entertainment, among the most ancient of arts, was delayed in producing historically identifiable personalities and, therefore, not surprisingly, women were even slower coming to the fore than men. They took no part in Greek theatre, for example, and those who went on the stage in Rome were rated as immoral, a sociological attitude which persisted for centuries. The Christian Church denied 'rights' to actors while the Far Eastern races more or less excluded theatrical people from 'respectable' society.

The earliest known actresses made their entrances in the late 16th century, after the Renaissance had begun to liberalise the other arts. Theatre companies (including ballet) were often family organisations whose players were usually related to actors or company managers, although it was common for female parts to be played by men. An Italian actor-author's wife, **Isabella Andreini** (Italian, 1562–1604) was the leading lady in the Gelosi Company and the most famous of the early recorded actresses. Her performances were greatly praised in many contemporary documents. She also produced seven children between acts, so to speak, as well as travelling from Italy to Paris with the company. The first French actress recorded by name was **Marie Venier** (French, fl 1590–1619), the daughter of an actor-manager. She, according to documents of her time, was beautiful and an accomplished actress, being at her best as a tragedy queen.

By then France was leading in theatrical practice and on the eve of its resurgence under Molière and Racine. A great French acting family of this period was that of **Béjart**, its women the most dynamic among them. **Madeliene Béjart** (1618–72) not only played leading roles but also helped to establish and, for a time, managed the finances of Molière's company. And **Armande Béjart** (1642–1700) who rumour declared was Molière's and Madéleine's own child, eventually married Molière for a brief and unsuccessful period and proved the best interpreter of his plays. Moreover she was to manage the company with such drive and acumen that in 1679 she could merge the Hôtel de Bourgogne's Company with her own. In so doing she obtained the collaboration of **Marie Champmeslé** (French, 1642–98), the creator of Racine's greatest parts as Iphigénie and Phèdre. Together they formed, by royal decree, the Comédie-Française and established French theatre as the force it remains to this day.

The first English actresses of note did not appear until the 1660s as the freer notions of the Restoration permitted them. Until then all women's parts were played by men. Of the company who played at Drury Lane Theatre **Nell Gwynn** (English, 1650–87) is the most famous because of her association with Charles II (see section on Mistresses and Courtesans), but **Mary Knepp** (English, d 1677) who was at her best in comedy, probably preceded her while **Anne Bracegirdle** (English, 1663?–1748) undoubtedly excelled her both as an actress, as a beauty and (for an actress) her quite astonishing virtue, and freedom from scandal. The last attribute cannot also be accorded to **Elizabeth Barry** (English, 1658–1713), graded by *The Oxford Companion to the Theatre* as 'the first really outstanding English actress' who created over a hundred famous roles and was heavily tainted by scandal. English actresses also toured and **Mary Stagg** (English), of whom little is known except that she and her husband ran a theatre in Williamsburg in 1716 and she gave dancing lessons, became in the 18th century, the first known actress in what was to be the USA.

Carolina Neuber

One of the earliest recorded German actress-managers was **Carolina Neuber** (German, 1697–1760) who ran away from home to join the theatre and learnt her art with a travelling company. Under Johann Gottsched's direction she played almost as often in 'breeches' as in female dress – a quite common practice once women were generally admitted to the stage – and together they raised the standards of acting and presentation throughout Germany. Good taste, discipline and meticulous learning of parts replaced the haphazard anarchy of rough improvisation. But whereas Gottsched preferred to present plays which the public wanted and from which he could earn a living, Carolina Neuber was in favour of breaking new ground. In 1739 they parted, she to raise her own company staging advanced ideas of her own, the pair of them to indulge in a campaign of vilification of each other. Misfortune dogged the Neuber Company; it had few profitable successes and failed in 1760. She died in poverty and was denied burial in holy ground.

Ballet in its modern form first found expression in Italy, as the natural decendant of medieval mime, and was introduced lavishly into France in 1581 by **Catherine de Médicis** (see section on Statecraft and Politics). For the next century ballet developed mainly in the courts of Europe and found its strongest expression in France under the auspices of Louis XIV and his mistresses (see section on Mistresses and Courtesans) in parallel with the advance of the theatre. However, the dancers were hampered by ponderous, full-length skirts and ordinary shoes and it was not until professionals replaced the court amateurs that striking innovations were made.

Marie Camargo (Belgian, 1710–70) performed from the age of 16 with the Paris Opéra, and using the experience gained by dancing in 78 different ballets and operas, created greater freedom of movement by shortening her skirts, to expose the ankles and discarded the slipper's heel. Then she could execute the steps previously only performed by men – the *entrechât* and the *cabriole*. In so doing she gave women in ballet, with their lightness of charm, an advantage over men – a position they have virtually held ever since. Her contemporary, **Marie Sallé** (French, 1710–56), celebrated both in England and France, also made innovations by dispensing altogether with full skirts and the almost compulsory mask, and applying a far stricter discipline in the integration of music with theme and movement, becoming, in fact, the first woman choreographer and a leader too. In this art women were constantly finding new methods of self-expression. **Anne Heinel** (German, 1752–1808), who joined the Paris Opéra in 1768, developed the *pirouette*, demonstrating how a reduction in the weight of clothing gave a freedom to dancing, while a further advance in ballet technique came from **Marie Taglioni** (Italian, 1804–84) who was the first to use *les pointes* (toe-dancing with special shoes) and turn, with genius, the ideas of the preceding century into classical ballet as it is now known.

Marie Camargo

Opera, theatre and ballet, of course, were closely intermingled. Among the most ambitious actresses of the Comédie-Française was **Claire Clairon** (French, 1723–1803), a child actress who later turned to opera and then reverted to the stage as understudy to another fine actress, **Marie Dangeville** (French, 1714–96). For her début in a leading role Claire Clairon chose the most difficult part possible – that of Racine's Phèdre – and accomplished it brilliantly. As she meticulously learned her parts and improved her stage technique, she also introduced into the theatre a touch of historical authenticity with her choice of costumes. In retirement she passed on her knowledge by publishing *Mémoires et réflexions sur l'art dramatique* in 1799 and by giving lessons. Another 18th-century actress was beautiful **Peg Woffington** (British, c 1714–60) who began acting in her native Dublin and came to dominate the stage both there and later in Drury Lane. She took humorous female parts and also defied competition for her portrayals of men. At the age of 22 she was a star; at 28 playing opposite David Garrick. An extremely spirited woman with many lovers, no man was allowed to dictate her career, and after three years of Garrick, both on stage and in bed, she struck out on her own, being popular with all – except her fellow actresses to whom her good nature did not extend. She was the only woman to be admitted to membership of the exclusive all-male Beef-steak Club.

Sarah Siddons

Sarah Siddons (British, 1755–1831) the child of an actor-manager made her first recorded appearance on stage at the age of 12 though she undoubtedly walked the boards long before that. In 1775 Garrick invited her to play in his company at Drury Lane, but her unsure first appearance on 29 December, portraying Portia, was a failure. The critics hammered her and continued to do so. She returned to the provinces to perfect her technique.

In Bath, the centre of fashion and 'the Second Capital' of England, Sarah Siddons became queen of the Theatre Royal and this was the base for her travels to theatres elsewhere until, in 1780, Richard Sheridan, who replaced Garrick, asked her to play once more at Drury Lane. She finally accepted the invitation in 1782 and in October reappeared in London as Isabella in *The Fatal Marriage*. Despite stage-fright she took the audience by storm and from that day was acclaimed a tragic actress without equal.

Horace Walpole described her as of '. . . good figure, handsome enough, though neither nose nor chin according to the Greek standard. . . . Her hair is either red, or she has no objection to it being thought so, and had used red powder. Her voice is clear and good . . . her action is proper, but with little variety.' But she obviously impressed and in 1783 became elocutionist to the royal children in addition to her acting. Tragic roles were her forte and, with her dignified figure, she mesmerised packed houses as 'the greatest tragic actress'.

Sarah Siddons retired in 1812: at a memorable 'final' performance as Lady Macbeth, it was decided to stop the play after the sleep-walking scene, the audience being so moved. This was not the end, of course. Most great performers reappear after retirement, but the magic had departed. Gradually she was allowed to fade away.

'One of the greatest actresses France, or perhaps the world, has ever known' is the way *The Oxford Companion to the Theatre* assesses **Elisa**

Rachel (French, 1820–58) though this kind of eulogy is hard to substantiate at a distance in time. She benefited, of course, from the more sophisticated plays which were performed before better-educated audiences but it was in classical roles that she excelled. Her acting tours took her as far as Russia, in the East and America in the West. Overwork, aggravating her TB condition, caused her death.

Women behind the scenes have made some of the greatest contributions though, strangely enough, despite their impact on literature famous women playwrights are in short supply. **Aphra Behn** (see section on Literature) wrote *The Forced Marriage* in 1670 but a later woman playwright of note, **Hannah Cowley** (British, 1743–1809), contributed freshness to the stage with her first comedy *The Runaway*. Presented at Covent Garden in 1776, her comedies were among the first to be performed in America. *The Belle's Strategum* was last performed in London in 1913.

Also among important off-stage women, **Laura Keene** (British, *c* 1820–73) and **Catherine Forrest** (British, 1817–91), became the first two important actress-managers in America. Catherine Forrest undertook this dual career at the Metropolitan Theatre in San Francisco in 1853 and Laura Keene opened her own playhouse in New York in 1856. The latter's beautifully decorated theatre with its white and gold décor and gold damask upholstery housed a long run with *Our American Cousin* which, in addition to Laura Keene's policy of using American talent, established New York as the theatre centre of America.

Later came **Jessie Bonstelle** (American, 1872–1932) who was managing the Shubert's theatre in Syracuse when she was 19. After similar ventures in America and Canada she purchased the Playhouse in Detroit and was, in 1928, eventually able to make it one of her country's first Civic Playhouses. She also spotted and helped American actors and actresses of talent, for example **Katharine Cornell** (American, 1898–1974).

Annie Horniman (British, 1860–1937) was the vital impetus behind the British Repertory Theatre. She rebuilt the Abbey Theatre, Dublin and in 1903 opened it as the Repertory Theatre of Ireland, letting the Irish Players use it without cost for six years. It became a famous school for actors where new plays could be tried without a constant eye on the box-office. In 1908 she established at Manchester the first repertory theatre in Great Britain and with the fine group of actors who were drawn to her put on some 200 plays – over half of which were new. She also materially assisted repertory ventures in other British towns. Complementary to this, **Elsie Fogerty** (British, 1866–1945) with a dedication to elocution, founded the Central School of Speech Training and Dramatic Art – an organisation which has produced many fine actors and actresses, besides better public speakers. She was also one of those responsible for setting up the British Drama League.

Bestriding the period in which the cinema came into being alongside the traditional stage, was **Sarah Bernhardt** (French, 1844–1923). The illegitimate daughter of a Dutch Jewess by a well-educated young Frenchman (who settled a dowry of 100000 francs on her) she was educated in a convent and then entered the Comédie-Française in 1862

Sarah Bernhardt

where her potential as an actress was at once recognised and prematurely rewarded with the difficult title-part in Racine's *Iphigénie*. Suffering from lack of experience and appalling stage-fright she failed and for the next few years was relegated to smaller parts. With incredible industry and all-consuming dedication she mastered her profession and acquired an immense self-confidence which, when added to her faultless elocution and 'golden voice', could only lead to eventual success in costumed roles in the grand manner. Yet not until 1869 did she make her first big hit as the page in *Le Passant* (at various times she was to play 25 male parts) and then, almost at once, there came a standstill caused by the Franco-Prussian War in 1870. Moving into Paris shortly before the siege she organised a field hospital and dedicated herself to nursing the wounded both throughout the siege and during the dangerous days of the Commune.

In the aftermath of the war her career blossomed, reaching its peak of attainment in 1874 with her performance as Racine's Phèdre. As a star 'Divine Sarah' picked her parts carefully and, upon leaving the Comédie-Française in 1880 to form her own company, also chose her leading actors, some of whom joined the corps of lovers that studded her career. The birth of an illegitimate son by the Prince Henri de Ligne in 1864 she had taken in her stride, but her marriage to Jacques Damala in 1882 was a ghastly failure that ended in legal separation. In any case her relationship with people was almost invariably tumultuous, with brawls involving those fellow actresses and rivals who caught her ire. And while her salary was high (one US tour fetched in $194000), so too was her extravagance that generated repeated crises, compelling her always to work hard in order to support her high style of living.

In the art of self-publication she was supreme though denigrated by those, like Shaw, who preferred acting to be restricted to the stage. The famous parties for royalty, and the reception arranged for her in New York on the first of her eight rail tours in the 'Sarah Bernhardt Special' of the USA (three of them of the farewell type) were memorable as exercises in good management. To quote Henry James, she was too American not to succeed in America, but this versatile character also succeeded in England, South America, Australia and Egypt where she frequently appeared on tour. She persisted in playing the parts that suited her, took up sculpting at which she was outstandingly good, tried painting at which she was mediocre, went ballooning which was exciting as well as good publicity, and failed badly as a burlesque singer. As one of the first French film stars she was unhappy with the medium – 'those ridiculous photographed pantomimes' as she called them. But she made several in France (and thus we can still see her exaggerated gestures and declamations) and in *Queen Elizabeth* was the heroine in the first full-length film made in America, a box-office success even though she was a personal failure. She was a pioneer of the 'star system'.

Courage Sarah Bernhardt never lacked. After her right leg was amputated in 1915 she again toured the USA, clumsily stumping the boards. Short of money and, therefore, in harness to the end, the final collapse came on the eve of a dress-rehearsal a month before she died.

In the 19th century far more people went to see the circus – one of the most ancient forms of public entertainment – and music-hall, than any

Annie Oakley

AT REST

THE SERPENT DANCE

THE SPIRAL

Skirt Dancing
by *Loie Fuller*

other sort of theatrical display, and women were always to be found among the acts because circus acts have nearly always been family businesses. It is the sensational acts that are remembered – one such as that of **Madame Sequi** (French) who, in 1813, slid down a rope from 60 ft (18 m) enveloped in fireworks. Or the act of the sharpshooter of the circus, **Annie Oakley** (American, 1860–1926) of Buffalo Bill's Wild West Show. She once shot 100 out of 100 in trap shooting, could hit the edge of a playing-card at 30 metres (98 ft) and the end of a cigarette in her husband's mouth. Under 5 ft (1·5 m) tall, she was feminine and softly spoken off-stage, doing needlework between performances. Proudly she played before most of the crowned heads of the world and won an incomparable reputation in an act which bordered on vaudeville or music-hall. In fact **Loie Fuller**'s (American, 1862–1928) act was almost pure vaudeville even though, at one time, she worked for Buffalo Bill. She invented 'skirt dances' by twirling fine silk voluminous skirts while lit by changing coloured lights, which for her 'Fire Dance' came from below through plate-glass – an act once integrated with a performance of *Faust*. She was the first person to use luminous phosphorescent materials on a darkened stage and pioneered a more imaginative use of lighting for the theatre.

Stars who ruled the music-halls were known by their idiosyncrasies and the legs of the celebrated music-hall star, **Mistinguett** (French, 1875–1956), were the most highly insured in the entertainment world of her day. For some years she was also part-owner of the Moulin-Rouge where she entertained. On the British music-hall stage equally flamboyant personalities made their appearance – **Marie Lloyd** (British, 1870–1922), with her robust performances and strong character, took the fancy of the Press; **Florrie Forde** (Australian, 1876–1940) with her famous songs such as *Down at the Old Bull and Bush* and *Has Anybody Here Seen Kelly?* stormed audiences by downright force of hearty character. That the combination of lower musical drama and dance could ascend to affect profoundly the upper reaches of theatre, opera and ballet was frequently demonstrated by women. For example:

Ruth St Denis (American, 1877–1968), a vaudeville dancer, by chance came to study Oriental philosophy and dance routines with the result that she raised her technique to the height of ballet, an art which eventually assumed an idealistic religious direction. In 1906 she produced her Hindu ballet *Radha*, taking it on tour in Europe for three years and later, in the USA, she produced Egyptian and Japanese style ballet. In league with her husband she opened a dancing school which produced many well-known American dancers, including **Martha Graham**.

Lilian Baylis (British, 1874–1937) sang in music-hall, in South Africa in 1890 and for some years taught singing in Johannesburg – one of the first women to do so. But in 1898 she returned to England to help her aunt, **Emma Cons** (British) (the first woman member of the London County Council) run the Royal Victoria Coffee Music Hall – giving temperance entertainment which entirely suited both women's religious ideals. Cinema was sometimes shown but Lilian's long-term aim was the presentation of popular music, opera and theatre. From 1914, under the name 'Old Vic', and with her as sole manager, seasons of Shakespeare were performed, gradually ousting opera. So in 1931, Lilian Baylis who was an enthusiast with the ability to enthuse others, raised enough money to expand the Old Vic into North London by taking over the old Sadler's Wells Theatre site, building a new theatre and starting what amounted to a company devoted to opera and ballet. This has blossomed into a national organisation very much on the initiative of one of Lilian's closest collaborators, **Ninette de Valois** (see below). As a complement to the promotional work of Lilian Baylis there was the instruction given by **Italia Conti** (British, 1874–1946) who began acting in repertory but who found a vocation when, in 1911, she was asked to train children for *Where the Rainbow Ends*. This venture virtually founded her Theatre School which over the years trained Noël Coward, **Gertrude Lawrence** (British, 1898–1952) and Anton Dolin.

New dancing styles, however, came not only from the classical ballet, which systematically built upon well-founded techniques, but from women who yearned for freer expression and rejected the rigorous classical routines. The leading performer of new styles was **Isadora Duncan** (American, 1878–1927) who adopted natural movements to symphonic music while dancing barefoot, clad in flowing Grecian robes. Her reception during a European tour, beginning in 1902, was mixed. Paris was enthusiastic and subsequently people in the other capitals began to take her seriously, though many critics rated her eccentric. But to the Russian, Fokine, she was the inspiration which led to the revolution in classical ballet brought about by Diaghilev's Ballets-Russes in 1909. Isadora Duncan was somewhat accident prone. Frequently short of money to finance her fervid efforts to spread the art of dancing among the young, she moved from crisis to crisis. Her two illegitimate children were drowned in 1913; her marriage in 1922 to a Russian poet broke down; finally she was strangled when her long scarf became entangled in the wheel of an open car. There have been many imitators of her art:

Margaret Morris (British) who first appeared on the British stage in 1899, aged eight, and who John Galsworthy helped to form a troupe of six child dancers. Later John Ferguson the artist (whom she was to marry) taught her painting as a way of recording her dance techniques. They started the Margaret Morris Club as a sort of salon (see section on Mistresses, Courtesans and Salonnières) – a club which, backed by an orthopædic surgeon, gradually adopted a remarkable health remedial purpose for cripples.

Agnes de Mille (American) the choreographer of modern dancing who was still teaching and dancing in her eighties.

The most influential classical ballerina of the early 20th century was **Anna Pavlova** (Russian 1882–1931), a member of the Russian Imperial Ballet. Though Fokine helped establish her fame with the *Dying Swan*, she fell out of accord with the Diaghilev Ballet's mood, of which she was its first ballerina, and struck out with a company of her own, inexhaustibly touring all the major countries and dominating each performance by a fierce determination to display her art at its best. Though she wore herself out, she built well for the future. Her successor in the Ballets-Russes was **Tamara Karsavina** (Russian) who, with Pavlova employed

Anna Pavlova

Ninette de Valois

English dancers and settled in England, thus strengthening the struggling ballet of that country. Meanwhile **Alexandra Danilova** (Russian), another product of the Russian Imperial Ballet and Ballets-Russes, performed the same service in the USA and the other countries she visited, while **Rina Nikova** (Russian) who entered Palestine in 1925 after training in the Moscow Grand Theatre, became both prima ballerina and choreographer of the Palestine Opera, founder of the first Israeli School of Ballet, founder of the Yemenite Ballet in 1933 and eventually Director of the Biblical and Folklore Ballet in Jerusalem.

Devotees of British ballet revere **Ninette de Valois** (Irish) who first danced in revue and opera before joining Diaghilev in 1923. Quite soon she began to excel as an organiser as well as a dancer, and from dancing for the Camargo Society, running her own school of dancing (which **Marie Rambert** (Polish) a colleague in the Diaghilev Ballet helped found) and producing ballet both in England and Eire, she moved to join Lilian Baylis in 1931 to train the corps de ballet of the new Sadler's Wells Theatre – and took with her the best of the Camargo Society. In the capacity of Director, gradually assumed, and Choreographer, urgently developed, she built up the company which became the Royal Ballet. More important, however, was her selection and training, with the aid of Frederick Ashton, of many fine artists and an authentic 'English Ballet', with a style of its own. This she did despite the ravages of a war which, in fact, provided a vitalising spark to her dedication. Meanwhile Marie Rambert continued to run a small company specialising in 'modern' ballet.

In America, perhaps the most important woman of the theatre was **Rachel Crothers** (American, 1878–1958). She explored almost every aspect of drama ranging from walk-on to lead parts, through playwright, management, production, star-maker, to philanthropist on behalf of the stage community. Underlying her approach was a fierce demand for feminine equality – the titles of her plays, of which for a period of 30 years there was one a year in production, speak for themselves: *A Man's World* – a study of double standards in morality and written in 1909; *He and She*; *As Husbands Go*; and *When Ladies Meet*, which took a look at women's psychology. Nevertheless she did not permit her feminist ideals to overcome the professionalism which made her a moving force in progressive theatre. She was responsible for sponsoring many famous actors and actresses including **Maxine Elliott** (American, 1868–1940), **Katharine Cornell** (American, 1898–1974) and **Gertrude Lawrence** (British 1898–1952). During the First World War she founded Stage Women's War Relief, in the Depression guided aid to down-and-out actors and actresses and, in the Second World War, was one of the movers behind the famous Stage Door Canteen.

Motion pictures which first appeared as commercial productions in 1894 initiated a revolution in entertainment and the first woman to appear in a screen entertainment was **May Irwin** (American) who shared a kiss with John Rice in 1896 and so scandalised parts of the audience that the first demands for screen censorship were submitted. The leading motion-picture industry at first was France's where Léon Gaumont began production in 1896 and whose secretary, **Alice Guy-Blaché** (French) he put in charge of the artistic side. By 1900 it was she who was running the entire production side of a concern which, by 1914, had become the biggest film studio in the world and was already experimenting with sound and colour.

The first women to appear in films were not stars, of course, but small-part actresses earning minute salaries. In America the first to receive a contract was **Florence Turner** (American, 1888–1946) who signed for the Vitagraph Company in October 1907 having already had a success in a previous short film. A starting salary in those days was $25 a week and mostly the girls were anonymous, Florence Turner being known, for example, as 'The Vitagraph Girl'. Not all the actresses had her ability or that of **Mabel Normand** (American, 1894–1930): few could speak well and a great many depended upon their pulchritude and the directors artistic skill and patience to pull them through – a system which persisted for generations and covered a morass of artistic incompetence. **Alma Taylor** (British, 1895–1974) who was the first British film star to become famous, began in 1907, appeared as a star in *David Copperfield* in 1913 and by 1915 topped a popularity poll two places above Charlie Chaplin. She could act, however, and although the advent of 'talkies' in the 1920s shortened her career, she was among those who made a few talkies with reasonable success and went on, in 1935, to be one of the first television actresses.

Naturally it was to the established 'great' actresses to whom the film companies turned as they found their feet and expanded their activities. Apart from Sarah Bernhardt (see above) there were several more of her calibre who made the plunge and ended with the same sense of disenchantment. **Alla Nazimova** (Russian, 1879–1945) had appeared on Broadway in 1905 and enchanted audiences by her acting and dancing (she was a superb interpreter of Ibsen), but although she made many successful films (the last in 1944) and in the 1920s could earn a salary of $13 000 a week, she never felt as happy on the screen as on the stage. It took a fresh generation to create a new breed of entertainer.

Of these the dominant woman of the motion-picture industry was **Mary Pickford** (Canadian) who first trod the stage at the age of five and began an acting career in roadshows that led to her first child-star part on Broadway. Beginning work for the cinema in 1909 as an extra for a salary of $5 a day she came under the direction of the celebrated D. W. Griffith, though by leaving the stage she was said to have 'tainted herself'. She went back until in 1912 when, again for Griffith, she took part in a film *The New York Hat*. After that she stayed with cinema and quickly built a reputation as a talented actress who 'lived her parts and knew her mind', one who refused to exaggerate, would not be 'directed' unless it suited her and who, ably advised by her mother, was a tough business-woman committed to making a fortune from the star system then beginning to evolve. Refusing to stay on contract to any particular studio and taking advantage of a swiftly growing popularity with audiences, she forced a sharp increase in her own salary which communicated itself in proportionate rises for all the other stars. Her child-star image went with her from stage to screen: little girl parts in such films as *Cinderella* in 1914, *A Poor Little Rich Girl* and *Rebecca of Sunnybrook Farm* followed

Mary Pickford

each other with implacable regularity until she rebelled in 1918 and played, with success, dual parts in the tragedy *Stella Maris*. After that she mixed light roles with serious ones, but in the meantime, as a rich woman with command of almost any salary she cared to name, she had, in 1916, formed the Mary Pickford Film Corporation. In 1919, in company with Griffith, Charlie Chaplin and Douglas Fairbanks (who was to be her second husband) she formed United Artists. At this time she was earning $1 000 000 a year and working incredibly hard, 15 hours or more a day, acting in the films she directed besides running, in detail, the company she had formed. For Mary Pickford was much more than a star: she was mistress of every detail of the cinema industry, and a superb spotter of talent too.

By 1932, among the richest self-made women in the USA (her fortune has been guessed at $50 000 000), she had made more than 200 silent films and 4 talkies. Though the successes continued to be mainly the little girl sort that had made her 'the World's Sweetheart', in talkies she did not do so well. She decided to retire 'while I am at my peak', but also because the fans were turning away from the older woman, and busied herself with a vast variety of business enterprises and charity ventures, though making one more talkie, *Coquette*, in 1935. She continued to hold an interest in United Artists until 1956, sold War Bonds in a big way and wrote four books, mostly of an autobiographical nature, and now lives the life of a recluse.

The advent of talking films brought a new challenge to the cinema world. The first woman to play in a 'talkie' scene of a full-length film was **Eugenie Besserer** (American) with Al Jolson in the first partial talkie, *The Jazz Singer*, in 1927. Many of the actresses did not have good speaking voices. There were strong doubts if **Greta Garbo** (Swedish) with her husky voice could make the transition, but in fact she was among the few 'greats' who did so triumphantly with *Anna Christie*, made in Hollywood in 1930. Greta Garbo, however, who had made her first silent in Sweden in 1922, had received proper dramatic training in Stockholm and had real talent and genuine personality besides beauty. She did things before the camera which directors could not improve upon, and at one time earned $300 000 for a picture.

Perhaps the most talented woman film producer and editor (of whom there are very few) was **Leni Riefenstahl** (German) who began her career as a dancer, took her first star part in *The White Hell of Pitz Palü*, in 1929, brilliantly directed *The Blue Light* in 1932 and then came to notoriety as the result of writing and producing *Triumph of the Will* – the record of the Nazi Nürnberg Rally of 1933. With the encouragement of Hitler and despite the hostility of Goebbels, the Nazi Propaganda Minister, she engineered a masterpiece even if it was long-winded and repugnant to those who hated Naziism and was to cause her persecution after the Second World War. With *Olympiad* in 1936 she confirmed her ascendancy with what is still the finest film record of an Olympic Games.

The second largest film industry in the world grew up in India after 1912, but there the actresses were inhibited because they would be 'publicly branded'. Only prostitutes played on the stage and kissing, then as now, was forbidden. The first to break down prejudice was **Kamala** (Indian) followed in 1919 by **Mrinalini** (Indian), the daughter of a pioneer producer, D. Phalke. Mostly Anglo-Indian girls came forward, such as **Effie Hippolet** who took the name **Indira Devi**. But when 'talkies' arrived the best speaking voices came from highly educated women and so the first Indian woman film star of royal blood – **Zubeida**, daughter of the Muslim Nawab of Sachien – made her début aged 12 and was later joined by two sisters and her mother, Begum **Fatima**, who became India's first female film director.

The most versatile of early Indian film actresses was **Devika Rani Chaudhury** the daughter of a senior army surgeon. She trained as an actress in London and married a struggling director. Together, in 1930, they made India's first talkie *Karma* – in both English and Hindi. Devika Rani went on to found Bombay Talkies Ltd in 1934 but, far more important, opened a way for Indian women's emancipation. Female stars would soon be socially equal to statesmen of world renown.

A paradox of Indian women's status was revealed within the embryo film industry. They were divided into three categories and paid accordingly.

Classification	Daily Wage	Type of Part played
Ordinary girl	Rupees 5	Crowd scenes and the like
Decent girl Class C–A	Rupees 10–20	Middle-class scenes
Super-decent girl	Rupees 25–40	High Society scenes

Nevertheless, even the lowest rate was higher than that payed to servants in the 1930s. By the 1940s stars earned scores of thousands of rupees per film. In 1973 a top star might receive as much as Rs 600000 per film and make six a year.

In Japan films were first produced about 1920 and suffered, as did those in India, because women's parts were played by men. Nevertheless the first female film stars appeared in a matter of a few months, one of them being **Sumiko Kurishima** and in due course **Kinuyo Tanaka**, a leading actress, became Japan's first woman film director.

The Russian film actresses followed the world-wide trends. For example, **Vera Kholodnaya** took to the cinema from ballet, **Sofiya Giatsintova** came to the stage via the Moscow Arts Theatre in 1911, playing in and producing Shakespeare and Ibsen and then went on to produce films of Ibsen – *Nora* and *A Month in the Country*. And **Marina Ladynina** who was at first a school-teacher, played as a variety artiste, a screen actress and as a serious actress with the Moscow Arts Theatre from 1933 to 1935, won no less than five Stalin Prizes. In more recent years **Maya Plisetskaya**, a member of the Bolshoi Theatre since 1943 who danced all the principal ballet roles, touring widely, in 1968 turned to films to play Princess Betsy in *Anna Karenina*. She is in fact the latest of the great Bolshoi ballerinas, a worthy successor to **Galina Ulanova**. The latter began to study at nine under her mother **Maria Romanova** (a ballerina herself) and eventually toured the world with the Bolshoi and became the winner of four Stalin Prizes plus the Order of Lenin.

Show business is an exacting profession which drains its members both physically and psychologically. Hours of work and travel are long. Radio and television (which readily accepted professionals from other mediums) increase the entertainment population and attract the stars of

Ulanova

Ingrid Bergman,
a talented star of stage,
cinema and television

stage and screen. The greatest of its 'greats' are those who fight to turn in consistently good performances throughout protracted careers, who develop and revitalise their art even as they grow older and who also contribute to the running and well-being of a profession which survives at the whim of the public. Ulanova was long-lasting and so has been **Margot Fonteyn** (British) the Sadler's Wells and Royal Ballet ballerina whose performances matured as she neared her fiftieth birthday and who continues to captivate her audiences. Among the staunchest fighters has been **Sheila van Damm** (British) who kept the London Windmill Theatre with its non-stop Revuedeville in business throughout the Second World War despite the bombing, and only succumbed to quite irresistible financial pressures when forced to close down. She made her name, too, as a motor rally driver.

Ethel Waters (American), the negro woman who endured terrible poverty as a child, was compelled to marry at 12 and yet by 17 was making a living on stage to become the first woman to sing *St Louis Blues*. From downtown night-club singer she advanced as star in the most fashionable clubs of New York and was famous for *Dinah* and *Stormy Weather*. At the same time she moved into all-negro revue in 1927, and this finally led her to a complete transformation when she undertook drama on stage and cinema in *Cabin in the Sky* in 1940 and 1943 respectively, thrilling her audiences with an unsuspected artistic intuition. Yet Ethel Waters has drunk deeply of life and was readily involved in the struggle for equality, be it racial, sexual or within her profession. In the racially orientated film *Pinky* she underlined her militant work for the Negro Actors' Guild and Actors' Equity.

The popular queens of stage and screen continue to be the stars who regularly thrive upon glorification – with or without outstanding ability. The creative women of show business are those who combine acting talent with the personality and taste to present the stars in acceptable style to the public while achieving advances in the state of the art. Few among directors and managers have done more in this respect than **Joan Littlewood** (British) who has founded three experimental theatre groups in her career, including the well-known Theatre Workshop in 1945. A BBC producer in the Second World War, she later toured extensively and began investigations into the integration of song and dance with drama. Moreover these experiments found approval with audiences – *A Taste of Honey* (by **Shelagh Delaney** (British)), *Fings Ain't Wot They Used T'be* and *Oh What a Lovely War* have won international showing.

The discovery of new places is a common concept of the aim of exploration. Hence the names of famous European explorers are chiefly associated with travel. The feats of those who, since the 18th century, searched deep and at great personal risk into the hinterlands of Africa, South America and the Arctic and Antarctic overshadow the less-renowned deeds of those who regarded exploration as a scientific examination of a limitless range of geographic and ecological subjects. Humility suggests, however, that what might seem to be a dramatic find by one person in what was, to him, unknown territory could merely be recognition of the local inhabitants' everyday scene. Discoveries are not the sole prerogative of white people. In this sense, therefore, many publicity-conscious explorers whose achievements are measured by long journeys in dark countries and little in the way of scientific record, contributed negligible information compared with the dedicated people methodically collecting information.

So, though women played only a small part in the Grand Explorations such as thrilled the world in the 19th and early 20th centuries, their contribution to systematic study has been none the less important as this section and that on Science and Medicine show.

Objective analysis after careful observation is vital. A Spanish nun **Etheria** (or **Aetheria**) journeyed through the Middle East, towards the end of the 4th century, recording detailed descriptions of the year's daily liturgical activities in Jerusalem, especially of the re-enactment on location of the Palm Sunday procession and other events during Holy Week leading up to Easter Day – a practice new to her. Her writings have shown scholars that the impetus to change the widespread Christian

way of merely fasting for a week before Easter into symbolic enact-
ments actually emanated from Jerusalem itself. But it was not until
much later that women became involved in scientific work in its modern
sense. **Maria Graham** (British, 1785–1843), on becoming widowed
during a voyage to Chile in 1822, spent a year there investigating
the country and keeping a journal of her findings that is considered
one of the most valuable records of this period in the history of the
developing republic. She was present when Valparaiso was largely
destroyed by earthquakes and timed, recorded and noted their
symptoms. In addition she brought back to England many plant seeds
and roots which she had collected.

Botany, being among the earliest scientific subjects taught to women,
stimulated them to wider as well as closer examination of specimens.
Marianne North (British, 1830–90), discovered plants and painted or
drew them in a scientifically, extremely accurate manner while journeying in Syria, on the Nile, in Sicily, North America, in the West Indies
and Brazil, in Japan, Borneo, Java, Singapore, Sri Lanka and India.
She painted hundreds of pictures, preferring to dedicate herself to this
work in solitude in jungle huts rather than be fêted by the local hierarchy.
Then she paid for the building of a gallery at Kew Botanical Gardens
that was opened in 1882 and still contains about 800 of her works.
One previously unknown tree she had drawn, the Capucin, was subsequently named 'Northea' after her and she is also commemorated by
the *Crinum northianum*, the *Kniphofia northiana* and the *Nepenthes
northiana*. But in the 19th century many people seemed to travel more
for the sake of doing so. The first female Fellow of the Royal Geographical Society, **Isabella Bishop** (British, 1831–1904) journeyed
extensively in Australia, western USA, Persia, China, Malaysia, Indo-
China, Turkey, Korea, Hawaii, India, Kashmir, Japan, Manchuria and
Morocco, climbing volcanoes and mountains, crossing deserts, wading
swamps and hacking her way through jungle. To pay her way she took
jobs as a cowboy, a missionary and a cook. Usually she travelled alone.
But dramatically staunch though her determination was it cannot be
claimed that she contributed much else in the way of achievement.

For sheer endurance **Florence Baker**'s (Hungarian, *c* 1836–1916) life
must take some beating, however. At seventeen years, as she was about
to be sold to a Turk by her ex-nurse, the renowned explorer, Samuel
Baker, bought and took her as his wife on all his major travels. They
searched for the source of the Nile and had been given up for dead when,
after many harrowing hardships, they finally regained contact with
civilisation to give details of one of the sources of the Nile – Lake Albert.
And when he returned to the Equatorial regions of the Nile, and was
given command of a military expedition to stop slave-trading, she still
remained his constant companion and partner throughout many
dangerous excursions. They later visited India, Japan and America.

It is easy, of course, to be mesmerised by the exploits of the well-
advertised explorers such as **Fanny Workman** (American, 1859–1925)
and forget that a great many of the women who accompanied their
families into the colonial territories opened up by European peoples
were genuine explorers. For example the first settlers in the USA, and
several of those who accompanied the frontiersmen probing westward

over the succeeding centuries in the van of the great emigrations to come, were often explorers in the purest sense of the word. Nevertheless Fanny Workman and her husband catch the eye for having organised extended expeditions to the Middle East and India in the 1890s and for climbing Himalayan mountains. They made sure of recognition by lecturing and publishing five well-documented books as records of achievement, claiming among other things a woman's record height at that time of 23 300 ft (7101 m) on one of the Nun Kun peaks in 1906. Moreover it was she who mostly contributed the main scientific data and she who seems to have driven hardest in going to places where white women had not been before, combating, thereby, the 'sex antagonism' of male scientists and mountaineers whom she claimed to detest and abhor.

The search for botanical subjects continued to drive many women to explore. Studies compiled in central Asia, the Crimea, Urals, Caucasus and Pamirs by **Olga Fedchenko** (Russian, 1845–1921) are standard to this day.

Supreme among explorers are those who looked for scientific rewards and of these **Mary Kingsley** (British, 1862–1900), the daughter of the anthropologist George Kingsley (a younger brother of the author Charles), was outstanding. Until aged 31 there was no question of her leaving England since she was compelled to look after her mother and brother. But her parents' death instigated her voyage to the Congo in 1893 in an endeavour to finish her father's work. Largely self-taught in the German language, besides scientific matters, she aimed to examine 'fish and fetish', as she put it, when describing her search for freshwater fish, native religion and law. She saw no reason to lower her personal standards while travelling, even though she entered appallingly squalid and dangerous parts. Dressed in black skirt, high-necked blouse and a tight-fitting hat, her principal weapon was an umbrella, her manner that of a Victorian matron out to Sunday afternoon tea. With inexhaustible industry and an insatiable quest for knowledge she survived by incredible luck as well as fortitude. While at sea she learnt navigation and cargo stowage and practised the former as pilot of a 2000 ton (2204 tonne) ship off the African coast. When she fell into a 15 ft (4·5 m) deep animal trap, with ebony spikes set in the bottom, she was saved from serious harm by the voluminous, tucked-up folds of her heavy skirt. Only a few of her many adventures found their way into her highly readable book, *Travels in West Africa*, published in 1897. The more hair-raising ones were omitted either because it was felt they might be too upsetting to the public at large – or simply because they would not be credited. For by then she was a celebrity.

In fact she had made a quick visit home in 1894 with enough fishes, beetles and insects to warrant a donation from the British Museum to buy an expensive collector's outfit and then dashed back to the Congo again, in 1895 to ascend the Ogowe River, thus entering totally unknown territory. Her aim was to study the Great Forest tribes, known to be ferocious cannibals, and she travelled as a trader to gain the people's confidence. To a certain measure her safety depended upon looking 'unusual', her subsistence was drawn from living off the country and among the people. This was itself perilous and could lead to strange hospitality. Once her hosts provided her with a hut containing some

Mary Kingsley

Evelyn Cheesman
in a Papuan forest

stinking bags which when emptied into her hat turned out to contain 'a human hand, three big toes, four eyes, two ears and other portions of the human frame'.

By the time she came home in 1895 she had drawn the firm conclusion that European culture should not be imposed on Africans and that good government must have a thorough understanding of the African religions, laws and customs. To this end she wrote *West African Studies* and advised and argued her case with people of influence, though gaining little more than greater public awareness of the problems. Unavoidably, therefore, she remained disillusioned by the attempts of the missionaries to alter the African moral standards and of the politicians and traders who exploited the natives, for she asked for understanding of primitive people from people whose limited understanding could not visualise the problem. Mary Kingsley found it impossible to return to Africa for another five years despite her yearning to do so: home ties, book-writing and public engagements prevented it. And tragically when at last she went back in 1900, to nurse Boer prisoners in South Africa, she contracted and died of the enteric fever from which her patients suffered.

Another woman who went alone among cannibals was the entomologist **Evelyn Cheesman** (British, 1881–1969) who spent much of her life studying and collecting tropical insects for scientific purposes. She visited the New Hebrides group of islands in the Pacific, the Melanesian islands to their north-east, the Marquesas Islands and the Galapagos Islands, and also spent a year in the interior of New Guinea where she collected 42000 insects plus such creatures as parasitic worms, leeches, reptiles, spiders, moths and molluscs for the British Museum.

She remained unharmed by the cannibals partly because, unknowingly, she had chosen as her first guide a boy who was supposed to be mad and had committed murder. The natives considered that her magic must be extraordinarily strong to withstand these bad spirits and also that her strange collections could only be the elements for powerful sorcery. So she was doubly assured of their respect, though extremely careful, too, to observe the taboos or superstitions of these Stone Age savages in order not to push her luck too far.

Because of an innate sense of sociology, in which connection she published many authoritative books prior to 1916, and a liking for travel **Elsie Parsons** (American, 1875–1941) mother of six, was led to study the American Indians as well as a miscellany of other American coloured races. This examination of people after 1915 led her from Massachusetts to Arizona and thence to New Mexico, Peru, Ecuador and the Caribbean. In addition to her sociological works, such as *The Old-Fashioned Woman* (an argument against sex-taboos published in 1913) she wrote reports on the Zuñi Indians, in 1915 and 1916, that were the forerunners of her numerous works resulting from ever-wider travels. From 1923 to 1925 she was President of the American Ethnological Society and, at the time of her death, President of the American Anthropological Association.

When the treasures of Egypt were being enthusiastically examined and (sometimes) looted by the world's collectors, the anthropologist **Winifred Blackman** (British, d 1950) instead spent 15 years travelling the country studying folklore from the ancient story-tellers and gaining the people's confidence by healing the sick with modern medicines. At the same time, however, she watched the magicians, their seances and healings. The latter were brought about generally by charms allied to drugs, specimens of which she sent to the Wellcome Historical Medical Museum in London where they were analysed and proved, in most cases, to be of use for the purpose prescribed. She also collected about 150 tattoo designs, some of which could be traced back to about 2000 BC and which were currently being worn as cures for ailments.

Arctic journeying, to explore and collect botanical specimens, was undertaken by **Isobel Hutchinson** (British, b 1889) who visited Greenland and Alaska to collect plants for the Herbarium at Kew, and to buy Eskimo crafts for the Cambridge Museum of Ethnology. She travelled from Nome, in the Seward Peninsula of Alaska, northwards round Cape Prince of Wales, round Point Hope, past Barrow and then by dog-sledge across the rough sea-ice and tundra back into Canada, buying from the Eskimos and collecting from the surprising variety of plants when she could.

Yet the longest walk by any woman may have been that taken by **Gertrude Benham** (British) who spent more than 30 years walking the world. In the course of her journey she climbed more than 300 peaks of 10 000 ft (3281 m) or over, visited Switzerland 17 times, made her first visit to the Canadian Rockies in 1904 and, in 1909 was the first woman to climb the 19 700 ft (5667 m) Kilimanjaro. In 1908 she tramped across South America from Valparaiso to Buenos Aires (the only time in her life she was robbed) and then in 1913 walked across Africa from west to east. Gertrude Benham travelled alone (using porters only when essential) to every part of the British Empire except Tristan da Cunha and some small islands. Seven times she went round the world. Never once carrying a firearm but always taking a Bible, a pocket Shakespeare, *Lorna Doone*, Kipling's *Kim* and her knitting, she accomplished her travels for under £250 a year! She shunned publicity and, therefore, avoided fame, but gave her collection of curios to Plymouth Museum.

Gertrude Benham

Alexandra David-Neel

The first white woman to visit the forbidden city of Lhasa in Tibet was **Alexandra David-Neel** (French). She studied Oriental philosophy and religions and in 1910 went to India to carry out Oriental research for the French Ministry of Education. Three years later she made short clandestine trips across into the forbidden Tibetan territory and also visited Burma, Japan, Korea, China and the Tibetan country under Chinese control that was open to foreigners. Everywhere she imbibed the mystic and philosophical teachings of the people and for two years lived the life of a hermit in a cave.

Her first clandestine visits to Tibet were intriguing and soon led to an abortive attempt at deep penetration. Finally, however, she reached Lhasa (staying there two months) by travelling for four months on foot in the grip of winter, disguised as the old Tibetan mother of her adopted son, Yongden, who accompanied her. By playing the role of the initiated wife of a lama-magician she gained respect and a measure of safety among poor people, but since they carried little with them they only narrowly escaped starvation and freezing to death. Alexandra David-Neel was made a Knight of the Legion of Honour, received a Gold

Medal from the Paris Geographical Society and the Dupleix Medal for Explorers.

With the coming of motor cars and aeroplanes, exploration (in the dramatic 19th-century sense) virtually came to an end. Field-studies became more specialised, systematic and scientific and, therefore, less eye-catching to the newspapers. On the other hand they began to demand increased resources and such great financial backing that the individual was forced to give way to group efforts supported by extensive mechanical aid – often with State assistance. Yet women still found their place in many adventures, some travelling by traditional means and others more exotically.

Freya Stark (British) travelled through the Lebanon and Syria on a donkey in 1927 and in 1929 explored the wild and remote parts of Persia, including the Assassin strongholds.

Myrtle Simpson (British) was one of a team of three who, in 1969, failed in an attempt to reach the North Pole but in the process, became, probably, the first woman to trek across the North Polar ice-cap. She has also taken part in experiments to fit 8 'days' of 21 hours each into an ordinary week in both Arctic and tropical conditions (in Spitzbergen and Surinam). When on trek with her husband, it is she who carries out the scientific research.

Valentina Tereshkova

Valentina Tereshkova (Russian) was the first and so far only woman to enter space, in 1963 (see section on Ships, Motor Vehicles and Flight) in what was converted into a supreme example of propaganda exploitation backed by the full resources of a State.

Ideally the true philosophy of exploration remains, as Freya Stark believes, in toleration; in accepting other people's beliefs as being as valid as one's own; in realising that basic values are common to all people, irrespective of creed or colour. Above all, without preconceived ideas, to give an unambiguous, accurate and concise assessment of discoveries.

19

WITH SHIPS, FLIGHT AND MOTOR VEHICLES

Whatever else men may sometimes say in denigration of women, only rarely do they accuse the opposite sex of cowardice. When the need has risen, women have invariably demonstrated their courage (how many men would cheerfully experience childbirth?) and have been to the forefront in indulging in new and potentially dangerous ventures. Though their names do not prolifically appear in the annals of seafaring, airmanship and motoring, they have travelled by those means since boats first sailed, balloons first rose into the sky and automotive vehicles first ran. Few women of note, however, have been directly responsible for designing and building ships, aircraft or motor cars and, therefore, in these spheres, where men have been and remain absolutely supreme, the sum of women's achievement is deeds of bravery, along with tasks of strict utilisation, in addition to those of exhibitionism.

WITH SHIPS

The apotheosis of feminine bravery at sea was performed on 7 October 1838 by **Grace Darling** (British, 1815–42) in rowing through heavy seas to rescue survivors of the steamship *Forfarshire* where it lay wrecked on the rocks near the Longstone Lighthouse, of which Mr Darling was Keeper. Grace Darling spotted survivors and with her father made one trip to the wreck, bringing back one woman and four men. Mr Darling then returned with two of the survivors to rescue four more men. At first close scrutiny was focused upon the scandal of the ship's unsea-worthiness and only later was Grace Darling exploited to deflect public anger. The news media, and those in search of a quick profit by painting this simple girl's picture and promoting her as a circus or music-hall act, applied fearful pressures which eventually broke her health. On the other hand **Ida Lewis** (American, 1842–1911), the daughter of the lighthouse-keeper at Lime Rock, Newport (and eventually the holder of that office herself) achieved far more – and was also more rugged. She rowed four men to safety sometime in 1858/9 after their boat had capsized and was responsible over a period of 48 years for saving something like 15 lives at sea. She was an immensely strong oarsman who, like Grace Darling, attracted enormous publicity – but in her case without fatal effect.

Ida Lewis

Rowing is not among the sports followed by many women (they did not form clubs until the early 1920s) and yet the first woman to be part of a small (20 ft (6 m)) boat crew crossing the Atlantic Ocean, **Joanna Crapo** (British) acted as an oarsman. The advent of fast motor-boats at the end of the 19th century instigated motor-boat racing – in those days sometimes called 'botoring' – and the first woman to distinguish herself as a botorer was **Dorothy Levitt** (British). In 1903 she won her first race at Cowes and demonstrated her Napier boat before the King. (See also under Motor Vehicles below.)

Superstition has often ruled against women as professional sailors (see however, sections on War and Crime) and so the first woman to become a sea-captain, **Anna Shchetinina** (Russian), has been a long time appearing. She applied for her ticket in 1928 at Vladivostok and went through the full curriculum of seafaring instruction. By 1935 she had qualified and was sent to Hamburg to take command of the diesel-ship *Chavicha*. On the eve of war in 1941 she entered the Navigation Department of the Leningrad Institute of Water Transport Engineers and since then has trained hundreds of sailors, becoming Head of the Department in due course. As a summer pastime she has sometimes captained voyages in ships crewed by her students, one such journey taking her round the world. Like the first seagoing woman radio officer, **Dallas Bradshaw** (Canadian), who qualified in 1970, she helps dispose of the old seamen's contention that women at sea are unlucky.

And like men there are women who sail the world single-handed – the first to cross the Atlantic being **Ann Davison** (British) in 1952/3, though she stopped off *en route* and, therefore, took 454 days from Plymouth to Miami in her 23 ft (7 m) *Felicity Ann*. The first woman to sail the Atlantic non-stop single-handed, travelling from east to west in the 33 ft (10 m) yacht *Aziz* in 44½ days, was **Nicolette Milnes-Walker** (British), a research psychologist who gave up her job to make the voyage in 1971. In her book she admits that the voyage was essentially selfish.

The Pacific Ocean has its female conquerors too, **Sharon Adam** (American) being the first woman to sail it single-handed in the 31 ft *Sea Harp*, taking 75 days in 1969, from Yokohama, Japan, to San Diego. While the first woman to cross in a rowing-boat (the 35 ft (10·6 m) *Britannia II*) was **Sylvia Cook** in company with John Fairfax. Their voyage from San Francisco to Hoyman Island lasted, with stops, from 26 April 1971 to 22 April 1972. At times, due to injury from a shark to John, it was Sylvia alone who was fit to row. They survived many perils.

FLIGHT

Madame Blanchard

The first woman to go aloft in a tethered balloon (a year after the first flight of all) was the **Marchioness de Montalembert** (French) on 20 May 1784, but it was Madame **Thible** (French) in company with Monsieur Fleurant who, a fortnight later, became the first woman to make a free flight, rising to 8500 ft (2789 m). At the end of June 1785 **Letitia Sage** (British) (weight 200 lb (94 kg)) went aloft in London and eventually descended near Harrow, none the worse for the adventure though one man was excluded from the original party because of her excessive weight. After this women were quite frequently involved with the publicity aspects of flying. The first to lose her life in an air crash, Madame **Blanchard** (French), had taken to ballooning as an escape from noise, but rather stretched her luck by giving a firework display while airborne in 1819. The balloon was filled with hydrogen! On the other hand, Madame **Gamerin** (French) made a practice of destroying her balloons in flight, escaping by parachute. But gradually women began to take the controls of aircraft; the first to pilot an airship solo was an actress, **Aida d'Acosta** (American), who flew the smallest Santos-Dumont ship (No. 9) a distance of half a mile in 1901. And after the first aeroplane achieved man-carrying, powered, sustained flight in December 1903 and the first woman flew in one, as a passenger – **Thérèse Peltier** (French) in 1908 – it was she who almost immediately became the first woman to fly solo – without qualifying as a pilot. That honour fell to another Frenchwoman, Madame **de Laroche** who received Pilot's Certificate No. 36 in 1910 and was killed in a crash in 1919. She lasted longer than a great many men and several women too. For example, in 1910 the first British woman to fly solo, **Viola Spencer**, who was also a professional parachute-jumper, never qualified as a pilot since she was killed while parachuting a few weeks later. Hence the first British woman to qualify as a pilot was **Hilda Hewlett**, who quickly became an instructor and taught her naval officer son to fly in 1911, thus becoming the first and possibly only woman to teach a naval airman how to fly – he being one of the first officers of the Naval Wing of the RFC. (For women's part in air warfare see section on War.)

They were a little slower in the USA. There the first woman to receive a

Pilot's Certificate, who also became the first woman, in 1912, to pilot an aeroplane across the English Channel, was **Harriet Quimby** (American). She learnt to fly in secret for fear it would interfere with her career and was more successful than **Julie Clark**, the first American woman to be killed in an aeroplane crash, who qualified in May 1912 and died a month later.

Soon women began making records. **Adrienne Bolland** (French) became the first woman pilot to cross the Andes (where the lowest peak is 14000 ft (4267 m)) in April 1919 employing an aeroplane with its single 80 hp engine from her joy-riding company in a journey that took seven hours. This feat demonstrated woman's ability to stand cold at high altitudes, also without access to additional oxygen supply, and yet practically coincided with a severe retrograde act by the International Commission for Air Navigation when it banned women from taking part in commercial aviation. The regulation for taking the commercial B Licence was drafted to stipulate that the pilot must be a male, this being the opening phrase in the paragraph dealing with physical qualifications. It cost Adrienne Bolland her licence and the money she had invested in her company. More than that it angered enthusiastic women aviators besides those politicians with declared approval for professional women. Fortunately the most forceful personality behind British and, indirectly, world's women's aviation was at this time **Sophia Heath** (British) (see also section on Sport), who as a pilot made it a primary aim to improve air safety and reliability. She fought in 1926 against the International Commission's ban and demonstrated women's capability by passing the necessary medical and aptitude tests (during her menstrual

Thérèse Peltier

period) and, by qualifying in navigation, meteorology, engine-fitting, rigging and the theory of flight, she convinced the doubters. Then, she attacked records, as the first woman to fly solo from South Africa to England between 12 February and 17 May 1928 and, for example, in a single day with six refuellings, taking off and landing at 50 different airfields and 17 'likely' landing-fields in England. Later, prior to suffering serious injury in a crash, she became, perhaps, the first woman airline pilot of all time, in the employ of Royal Dutch Airlines.

The greatest challenge in aviation during the post-First World War years was the conquest of the Atlantic Ocean, which was first flown non-stop by men in 1919. But thereafter many more men and women were to fail in the attempt. The British-born Princess **Anne Lowenstein-Wertheim** was lost in 1927 and **Elsie Mackay** in 1928. In 1927 **Ruth Elder** (American) – who had only just learnt to fly – was rescued from the sea when only 600 miles off the Irish coast. Each of these women was in company with a male pilot, as in 1928 was the first woman to fly the Atlantic, **Amelia Earhart** (American, 1898–1937) (see below).

Professionalism was the keynote to success in aviation, the first woman to fly 'blind', Lady **Bailey** (British, 1890–1960), in 1928, was also the first woman to make a return solo flight between England and Cape Town, though the outward flight took nearly two months and the return even longer since it incorporated an air tour of Africa. Already, flying was becoming a more accepted part of life. In 1930 United Airlines began the first coast to coast all-air passenger service across America and in May employed **Ellen Church** (American) a nurse, who had become the first stewardess in a flight from San Francisco to Cheyenne.

  The greatest British pioneer airwoman was **Amy Johnson** (1903–41), a BA in Economics. While earning only £1·50 a week as a typist she learnt to fly and, perhaps as important, how to service aircraft. Reluctantly her father backed her intention to become a commercial pilot, but in 1930 she persuaded a wealthy backer to sponsor an attempt to fly solo from England to Australia. In the event she took 17 days and, but for minor damage received in a forced landing, would have probably beaten the record. As it was she did beat the record from England to India. The desire to beat records spurred her on. In 1931 she flew in a light aircraft from London to Tokyo via Moscow in 80 hours; in 1932 she beat the record from London to the Cape (held by her husband) and then the record for the return journey. She was to remain in aviation until the Second World War, flying against time and in races and acquiring enormous expertise, but was lost at sea while ferrying an aeroplane.

But it was Amelia Earhart who became the greatest pioneering airwoman, though it was not until wartime nursing in Canada brought her into contact with pilots of the Royal Flying Corps that she sensed her purpose in life. Enthused by them she took a short course in engine mechanics in 1919 and the next year made her first flight. In 1921, after taking lessons from **Neta Snook** (one of the earliest American female pilots) she went solo. At first records were her aim too; the following year she beat the official woman's altitude record at 14 000 ft (4267 m)

Amy Johnson in Jason on the way to Australia

Amelia Earhart after her first Atlantic crossing

in a Kinner Canary and for the next six years alternated for work between a barn-storming pilot of Kinner aircraft and as a social worker. Fame – and there is no reason to think she at first sought it – passed her by until 1928, when she was selected, as much for her charm as her aviator's prowess, to accompany two men in an Atlantic crossing. During the 20 hour 40 minutes flight she merely kept the log – nevertheless she was the first woman to fly the Atlantic and overnight became a national figure.

Although Amelia Earhart's subsequent career became studded by adventurous endurance flights it must never be forgotten that the role she adopted was that of a genuine aviation pioneer, not a sensation-monger. If her participation in the first Women's Air Derby from Santa Monica to Cleveland was a publicity stunt in 1929, her long flights in autogiros helped pave the way for the helicopter. She felt that women ought to do the same aviation work as men and she wanted to make aviation safer. Her solo crossing of the Atlantic in 15 hours in 1932 – the first by a woman – demonstrated these things. It was her publisher husband, George Putnam, who publicised her adventures while she strove for improved airlines in her capacity as an officer of Luddington Airline. And after her first solo trans-Pacific flight from Honolulu to America in 18 hours 16 minutes and the first non-stop flight from Mexico City to Newark, N.J. in 1935, she took the post of Aeronautics Adviser to Purdue University.

It was Purdue which bought the Lockheed Electra monoplane in which Amelia Earhart and three men were to attempt a round the world flight as a test of mechanical and human reliability and endurance in 1937. The aircraft was referred to as a 'flying laboratory', its principal task to pioneer new air routes. In March a crash on take-off set the project back, but on 2 July, having already flown most of the route, the Electra ran out of fuel when it failed to locate Howland Island in mid-Pacific and was never seen again.

Record-breaking, nevertheless, spurred progress. **Jacqueline Cochrane**'s (American) life became absorbed by them. Moreover she had the skill and the charm to influence the all-essential backers for various expensive projects. With the support of industry and the Armed Services, for example, she was given the use, in 1938, of a Seversky fighter aircraft with which she won the Bendix Cup Air Race; in 1953 she was the first woman to fly through the sound barrier; and in April 1962, when 16 of her previous 33 records were still intact, put in a claim to the US National Aeronautics Association for 49 new records (the highest number ever claimed at once) for a series of point to point records in a flight by a four-engined Lockheed Jetstar from New Orleans to Germany. Finally, on 11 May 1964, she became the fastest woman pilot of an aeroplane with a speed of 1429 mph (2300 km/h).

During the Second World War, however, she had been placed in charge of a group of women pilots called the 'Women Auxiliary Service Pilots' (WASP). (Another such group for non-combatant flying was formed in the USA by **Nancy Love** (American) called the 'Women's Auxiliary Ferrying Squadron's (WAFS).) In Britain there was the Women's Air Transport Auxiliary in which **Joan Hughes** (British) was a pilot at 17 and became the only instructor on all types. War produced

Hanna Reitsch

Germany's leading woman pilot, **Hanna Reitsch**, whose first experience of flight was as a glider pilot in 1930 and first venture with powered aircraft in 1935. Thereafter she developed into a test pilot, one of her tasks being to fly a Dornier bomber into a balloon cable to see what the effect might be: it crashed. She was the first woman to fly a rocket-engined aeroplane – the temperamental Messerschmitt Me 163 – and in this too she crashed, as did so many other pilots. She is celebrated for undertaking a dangerous mission to Hitler's headquarters in Berlin at the height of the last siege in April 1945.

The first Russian woman jet pilot was **Olga Yamshchikova** who learnt to fly in 1931 and boasts the following among her other Russian women's firsts:

1933 First flying instructor.
First stunt flyer.
1935 One of three glider pilots in a sky train from Moscow to the Crimea and back. She flew in action during the war at Stalingrad while in command of a women's fighter regiment. To a Russian woman too, to **Lyubov Ulanova** in 1960, goes the credit as first woman to fly a jet airliner on scheduled services. She qualified as a pilot in 1940 and throughout the war flew cargo – much of it gold – out of Siberia. By 1973 she had over 17 000 air hours to her credit and three records, in June 1969, for closed-circuit distances, speed and altitude flying with an all-woman crew. She also became a member of the Latvian Parliament. Another sort of distinction, however, belongs to **Svetlana Savitskaya** (Russian), an engineer, who in 1970 won the World Aerobatics Championship, thus demonstrating outstanding precision besides verve in this performance of airmanship.

Russia also claims the first, and, so far, only woman in space – **Valentina Tereshkova** who went into orbit in Vostov 6 on 16 June 1963 and stayed up for 70 hours 50 minutes, completing 48 circuits. At once she became the most publicised woman in Russia and the world and continues to be the principal Russian symbol of feminine achievement. A textile-worker, she learnt to parachute in 1959 and later was taken into the space programme. After 1963 she was pushed up the ladder of responsibility to become a much-travelled Chairman of the Soviet Women's Committee and a member of the Central Committee of the Communist Party. While in no way denigrating her courage it is well to compare her space efforts, which were backed up by a vast nation's resources, with those early solo pioneer airwomen, named above, who did so much for themselves with so little to spare.

Some, indeed, are still pioneers. **Anne Burns** (British) became the first woman to win the British National Gliding Championship in 1966, a genuine individual feat of airmanship since glider pilots are entirely dependent on personal resourcefulness and judgment of conditions for staying aloft and are bound, moreover, to make every landing 'forced'.

But others, like Amelia Earhart, will continue in the attempt to make flight safer. **Violet Milstead** (Canadian), known as the 'Bush Angel', was the first to teach bush pilots and taught more than 100 to fly. She herself flew more than 50 types of aircraft and is quoted as saying, 'I'd rather be 2000 ft upstairs than eat, sleep or get married.'

Women will take an ever-more active part in aviation as it becomes yet more a part of everyday life. The traditional record-breakers will fade into legend. But some women still try for more bizarre records. For example:

The one who made the longest 'delayed' parachute drop in 1965 when she fell 46 250 ft (14 100 m) – **O. Komissarova** (Russian).

And the youngest solo pilot, **Betty Bennett** (American) who performed the feat in 1952 when only ten years of age.

MOTOR VEHICLES

Although the first 'horseless carriages' looked just that – a horsed vehicle deprived of its traditional motive power – their shape, sound and speed in no way deterred women from climbing aboard. It was only a matter of a few years before an adventure reverted to a novelty and finally the commonplace. Women quickly adapted themselves to motor travel and devised suitable dress for the occasion – the latter very important. One lady included a Colt revolver as part of her equipment.

The first English woman to manage and drive a motor-car is said to have been Baroness **de Lorenz** but women all over the world had long taken to this mode of transport and had already been riding motor-cycles.

During the Marseilles–Nice two-day event in 1898 Madame **Laumaillé** (French) led her class the first day and finally finished fourth – two places ahead of her husband, as the first lady racing driver. Perhaps unique among the early women motorists was **Dorothy Levitt** (British) (see also above). In 1903 (the year the Ladies' Automobile Club was founded) she had won the Motor-boat Championship of the Seas at Trouville, defeating all-comers, but as the first English woman to take part in public motor-car competitions, two years later, she won a road race at Brighton and set a woman's world record speed of $79\frac{3}{4}$ mph (128 km/h), raising it to 91 mph (146 km/h) in 1906 when the world's record itself was only 121·57 mph (194 km/h) in special conditions. In Germany in 1907 she dominated all women competitors and was fourth

Dorothy Levitt

out of 172 (both sexes) in the Herkomer Trophy Race, even though her car was of lower power than 42 competitors. But in addition to being a competitor in many hill-climbs, and in 1907 winner in her class in France, she wrote a delightfully chatty book called *The Woman and the Car* and sponsored the concept of the light car.

Typical of the many women who drove cars and lorries during the First World War, though outstanding for the extent of her personal achievements, was the adventurous **Gwenda Stewart** (British). At the age of 15 she learnt to ride a motor-cycle and drove an ambulance in the Balkans and with the Serbian Army in 1916. Then she took part in the Romanian campaign and drove a heavy lorry for the Russians (no mean muscular feat for a very slight girl). Always restless she rafted down the Yukon River after the war, but in 1925 returned to motor-cycling and secured the world's 24-hour record – the first woman to do so. Then in 1926 she took the world flying kilometre record at 186 km/h (51·5 mph) but in 1927 had a serious crash. After that she concentrated upon motor-car racing with emphasis on record-breaking: at one time she was the possessor of no less than 76 records. Though several times she crashed her nerve seems never to have been shaken even if those of people who watched her were (see below).

The first motor-race meeting had taken place at Brooklands in 1907 and the following year five women competed for the first ladies' race on the course – an event won by a length by Mrs **Locke-King** (British), at an

Gwenda Stewart

Lee Breedlove

average speed of 50 mph (80 km/h). But it was not until Madame **Jennky** (French) became the first woman to win a major European hill-climbing competition at Gaillon in 1927 that women again began to vie strongly with the men for honours in speed and endurance.

In 1928 Mrs **E. Thomas** (British) held the ladies outer lap record at Brooklands with a speed of 120·88 (193 km/h) – barely 10 mph (16 km/h) less than that achieved by men at that time.

In 1929 Mrs **Victor Bruce** (British) won the Montlhéry 24-hour race, covering 2149 miles (3434 km) at an average speed of 89·57 mph (144 km/h).

In 1935 **Kay Petrie** (British) lapped Brooklands at 134·2 mph (214·4 km/h) (the ultimate record was only 143·44 mph (229·5 km/h when set that year) only to see it smashed next day by Gwenda Stewart with 135·95 mph (217·5 km/h). But at that the organisers took fright and they promptly forbade women to attempt the record. It has to be admitted that some were a trifle accident prone. But record-breaking continues and in 1965 **Lee Breedlove** (American) took the women's land speed record in a jet-propelled car at Bonneville Flats, USA, with a speed of 335·07 mph (539 km/h) over 1 km (0·62 mile).

Mostly however, women continued to compete against each other in ladies' classes rather than against men, although this practice is gradually falling into disuse, particularly in rallies.

The most successful French woman in rallying has been **Claudine Trautmann** who won the Ladies' Championship nine times, post 1960, and many events besides. She had the distinction of being appointed a works driver by Citroën. And the most successful of all lady drivers has been **Pat Moss** (British). She has consistently beaten the men, taking the Liège–Rome–Liège Rally in 1960, in partnership with **Ann Wisdom** (British) as well as the Tulip and German Rally in 1962 and the Sestrière Rally. And these are far from being alone in her list of successes.

Despite the traditional sneer applied to women's skill as drivers, one insurance company offers a 30% lower rate to women than to men – not that this necessarily reflects a safer record by women. It could be that, statistically, men are more often at higher risk than women because they have to use cars in bad weather conditions when women might easily decline to venture out. The insurance companies, not surprisingly, are reluctant to give detailed accident figures to the general public. Safety – the desire to arrive – ought to be the criterion of motoring though woman's ability to achieve this, compared with man's behind the wheel, will no doubt remain the subject of hot debate in the years to come.

20

AS SPORTSWOMEN

Apart from an almost rigid exclusion of women by men from sport in ancient times the feminine sex has, until recently, been partly inhibited from involvement by the difficulties imposed by dress. Light Grecian robes and the equivalent of the bikini top would not have imposed many restrictions upon movement, but the creators of the Olympic Games would have nothing to do with women in the arena and even denied them (with the exception of the priestess of Demeter Chamyne) the right to watch. The Romans went further in 393 BC and prohibited the Olympic Games altogether though they at least permitted women to take part in chariot races and to watch games. But, of course, in those days athletics were closely related to politics, religion and war-making (cynics are entitled to ask if things have changed very much in the interim) rather than as a way of relaxing and fostering innocent competition. But that was not the only hindrance to women's participation since, as women acquired more time for indulgence in sport, the Western etiquette which forbade exposure of an ankle prevented them from producing sufficient mobility to compete on anything like equal terms with men even had their physique been equal to that test.

Probably the first sport taken up in any magnitude by women was archery, though their intention may have been more as a means of self-defence than competition. The legendary Amazons were said to be archers (see section on War) and all British monarchs up to and including Queen **Victoria**, learnt the art. The longest reign as a British champion in any sport is 41 years which was achieved by the archer **Alice Leigh** (1855–1948) who first won the Championship in 1881 and for the final time in 1922. It was first included as a women's competition in the Olympic Games in 1904 (though later dropped) when women of the USA won all three events, **M. Howell** being the winner in both the Columbia and National rounds. Women's archery returned to the Olympic Games in 1972, very much as the result of lobbying by **Inger Frith** (Danish), the President of the International Archery Federation.

The successor to the bow, the gun, has its female adherents and the most famous woman shot in a sport dominated by men was **Annie Oakley** (American, 1860–1926) (see section on Stage and Screen). Nevertheless, the smallest group on record for bench rest shooting by either sex is to the credit of **Mary De Vito** (American) with 7·68 in (194 cm) at 1000 yd (914 m) in 1970 while the only woman to win the Queen's Prize at Bisley (which has been awarded since 1860) was **Marjorie Foster** (British, 1894–1974) in 1930 with a score of 280 (the record held by men is 293).

The oldest of the popular sports in which women have taken a leading part is golf. In the mid 16th century **Mary Queen of Scots** (1542–87) played it at St Andrews and ladies continued to swing a club in the ensuing years in many countries. Yet it was not until the 19th century that golfers in Scotland began to form the organisations which led to modern international golf. In 1810 a ladies' prize was offered at Musselburgh Golf Club; in 1872 a Ladies' Golf Club was founded at St Andrews, and in 1893 the Ladies' Golf Union was formed to govern their game. Then in 1894, the United States Golf Association was formed for both men and women's golf and soon after that the game took on international scope, though the first woman golfing champion in the world had already been **Margaret Scott** (British) who won the British Women's Championship in 1893 and one of the two sports first played by women in the Olympic Games of 1900 was golf when **Margaret Abbot** (American) became the first women's Olympic Champion against five competitors.

Croquet is another game which has long been played by women and one of the few in which skill rather than physical strength is the criterion. In fact the unsurpassed holder of the most championships remains a woman, **Dorothy Steel** (British) who won 31 titles (15 of them as Women's Champion) between 1919 and 1939.

Dorothy Steel

Women are not normally associated with the physically violent sports though in the 18th century in England, when prize-fighting for men was becoming popular, Mrs **Stokes** (British), a renowned prize-fighter at the top of her form in 1725, drew great crowds. Female boxing, and wrestling too, are still staged, though rather more as a bizarre spectacle than a genuine sport. In the same way they only occasionally play Rugby and Association football and other derivatives.

The sport in which women first made a great impact was lawn tennis, though not until 1874 when it acquired a standardised form after Walter Winfield designed 'a new and improved portable court'. Then the failing All England Croquet Club (which admitted women) diversified its interests and began tennis tournaments at Wimbledon. It quickly spread and was introduced into the USA, it is said, by **Mary Outerbridge**

Hazel Wightman presents her cup to the winning USA team which include second from left *Doris Hart*, second from right *Shirley Fry* and right *Louise Brough*

who had seen British Army officers playing it in Bermuda in 1874. Ten years later **Maud Watson** (British) became the first women's tennis champion out of 13 competitors at Wimbledon, and the first US women's champion was **Ellen Hansell** in 1887. Along with golf, it was one of the first games played by women in the Olympic Games of 1900. Thus **Charlotte Cooper** (British) became the first woman to win an Olympic Gold Medal when she took the singles. A leading advocate of women's tennis was **Hazel Wightman** (American, 1887–1974) who won 48 US titles between 1909 and 1954, inaugurated the Wightman Cup competition between the USA and Britain and referred to the game as 'a channel of intensified life'.

The only two women to achieve the Grand Slam by winning Wimbledon, the US, French and Australian titles in one year have been **Maureen Connolly** (American, 1934–69) in 1953 and **Margaret Court** (Australian) in 1970, the latter also being the current holder of the record for highest earnings in a season – over £80000 in 1973. The youngest ever Wimbledon Champion was **Charlotte Dod** (British, 1871–1960) who was 15 years 8 months when she won in 1887.

Table tennis also has its stars, the greatest number of world singles titles by any player belonging to **Angelica Rozeanu** (Romanian), who won six between 1950 and 1955 and the greatest number of world titles won by any player is 18 going to **Maria Mednyanszky** (Hungary) between 1927 and 1935. This sport can probably claim the youngest of any international player for in 1958 **Joy Foster** (Jamaican), then aged eight, became both her country's singles and mixed doubles champion.

It was from the races held at fairs and during local festivals that women's athletics took root. Then schools adopted races for girls, particularly in the USA. The first modern athletics meetings for women seem to have been held in 1904 in Germany, though it was another ten years before they acquired a recognised organisation. Nevertheless the earliest mention of a women's world record dates from 1910 when **E. Macbeth** (American) ran 50 yards in 6 seconds. Formal organisations were much slower in appearing. The first were formed almost simultaneously in France and Austria in 1917 – separated though the antagonists were by war – and lead towards a common goal, the founding in 1921 of the Fédération Sportive Féminine Internationale by Madame **A. Milliat** (French) who also takes credit for the original French organisation and for running the first truly international meeting for women in Monte Carlo in 1921 and the first Olympic Games for women in Paris in August 1922, after the Olympics Committee had refused women a part in the Games. At the same time women were beginning to dress more fittingly for the sport: **Elaine Burton** (British), who won the 100 yards dash at the British Northern Counties Championship in 1919 (and later became a Member of Parliament) was the first woman to compete in shorts and spiked shoes. Most athletics records change frequently but those in weight-lifting are slow to topple. The greatest lift by a woman, 3564 lb (1616 kg), was achieved by **Josephine Blatt** (American, 1869–1923) in 1895 using a hip and harness lift and the highest competitive two-handed lift by a woman, 392 lb (177 kg), by **Jane de Vesley** (French) in 1926. The greatest overhead lift by a woman is 286 lb (129 kg) by **Katie Sandwina** (German, 1884–1952). Weighing in herself at 210 lb (95 kg) she is said to have shouldered a 1200 lb (544 kg) cannon off the tailboard of a wagon in Barnum and Bailey's Circus.

It was in gymnastics that the most Olympic medals to be won by any competitor of either sex in any sport was achieved by **Larisa Latynina** (Russian) who between 1956 and 1964 took 18 (9 Golds, 5 Silver and 4 Bronze).

A game light-heartedly associated by many men with women, and yet played rather more by men, is field hockey. Its antecedents are to be found in ancient Persia though its modern form dates from about 1875 in England with women beginning to participate in schools, and forming their first club at East Molesey in 1887. The first national Association appeared in Ireland as the Irish Ladies' Hockey Union in 1894 and the first international game was played between Ireland and England in Dublin in 1896. **Constance Applebee** (British) a physical educationalist, took the game to the USA in 1901 where it has since become the most popular outdoor sport for women. The International Federation of Women's Hockey Associations was formed in 1927 but as yet, although

Larisa Latynina and
Gertrude Ederle

there are women's international matches, there is no women's competition in the Olympic Games. It is, unfortunately, almost a tradition of women's hockey that each innovation in the rules by men, in their attempts to improve the game, is seemingly regarded with suspicion by women who almost invariably delay its introduction.

The sport in which, perhaps, the most innovations have been made by women is that of competitive swimming. The first women's world record went to **Martha Gerstung** of Germany in 1908 in the 100 metres freestyle and the first women's participation in Olympic swimming took place in the Games of 1912 with **Fanny Durack** (Australian) taking the Gold Medal for the 100 metres freestyle, Great Britain winning the 400 metres relay and **Greta Johansson** (Swedish) winning the high diving. In 1917 **Charlotte Boyle** and **Claire Galligan** (both American) of the New York Women's Swimming Association, against the advice of the experts, experimented with the six-beat crawl (as opposed to the preferred four-beat) and in 1918 beat all records with the result that they were copied with even greater success by the men. This New York association produced some truly remarkable women. One of its members, **Gertrude Ederle** (American), was the first woman to swim the English Channel, for which she received a ticker-tape welcome in New York City. She won her first international race at 14, set many women's world records in freestyle swimming up to 880 yards and swam the Channel on 6 August 1926 in the then world record time of 14 hours 39 minutes. In the Olympic Games of 1924 she won a Gold and two Bronze medals out of the five racing events then open to women, but in 1926 she turned to instruction and also became an adviser on fashion. However, the most world records belong to **Ragnhild Hveger** (Danish) and amounted to 42 in the period 1936–42, and the fastest official crossing of the English Channel by a woman was made in 1973 by 16-year-old **Lynne Cox** (American) in 9 hours 36 minutes – only 1 minute slower than the fastest man. As a record of female endurance in water there is the swim of 200 metres in 7 minutes 53 seconds in water at 1·5 °C by 53-year-old **Jenny Kammersgard** (Danish) in 1972.

Mountaineering has attracted women from the earliest of times if only as a way to safety when threatened by enemies in the valleys. In the section on Exploration some of those who climbed for scientific purposes are mentioned. As part of a competitive sport, for individual, sectional or nationalist reasons, women have also played a part, one of the most remarkable among them being **Annie Peck** (American, 1850–1935) whose motivation was to set foot where no man had stepped before. Beginning on nursery slopes in Europe in 1885 she climbed the Matterhorn in 1895 – dressed in knickerbockers, tunic and felt hat tied by a veil. In 1904 she was the first to climb Mount Sorata (21 300 ft (6492 m)) in Bolivia, a remarkable feat without oxygen, and in 1908 Mount Huascaran (21 812 ft (6644 m)) in Peru – though one of her male companions tactlessly set foot first on the peak. She was a founder of the American Alpine Club.

Among the prizes in the first recorded chariot race was 'a woman skilled in women's work' and it is only recently that women have started to take over the professional reins of horse-racing. As yet a man as a prize has not been offered. The first woman allowed to hold a licence to train race-horses for the flat in England was **Florence Nagle** (British) in 1965, although prior to that several women practised while the licence was held for them in a man's name. The first women to ride under Jockey Club rules in England mounted the saddle in the Goya Stakes in May 1972 at Kempton Park. There were so many applicants for the honour that lots had to be drawn for the 21 places and the winner was ridden by **Meriel Tufnell** (British) who later became Ladies' Champion Rider for 1972. The only thing notable about these events is their delay in actuation. Women have ridden in races as amateurs in most countries for generations, but racing history was made in March 1974 when **Anna-Marie la Ponche** (French) became the first woman rider to win against professional jockeys in Europe.

In equestrian sports women now compete on equal terms with men, their principal inspiration being **Pat Smythe** (British) who was a member of the British team in 1947 when aged 19. Eight times British Ladies' Champion and European Ladies' Champion in 1957 she was the first female member of a team which gained an award (Bronze) in the Grand Prix (jumping), in the 1956 Olympics.

Women have long been associated with bull-fighting, usually on horseback, but it was only in 1908 that they were forbidden to fight on foot in Spain. In Mexico they are allowed to take part on foot and in many countries are regular participants in the ring. Perhaps the most famous of modern female bull-fighters is **Conchita Cintron** (Portuguese American) who by the age of 21 had killed 400 bulls on foot. She celebrated her marriage to a Portuguese nobleman by retiring from the ring with a flourish – killing her last bull in Spain when on foot and thereby laying

Pat Smythe on Flanagan

herself open to arrest; however she was reprieved by the enthusiasm of the crowd who might otherwise have lynched the ring president. She eventually raised six children, became a celebrated dog-breeder and also a diplomatic attaché. The first modern woman permitted to fight bulls in Spain was **Maria de los Angeles** in 1973 when it again became legal.

As the combustion engine superseded horse-power women were very close to men in their attempts for speed records on four wheels (see section on Ships, Flight and Motor Vehicles). On the eight wheels of a pair of rollerskates, however, it is a woman, Miss **A. Vianello** (Italian), who holds the highest number of world speed titles for either sex, with 16 between 1953 and 1965. The older sport of skating on ice had been popular for many centuries before the first recorded women's ice-skating races of 1805 at Leeuwarden in Holland. The first women's world champion figure skater was declared in 1906 when **Madge Syers** (British) took the title and went on to repeat her triumph in 1907 as well as in the first winter Olympics of 1908 against six competitors. In the other winter sport of skiing the greatest reported aggregate elevation descended in 12 hours is 416000 ft (126796 m) and **Sarah Ludwig** (American) as one of a team of three achieved this on 16 February 1974. It is also interesting that the most world titles held by either sex can be claimed by **Christel Cranz** (German) who won 12 (four Slalom, between 1934 and 1939, three Downhill, between 1935 and 1939, five combined, 1934–9). She also won the Gold Medal for the Combined in the 1936 Olympics. Only two ski-bobbers have retained their world championship and both were women, **Gerhilde Schiffkorn** (Austrian) – 1967 and 1969; **Gertrude Geberth** (Austrian) – 1971 and 1973.

There are few sports in which women, unaided, have yet proved their physical capability to compete consistently on fully equal terms with men. A male champion will almost invariably defeat his female counter-

Sophia Heath

part. Nor have many women made much impact upon the sporting world outside their own particular sphere. One of the most effective advocates for women's sport was **Sophia Heath** (British, 1896–1939) who, apart from being an influential aviator (see section on Ships, Flight and Motor Vehicles), was one of the founders of the Women's Amateur Athletic Association of Great Britain in 1922, was frequently a member of international women's teams (without ever winning) and, above all, was the only woman to attend and give evidence at Prague in 1925 on the question of the advisability of women's entry into Olympic athletics – a study which culminated in women's first participation in athletic events in the Olympic Games of 1928.

Perhaps the most versatile and successful woman in sport was **Mildred Zaharias (Babe Didrikson)** (American, 1914–56). In girlhood she was superior to her contemporaries in athletics and at the age of 16 became an All-American basket-ball player, national champion at baseball and javelin-throwing; at 17 champion at baseball-throwing, long jump and 80 metres hurdles with similar titles in 1932 and that culminated in her capture of the Gold Medals for 80 metres hurdles (11·7 seconds) and the javelin (143 ft 3½ in (44·5 m)) at the Olympics. After that she turned professional to give athletic exhibitions and also began to learn golf. Rapidly she developed into a most powerful and graceful player, the top woman exponent of the game in the USA. She set a record in 1947 by winning no less than 17 separate championships, including that of British Amateur Champion which made her the first American to take the title. She was operated upon for cancer in 1953 but came back to win the US National Open and the All American Open tournaments the year after. In 1956, however, cancer won.

Sport means money, big money to its top exponents and many present-day players, particularly of professional tennis, are rich from the game and its pecunious sidelines. The greatest fortune amassed by an individual in sport was the £17 000 000 estimated to have been earned by **Sonja Henie** (Norwegian, 1912–69), the ice-skating star. She was thrice an Olympic champion (1928, 1932, 1936) and for ten consecutive years

The first woman up
Everest, *Junko Tabei*

(1927–36) Women's World Champion – which, as a record, remains unbeaten. After turning professional she acted as a promoter of her own ice shows and also starred in 11 films.

In this respect, therefore, sport has had its emancipating influence upon women by giving them access to self-earned, independent financial means as well as the fame which accompanies success at international level. It is worth bearing in mind that women have not been unsuccessful at personally negotiating higher rates of remuneration for themselves in the world of professional sport, a process which will evolve further the more they continue to play in a crowd-attracting style, no matter the game involved. Sheer determination, too, must have its reward as for example the feat of **Junko Tabei**, a member of the Japanese women's mountaineering team who, in company with a male Sherpa, became the first woman to reach the peak of Mount Everest (29082 ft (8840 m)) on 17 May 1975 even though, a few days previously, the expedition had lost some of its equipment as the result of an accident.

Babe Zaharias

JILLS OF ALL TRADES.

In the "Our Daughters" correspondence in the *Daily Telegraph*, a "Father of Six," says, "As yet we have no women architects, farm bailiffs, bill discounters, cab drivers, civil engineers, barristers, coalheavers, railway surveyors, dentists, engine drivers, farriers, boiler-makers, fitters, shepherds, shipwrights, solicitors, and commercial travellers."

MADAM,—I am a father of eight daughters, and, on reading the above, my eldest, Annie, at once decided on being an architect. She has bought a T-square, and a pair of compasses, and should Government want more law-courts, etc., she is quite ready to begin.

My next, Bella, having dark eyes, thinks a barrister is the best profession for her, as the wig will set them off to advantage. She is now quite prepared to receive any amount of briefs.

Rosa, my third, has turned railway surveyor. Not having a dumpy-leveller, or theodolite, and not knowing how to use them if she had, she surveys the railways at a safe distance with her opera glasses.

Sarah, my fourth, says she will be a shepherd, and dress like those at the Gaiety *Frankenstein*, to which her mamma says, "No! shepherdess or nothing!" She is now tending a Lowther Arcade sheep in the back garden.

Clara, my fifth, is not ambitious, and has fixed her mind upon coal-heaving. She has made a neat costume of black satin and a sack of corded silk, and practises hard all day in the coal-cellar. You should hear her cry, "Be-low!"

Flora and Florence (twins) are farriers. I purchased an anvil for them, and they have nearly made a horse-shoe, singing the while "The Anvil Chorus." All that is wanted now, they tell me, is a few holes bored in it and a horse to put it on.

And Dorothy, my youngest, having a remarkably strong wrist, has turned dentist. She bribed the page with sixpence to let her extract a few molars. The boy accepted the bribe; spent it, and now says, "Be blowed if he will!"—Yours, Benjamin Brown.

The adornment of the body by clothing, jewellery and cosmetics has evolved slowly from primitive beginnings. The fact that in recent times discoveries have been made of living, naked primitive people hardy enough to live in cool and breezy uplands but who, nevertheless, had their bodies intricately painted, rather suggests the theory that cosmetics may have been worn by early man before either jewellery or clothing. The use of jewellery is believed to be derived from the wearing of amulets to ward off the evil eye. There are several theories regarding the origins of wearing apparel – one is for warmth, another that man developed in warmer countries and that clothing was first used as protection against insect bites. Or it could be on the lines that he who killed a tiger wore its skin partly as a deterrent to a potential human enemy by demonstrating the magnitude of his strength, and partly through the superstition that, by doing so, he absorbed some of the dead animal's qualities. Whichever theory or joint theories are correct it could not have taken man long to realise that the wearer of the most magnificent skin of the fiercest animal cut the finer figure.

In the Middle Ages a woman could still live her whole life in a village without seeing a change in style of dress. But, by travelling just a short distance, variations would be observed. Among the rich, fashion changes and styles were communicated by sending dolls dressed appropriately; this started as early as the 14th century when dolls were sent from Paris to the courts of Europe to acquaint them with the latest designs in the French court and thus create a market for French fabrics.

In the 18th century the most famous dresser of these dolls was **Marie-Jeanne Bertin** (French, 1744–1813), better known as 'Rose Bertin', of very humble background who, by luck, flair and ambition, made her way so successfully that she was presented to Marie-Antoinette. At this time Marie-Antoinette had been criticised by her husband, Louis XVI, for not paying sufficient attention to her appearance. Rose Bertin altered that to such an extent that Marie-Antoinette then became criticised for her extravagances and ridiculed for her exaggerated headgear. Meanwhile, Rose Bertin was given the entrée into the royal ante-chamber and paid more than a Secretary of State, her clients also including the Queens of Spain and Sweden. At the Revolution she fled the country but continued to supply the Tsarina of Russia and the Queen of Spain, among other clients.

It was expanding communications and the mass introduction of sewing-machines after 1850 that caused universal changes in dress style among the mass of the population. Fashion, in the modern sense of the word, was born. Fashion plates (many of them coloured) in women's magazines brought to the attention of every fashion-conscious woman the latest innovations in dress. As a result styles came to be widely copied. Fashion magazines came into being from about the mid 19th century; for example *Harper's Bazaar* was started in America in 1867 with **Mary Booth** (American, 1831–89) as its first Editor.

A yet more constructive approach to bringing fashion into the home was made by **Ellen Demorest** (American, 1824–98) who conceived the idea of mass-producing accurate dress patterns and distributing them as an attachment to a quarterly magazine (launched by her husband in 1860), called *Mme Demorest's Mirror of Fashions*. At the same time she opened a shop on Broadway and rapidly built up a reputation as the dominant figure in American fashion design. The Demorests prospered and made a point of providing as much employment as possible for women: in 1876, for example, 3 000 000 patterns were distributed, priority being given to women as their selling agents and work-force. But the Demorests never patented their invention and in due course were overtaken by a competitor, Ebenezer Butterick and his patterns. A close colleague of Ellen Demorest was **Jane Croly** (American, 1829–1901), an excellent fashion journalist who was known as 'Jennie June'. A staunch feminist, she tackled a wide range of subjects on their behalf on the pages of magazines. She attacked long skirts, hoops and crinolines and tried to guide American women's shopping along rational lines – abhoring the chatter of '. . . women's eternal discussion of the trimming of a dress or a bonnet'. In 1868 she became the originator of the women's club, Sorosis, and its second President in 1870.

The first mannequin was **Marie Worth** (French). Her husband, the Englishman Charles Worth, designed expressly for her in the 1850s, but when she wore the dress to the store 'Gagelin and Opigez' in Paris, where both worked as assistants, her clothes attracted inquiries from customers. The firm was persuaded to allow Worth to open a small dress-making department and this became such a success that, in 1858, he opened his own shop. Two years later Marie Worth displayed some of her husband's designs before the wife of the Austrian Ambassador who then wore one of the crinolines to a royal ball. The Empress Eugénie was so impressed that the next morning Charles Worth was appointed as the first *grand couturier*.

Publicity by the right people or in the right places was always essential to successful designers. A new method of travel, by bicycle, was made easier for women by **Elizabeth Miller** (British) in 1851 when she designed a pair of gathered knickerbockers. This style was adopted by the suffragist and reformer **Amelia Bloomer** (American, 1818–94) who, to her surprise, found them named after her. The first dress-display dummy, a natural evolution from the fashion dolls of previous centuries, was shown by **Madame Paquin** (French) at the 1900 Exhibition. Made in wax, it was in her own likeness and dressed in the latest fashion. But Madame Paquin was herself a great exhibitionist besides an able organiser and became the first female Chairman of the Paris *haute couture* dress trade. Contemporaries of hers, the **Callot** sisters (French) ran an important atelier that made lace blouses and gold and silver lamé evening dresses fashionable for many more people in the mass market.

And they helped teach **Madeleine Vionnet** (French, 1877–1975), the first *couturière* to create for individuals. Between 1900 and 1906 her lingerie collections were among the loveliest examples of the day. She claimed to be responsible for mannequins discarding corsets in 1907 and that her mannequins were the first to show in bare feet and sandals. Supreme with the use of soft biased fitting fabrics, she is considered by some as the greatest of all the Paris *couturières* and one of the most original designers ever known. Yet her models were not extensively bought by fashion buyers because of the great difficulty in copying the superb and intricate cut of her clothes. She was also original in her day for using quarter-scale figurines for all her first *toiles* – a trial garment.

Underclothing too began to change shape and alter fashion. The first patent for a brassiere was taken out by **Mary Jacob** (American) in 1914. As a New York debutante she hated the restrictive corseting still fashionable at that time and one evening, before a dance, helped by her French maid, constructed a brassiere out of two handkerchiefs and some pink ribbon. This she patented as a 'Backless Brassiere' the following year, made a few hundred samples which did not sell and lost interest. Later she suggested the idea to the Warner Brothers Corset Company and accepted their offer of $15 000 for the patent. Later estimates put her patent's value at $15 000 000.

A key link between artist and dress-designer, **Sonia Delauney** (Russian) opened her own shop in 1925 selling clothes of her own design made up in materials of her own creation. Having caused a sensation in the 'Art et Décoration' exhibition in 1925, she sold in quantity to America but was, unfortunately, financially ruined in 1929 by the collapse of the New York Stock Market.

For generations high fashion had implied immensely elaborate dress, a trend that had been over-emphasised by glamorous actresses, particularly those from Hollywood. Suddenly, as part of the Economic Blizzard, there came a demand for simplicity led by two great designers, themselves great rivals:

Gabrielle Chanel (French, 1883–1971), daughter of a peasant who was set up in business with a dress-shop by an English lover just before 1914, worked for the Red Cross during the war. She noticed that women were looking for simpler clothing when doing war work and therefore adapted men's clothing for women's use. Thus was founded the fashion house which in 1920 was to produce artificial suntan and, later, perfume (Chanel No. 5 made her a millionairess), charm bracelets and large, chunky items of costume jewellery. In the early 1930s she designed simple clothes for the Hollywood actress **Ina Claire** (American), and this gave a strong boost to the theme of simplicity by removing the 'class' distinction that was usually created by the more exotic fashions. Clothes such as 'the little black dress' and 'the Chanel suit' of the mid 1950s which were uncluttered, easy to mass produce and readily variable in detail, gave everybody the opportunity to appear 'in fashion' at reasonable cost. Moreover, unlike so many designers, she seems not to have minded being copied – rather to have encouraged it.

Gabrielle Chanel
in a Chanel suit

Elsa Schiaparelli

Elsa Schiaparelli (Italian, 1890–1973) the child of a professor brought up with scholars, worked as a film scriptwriter and translater besides doing a little sculpting before creating her first fashion designs after the First World War. In the mid 1920s she made her name by designing amusing but attractive, modernistically decorated sweaters, from which she moved to the design of sports wear and then originated 'separates' and the evening dress with a matching jacket – forerunner of the evening suit. From the flat, shapeless look of the 1920s she re-established emphasis on the waist and, in 1931, the built-up shoulder line which dominated the silhouette until 1947. Elsa Schiaparelli originated the first boutique in 1935 – a salon that epitomised her striking originality with the rope handrails of its winding stairs. Here were displayed sweaters, skirts, blouses, belts and other accessories previously scorned by the *haute couture*. Fashion for her was fun. She originated coloured wigs and designed outrageous hats; her buttons could be golden sovereigns or dollar signs, locks or lollipops, and she had material printed to look like overlapping newspaper cuttings – thousands upon thousands of yards of this was sold. Always open to new ideas, she became in 1930 the first of any *couturier* to use the zip-fastener and, later, the first *couturier* to use material from man-made fibres. She had a feel for the texture and colour of materials. She used tweeds, linens and heavy crêpes for evening wear. Until she came along colours of clothes were delicate and subdued; her colours were daring and brilliant. From her came 'Shocking' pink and in 1954 an autobiography, *Shocking Life*.

A businesswoman to the finger-tips, this dark-haired, brown-skinned woman matched a violent temper with calculated execution of ideas – be it in the design of some new creation, the quick exploitation of an unexpected fashion, or the improvisation of pinning together dresses in order to meet the deadline for a fashion show when the seamstresses went on strike.

Fashion shifts its favours and emphasis in accordance with the whims of the public guided by the publicists and the leaders of the fashion trade. For example, a comeback for natural fibres was brought about by **Sybil Connelly** (Irish) when the Philadelphia Fashion Group visited Dublin in 1950. They were impressed by the originality of her collection and the materials used. Indeed, her subsequent success meant a re-organisation of the production of Ireland's native materials – such as bawneen, a natural white woollen material, previously only used for tough country wear – and created what is now a thriving fibre export trade.

In 1946 **Vera Neumann** (American) with her husband and a partner started selling her designs of clothing, scarves and household linen under the name 'Vera'. Now she employs 25 artists, leaves the financial side of the business to others and has annual sales of over $20 000 000. In 1967 the business was sold to Manhattan Industries for $5 250 000 and in 1972, as President of 'Vera' and Director of Manhattan, she earned $82 000.

But for sheer growth of output **Mary Quant** (British) must stand supreme. In 1955, when only 21, she and her husband-to-be opened the boutique 'Bazaar'. Designing and cutting the clothes herself, they sold, with a few helpers, 100 dresses a month, a figure which soared dramatic-

Mary Quant and
her life style

ally through the application of sheer enthusiasm and hard work. Though Mary Quant admits to being 'hopeless' when it comes to remembering figures, in 1967 the organisation exported 30 000 dresses to France alone. The firm organises about 30 collections a year in numerous countries and has also entered the field of cosmetics, shoes (unsuccessfully), dolls, household linen and wallpaper and paints. Now, as an entrepreneur of fashion with a team of designers, cutters, machinists and excellent managerial backing, Mary Quant has established herself as a fashion leader in the modern world of mass production, the dominant name among the other most successful designers of ready-to-wear clothes such as **Hattie Carnegie**, **Pauline Trigère**, **Claire Potter**, **Anne Fogarty**, **Adele Simpson** and **Bonnie Cashin**.

Today social differences in Western dress are negligible. The days are gone when rich women dressed primarily to seduce (with fashion

Japanese women in
traditional dress

emphasis moving to accentuate a different part of the body when over-emphasis of some other area had ceased to allure) and when the peasants were attired for utilitarian purposes only. Now a high percentage of women lead an active life and require clothes that are flattering as well as practical – preferably finding both qualities in one garment or alternately buying separate garments for work and leisure.

Women have gone to the most extraordinary lengths to make their faces appealing to men. In the year 902 there was the first mention that Japanese women plucked out their eyebrows completely and then pencilled in new thin brows, generally about an inch above the natural line. Next they offset their whitened faces by blackening their teeth – the latter effect achieved with a dye produced from iron and powdered gall-nut soaked in vinegar or tea.

By Stuart times in England there were many 'Beauty Specialists' who advocated remedies for covering or curing spots and wrinkles. These ranged from the use of white lead mixed with white of egg to the **Duchess of Newcastle**'s remedy which was oil of vitriol or sulphuric acid to remove the top layer of skin completely and reveal (hopefully) new clear skin underneath. Positively dangerous practices such as these can be found in beauty hints up to the end of the 19th century; a book of household hints of that time gives a recipe which includes quicklime as its main ingredient to remove superfluous hair. The nauseating beauty aid using, for example, dog's urine (as **Mrs Boswell**, wife of the diarist, did to her husband's disgust), has mercifully now been abandoned.

There were also, of course, gentle perfumed concoctions which did no harm at all and some were even beneficial – it being a cream such as this which started the pioneer cosmetic manufacturer **Helena Rubinstein** (see section on Trade) on her career. **Florence Graham** (**Elizabeth Arden**) (see section on Trade) also started off with an old recipe; hers being given her by **Elizabeth Hubbard** who found it among **Jeanne Récamier**'s (French 1777–1849) (see section on Courtesans, Mistresses and Salonnières) notes on beauty. Both Helena Rubinstein and Elizabeth Arden put emphasis on hygiene and scientific research which completely changed the concept of cosmetics – and also made it big business. Women – and men – will invariably seek fresh fashions, fashions that are, in part, controlled by technology.

Indian woman in traditional dress (sari)

"Nobody else thought of it, I'm the first!"

Clubs are generally established for specific reasons and so perform different functions. There are clubs for women with specialised interests, with similar social backgrounds, for educational purposes, political motives or charitable ideals. Most of these clubs affect only local women but a few are world-wide, with proportional influence, and cover several or all of these aims. Perhaps the first woman to advocate a form of women's club was **Christine de Pisan** (French, *c* 1364–1430) in her *Dit de la Rose* in 1402, her aims being educational and the furthering of women's rights.

In those clubs with specialised interests members exchange ideas and co-operate to achieve their aims, a facility provided by sports clubs, those of the arts and of the professions. If membership becomes synonymous with joining a trade or profession then the function of the club would encompass the duties of a union today or a guild in history. In 18th-century England there were, for example, the Mantua-makers' Club in St Martin's Lane and the Milliners' Club near the Royal Exchange: it is quite likely that these could have been used as trade unions to improve marginally their members' working conditions. A forerunner of a specialised club concentrating on the arts was the regular gathering of a group of English literary ladies in the mid 18th century who invited speakers and exchanged ideas. The participants in these gatherings included **Fanny Burney**, **Elizabeth Carter**, **Elizabeth Montagu** and Mrs **Vesey** of whom it is said that when the last invited Benjamin Stillingfleet to talk to them and did not wish him to be put off by finery of dress, she told him to come in the ordinary worsted stockings he was wearing at the time – his blue stockings (see section on Literature). New professions opening up to women also brought their clubs. For example, so successful were the female American journalists in the next century that, in 1882 in Washington, D.C., the Women's National Press Association was inaugurated. So it was with sport and the first women's cricket club, the White Heather, was formed in England in 1887. Women had been playing cricket since the previous century but it was not until 1888 that the first two professional teams took to the field.

Clubs for women of similar social backgrounds started as imitators of the exclusive male clubs. There was the 18th-century English Ladies' Club which Walpole referred to as 'the female Almacks' and the later 'Alexandria', founded in 1883 which, copying the example of men's clubs, did not admit visitors of the opposite sex so that even the future King Edward VII was forbidden to enter when he called for his sister.

The strongest bastion of women's clubs is the USA where the club-woman abounds. Here can be found the exclusive male clubs' female equivalents, such as the Chilton Club in Boston and the Acorn Club in Philadelphia. In America there are also clubs of general membership, the first two, which started in 1868, being the New England Women's Club of Boston and the Sorosis of New York. **Alice Cary** (1820–71) a writer and reformer, was the first President of the latter; to which she made her one and only speech; one of its co-founders being **Jane Croly** (see section on Fashion) who also founded the New York Women's Press Club and was an active promoter of the Federation of Women's Clubs.

An unusual similarity of background, that of direct lineage to soldiers or others of the American Revolutionary period, is required for membership to the Daughters of the American Revolution, a society organised in 1890 (probably by **Flora Darling** (1840–1910)) and now numbering approximately 188 000 members. There are detractors who think this society too much like a potato plant – the only good of which is underground – but it does provide scholarships, support schools for underprivileged youths and preserves historical Americana which might otherwise be destroyed in the name of progress. Much more as a crusade as well as an important part of the general process of giving meaning to the emancipation of the negroes, were the efforts of **Josephine Ruffin** (American, 1842–1924), herself a negress, who began organising clubs in 1894 as part of her work in Boston to assist negro women's development and the acceptance of educated negro women within the community. Her Woman's Era Club steadily expanded, produced its own monthly paper (edited initially by Josephine Ruffin) and at a conference instigated by her became affiliated with other clubs into the National Federation of Afro-American Women. This later merged with another organisation to form the National Association of Colored Women. In due course there was opposition, for reasons of colour, to the Era Club's proposed membership to the General Federation of Women's Clubs and eventually the club expired. However, Josephine Ruffin, poorly educated yet highly intelligent and systematic, was always held in great respect and continued her community leadership.

An equally redoubtable founder of women's associations (in her case for the furtherance of the education and care of the poor) was **Grace Dodge**

A senior member of the DAR

(American, 1856–1914), whose family played a prominent part in running the Young Men's Christian Association. In 1880 she helped found the Kitchen Garden Association that later became the Industrial Education Association; in 1905 the Girls' Public School Athletic League, the same year in which she healed a split in the non-sectarian Young Women's Christian Association, becoming creator and President of its National Board in 1906 and setting the organisation on the course it has since followed. All her life she devoted herself to welfare work rather than the social life into which her family's standing gave her entrée. On her death she bequeathed about $1 500 000 to the causes she had supported.

Those well-known American institutions, college fraternities, were widely adopted by women when they were admitted as students to State-supported universities. The names of sororities, as women's fraternities are generally called, usually consist of a series of Greek letters; the first, the Adelphean, founded in 1851, later changed its name to Alpha Delta Pi. That of the Monmouth College, founded in 1870, is called Kappa Kappa Gamma. Sororities are usually secret societies so the sound of Greek letters seems somehow apt.

For sheer size and international aspirations, little challenges the Women's Institute which began at Stoney Creek, Ontario, Canada in 1897 as the result of a talk on 'domestic science and sewing' by **Adelaide Hoodless** (Canadian, 1857–1910) to a Farmers' Institute. She suggested the formation of a similar Institute for women; the women were enthusiastic and on 19 February 1897 a women's department of the Farmers' Institute was formed, to be renamed 'The Women's Institute of Saltfleet' – and six days later of 'Stoney Creek'.

   Basically a non-sectarian, non-political, rural organisation with the objects to promote the knowledge of home economics and child care, it concentrated from the first on home and rural crafts. Its motto was 'For Home and Country'. The idea spread abroad and the first WI in Britain was started in June 1915, at that town in Wales that takes the charming name of Llanfairpwllgwngyllgogerychwyrndrobwllllantsysiliogogogoch. Many women elsewhere were also feeling the need for a similar rural society. For example in Norway in 1898 the House-Mother Association started independently with objects that were almost identical to those of the Women's Institute. Gradually various societies from round the world affiliated into the Associated Country Women of the World, probably the largest non-political female association ever, with its 8 000 000 members in 283 different societies scattered in 68 different countries. Its aims are to promote international goodwill and understanding between the countrywomen of the world, to raise the standard of living of rural women and to be a forum for them on international affairs.

By the beginning of the 20th century women's politically motivated organisations had popped up like mushrooms and their aims were mostly equality and the vote. The first women's movement in Belgium, the League for Women's Rights, was started by **Marie Popelin** (see section on the Fight for Equality) in 1892, though it was not until 1910 that the first women's club in Belgium, the Lyceum, was opened (again

A meeting of
the Women's Institute

on Marie Popelin's initiative), so illustrating the difference between a loosely knit association with a political aim and the more intimate social club.

Two illustrations of loosely knit political associations, each growing from suffrage organisations are:

The League of Women Voters (US) which was founded in 1920 by **Carrie Catt** (see section on Fight for Equality) from the 2 000 000-strong National American Woman Suffrage Association. As one of its functions it gives a kind of political consumer association service on governmental candidates though, after presenting non-partisan facts on each candidate does not come up with a 'best buy'. It believes in political responsibility through informed participation and although only women may be members, its data and findings are available to all. (See also the section on Politics and Statecraft.)

The Fawcett Society (Britain) which was formerly the London Society for Women's Suffrage founded in 1866, was renamed in 1919 after **Millicent Fawcett** (see section on Fight for Equality). Its scope is world-wide as its object states: 'The Society stands for equal rights and responsibilities between men and women as citizens. Its principal object is the removal of all inequalities and discrimination based on sex, whether in law, practice or custom, and the promotion of equal opportunity in all spheres of work or other endeavour. It seeks to promote education and the dissemination of knowledge on the past and present position of women. . . .' and in aid of this last aim possesses archives which are treasures of information from the past. Its methods to end discrimination against women are responsible and democratic, its belief in equality demonstrated by its membership which is open to any person of either sex who wishes to see an end to female discrimination. Its membership is soberingly low.

Religions give birth to their own societies. For example Jewesses have their Women's International Zionist Organisation covering nearly 50 countries (see section on Religious and Social Reform). There is the Young Women's Christian Association, founded in England in 1855, which was a union of Christian ideals rather than of doctrine. One of its objects then was to found a home for nurses returning from the Crimean War and its aim 'to advance the physical, social, intellectual, moral and spiritual interests of young women' is undertaken in its work to provide cheap and secure accommodation for girls wishing to work away from home, and summer camps, recreation or educational facilities irrespective of the race or religion of its participants.

Far-reaching political results were obtained by the Women's Christian Temperance Union, founded in 1874 by **Frances Willard** (American 1839–98) (see section on Politics and Statecraft), by a systematic campaign to make compulsory the inclusion in the curriculum of American public schools teaching of the destructive psychological and physical effects of alcohol. Beginning with New York in 1884 this subsequently became law in every State of the US, later spreading to Canada (except Quebec and Prince Edward Island), Sweden, France and Ireland and of local option in Australia and South Africa.

   The good influence of this Union's constructive educational approach to alcoholism was somewhat counterbalanced by its campaign for State Prohibition Legislation which swept the country like a wave in the 1880s and 1890s and led to the introduction of National Prohibition in 1920. For in its wake came illicit liquor-running and a sharp increase in criminal activity and gang warfare.

When in 1885, **Mary Leavitt** (American, 1830–1912) of the WCTU established a branch in New Zealand and **Katharine Sheppard** (New Zealander) took on the 'Franchise' Department, they were not to know then that this department would be the first women's suffrage movement in the world to see its aim achieved (see section on Fight for Equality).

There are, of course, thousands of women's societies formed for the sole purpose of social work, hospital-visiting and other services to the community. These are generally small, localised organisations, but some operate countrywide such as the Royal Women's Voluntary Service in Britain which, as one of its duties, runs a 'meals on wheels' service, delivering hot midday meals to aged people.

The fact that women have managed to form and run so many useful and successful clubs is, in itself, an answer to those who facetiously claim that women are 'unclubbable'. Clubs are a way of combining for self-interest or for the pursuit of an aim. Is it just possible that the calumny heaped upon women's clubs is a measure of their success in helping to reassert women's position in society?

SOURCES AND BIBLIOGRAPHY

Our search for information in compiling this book has led us to many sources, both private and public. Private individuals have made many contributions and libraries have frequently supplied us with essential documents and volumes. In particular we wish to acknowledge the enormous contribution by the Library of the Fawcett Society with its outstanding collection of women's archives from all over the world, the Dorset County Library, the Library of the British Ministry of Defence, the British Museum, The New York Public Library and the Library of Congress, USA.

We have also received immense help from the information services belonging to many overseas countries, although perhaps it should be mentioned that it seemed sometimes that the volume of assistance rendered was not necessarily an index of their present state of feminine emancipation nor their determination to extend its influence in the future. A few did not reply to our questions at all.

Extensive searches through the pages of newspapers and periodicals were profitable while listening to radio and television broadcasts gave leads for further research – though we learnt to be wary of some allegedly authentic information from the media. A search of encyclopaedias of all sorts, particularly *Britannica* and *Chambers's*, provided a foundation to our work, along with recourse to the standard reference works about personalities – such as the various editions of *Who's Who, Who was Who* and Dictionaries of Biography.

The Bibliography below is a select list only, comprising those works which seemed particularly important as an whole, or which provided unique scraps of information. Those works containing facts about women are, of course, practically inexhaustible.

Anon *Daughters of New Bulgaria* (1969).
    Status of Women in Canada (1970).
    Some aspects of the promotion of Belgian Women (1969).
    The rise of the Women's Movement in Indonesia.
    Derechos Politicos Profesionales y de Trabajor de la Major (1961).
    New Horizons, 100 years of Women's Migration (1963).
    Nobel: The man and his prizes (1950).
Arntz, H. (ed), *Germany reports women's affairs* (1969).
Barnouw E. and Krishnaswamy, S., *Indian Film* (1963).
Blom, E. (ed), *Grove's Dictionary of Music and Musicians* (1954).
Bochkaryova, Y. and Lyubimova, S., *Women of a New World* (1969).
Bolton, S., *Girls who became famous.*
Bridgeland, M., *Pioneer work with maladjusted children* (1971).
Brownlow, K., *The Parade's Gone By . . .* (1968).
Brusselmans, A., *Rendezvous 129* (1954).
Burgess, A., *The Small Woman* (1957).
Clark, F., *The position of women in contemporary France* (1937).
Cleverdon, C., *The Woman Suffrage Movement in Canada* (1950).

Contini, M., *Fashion* (1967).
Dorland, W., *The sum of Women's Achievement* (1917).
Drinker, S., *Music and Women* (1948).
Ellet, E., *Women Artists* (1859).
Fairfax, J. and Cook, S., *Oars across the Pacific* (1972).
Garland, M., *The Changing Form of Fashion* (1970).
Gaskell, E., *Life of Charlotte Brontë* (1857).
Halsbard, R., *The Life of Lady Mary Wortley Montagu* (1956).
Harding, A. (ed), *Guinness Book of Car Facts and Feats* (1971).
Hargreaves, R., *Women at Arms* (1930).
Hartnoll, P. (ed), *The Oxford Companion to the Theatre* (1957).
Harvey, P. (ed), *The Oxford Companion to English Literature* (1973).
Haynes, A., *The Dagenham Girl Pipers* (1957).
Heath, Lady and Murray, S., *Woman and Flying* (1929).
Hurd–Mead, K., *A History of Women in Medicine* (1938).
Hurst, M., *No Glass Slipper* (1967).
Huxley, G., *Lady Denman, GBE* (1961).
James, E. (ed) and others, *Notable American Women 1607–1950* (3 vols) (1971).
Jarman, T., *Landmarks in the History of Education* (1951).
Jennings, V., *Rahel: Her life and letters* (1876).
Johnson, C., *Lives of the notorious pirates* (1962).
Keller, H., *The Story of my Life* (1902).
Lane, M., *The Brontë Story* (1953).
Langna, I., *Dictionary of Discoveries* (1960).
Lawrence, C. (ed), *Fredrich Froebel and English Education* (1952).
Leijon, A.-G., *Swedish Women–Swedish Men* (1968).
Levitt, D., *The Woman and the Car* (1909).
Lynam, R., *Paris Fashion. The Great Designers and their creations* (1972).
Manvell, R., *Sarah Siddons* (1970).
Meyer, A., *Woman's Work in America* (1891).
Middleton, D., *Victorian Lady Travellers* (1965).
Mitford, N., *Madame de Pompadour* (1954).
Morris, M., *My Life in Movement* (1969).
Osborne, H. (ed), *The Oxford Companion to Art* (1970).
Owens, C., *Women Police* (1925).
Peel, R., *Mary Baker Eddy* (1966).
Peterson, C. *The Bantam Story* (1970).
Petrova, L. and Sheviliova, E., *Together with Women everywhere* (1967).
Phelps, G., *A Short History of English Literature* (1962).
Pope-Hennessy, U., *Madame Roland* (1917).
Power, J., *Brave Women and their Wartime Decorations* (1959).
Puckett, H. W., *Germany's Women go forward* (1930).
Robertson-Scott, J., *The Story of the Women's Institutes* (1925).
Rowse, A. L., *The England of Elizabeth* (1950).
Sackville-West, V., *St. Joan of Arc* (1936).
Schiaparelli, E., *Shocking Life* (1954).
Scholes, P. (ed), *The Oxford Companion to Music* (1960).
Simpson, H., *The Women of New Zealand* (1962).
Singer, K., *The World's greatest women spies*.
Skinner, C., *Madame Sarah* (1966).
Smith, W. S., *Women's Franchise Movement in New Zealand* (1905).

Sparrow, W. S., *Women Painters of the World* (1905).
Standing, E. M., *Maria Montessori* (1957).
Stern, M., *We the Women* (1963).
Strachey, R., *Women's suffrage and women's service* (1927).
Strachey, R., *The Cause* (1928).
Taylor, W. (ed), *The Guinness Book of Air Facts and Feats* (1973).
Tiltman, M., *Women in modern adventure* (1935).
Trevelyan, G., *English Social History* (1942).
Valois, N. de, *Come dance with me* (1957).
Whitney, J., *Elizabeth Fry* (1937).
Wolf, J. B., *Louis XIV* (1968).

INDEX